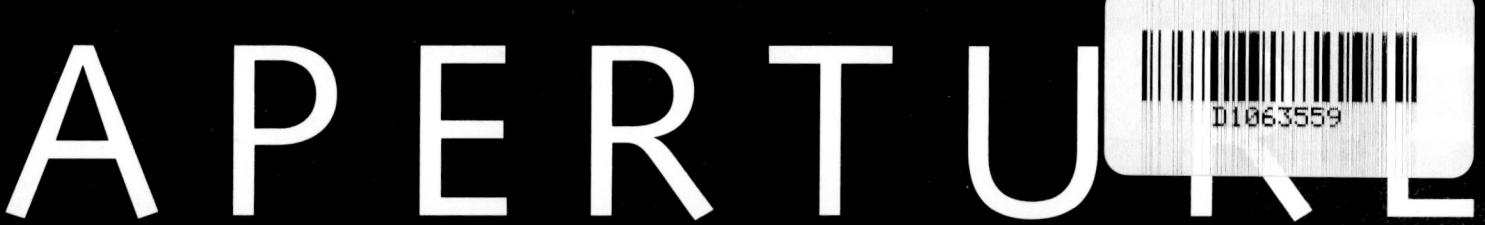

APERTURE

CONTENTS

Ran smack into snow storms in the Sierras, run over by dust storms in the desert, jumped out of the path of humungus snakes on the Navajo Reservations, knocked out by the heat in Death Valley, buried my face in the earth of Chaco Canyon, slept in ex-con hotels in New Mexico. All in all a quiet trip, wrote David Wojnarowicz in a postcard to his friend Jean Foos, in May of 1991.

To some viewers, the photograph of Wojnarowicz's face buried in the earth of Chaco Canyon resonates as an image of death, of loss, of powerlessness over his own AIDS-afflicted body. Others experience this image—as Wojnarowicz presented it to Foos—as one event in a series of interrelated events, a part of his journey that he chose (as he often did) to render visually. It is impossible to separate Wojnarowicz's life from his art; they intertwine synergistically and serendipitously, contesting hypocrisy and oppressive forms of authority. *Brush Fires in the Social Landscape* brings us the voice of this artist, speaking to and for a generation wrestling with issues of sexuality, identity, and the fragility of life.

Fervently anticensorship and an unsentimental advocate for AIDS awareness, Wojnarowicz was determined to make the private public. A seminal force behind a movement he wryly dubbed "Post-Diagnosis," his work flares with immediacy, embracing the repressed, the unspeakable, the intolerable, the marginalized. Wojnarowicz's life and work were driven by a desire for justice more than by any particular political agenda; he insisted upon challenging and dismantling what he termed a "pre-invented existence," which discriminates and imposes hierarchies on the bases of sexual preference, race, ethnicity, and gender.

Similarly, the innovative nature of his work defies traditional concepts of photography, stretching our notions of the medium's possibilities. Often juxtaposing text, paint, and collaged elements with photography, his works animate ideas and images, playing them off one another both ironically and meta-phorically. Experiencing Wojnarowicz's art is like being in the wake of a dream—or perhaps a nightmare. There is a complex tension between conscious and subsconscious, intuition and intention, sexuality, spirit, emotion, and intellect. The lasting imprint is a poetical fusion of provocative cadences.

Aperture first approached Wojnarowicz about publishing a book after a reading he gave in the winter of 1991 at our Burden Gallery, in conjunction with the publication and exhibition, "The Body in Question." Months later, during a visit with him in the hospital (where he was about to have an operation that was to help him through one of the many gruelling manifestations of AIDS), we talked again about the book, and planned to work on it together as soon as he was on his feet again. Unfortunately, this never happened. Wojnarowicz died of AIDS in July 1992.

Knowing of Wojnarowicz's interest in the publication, and with the remarkable support of Tom Rauffenbart (his lover, and now executor of the Wojnarowicz estate), we decided to proceed—sadly, without the benefit of Wojnarowicz's collaboration—with this project, publishing it as both a book and an issue of *Aperture*. Not since Aperture's earliest years—before there was a book-publishing program—has an issue of the magazine been entirely devoted to the work of one contemporary artist. We have taken this opportunity now to bring Wojnarowicz's work not only to his many followers, but also to those of our subscribers who initially might not have been inclined to notice and appreciate his extraordinary, significant vision.

Our task in this was not simply an art-historical one. The nature of Wojnarowicz's work demanded that we address who he was, how he lived, as well as what he created. And so Aperture drew together an immensely talented team of many of Wojnarowicz's friends and fellow artists, beginning with Tom Rauffenbart and painter Jean Foos. Working with Wojnarowicz, Foos had designed an earlier catalog for his exhibition "Tongues of Flame"

Opposite: UNTITLED, *from the "Sex Series," 1988–89, Gelatin-silver print, 20 x 24"* (organized by Barry Blinderman). She agreed to design our publication as well, and her acute understanding of Wojnarowicz and his work is evidenced through these pages. We then asked Lucy Lippard —a writer, thinker, and activist whom Wojnarowicz especially admired and respected—to write a social-political-art-historical portrait of the artist to serve as an introduction. At the same time, we interviewed writer Fran Lebowitz, who was extremely close to both Wojnarowicz and his dear friend and mentor Peter Hujar. She speaks of the rage, vision, and humanity that fueled Wojnarowicz's art and life. The gathering of voices grew as other friends and collaborators—Vince Aletti, C. Carr, David Cole, Karen Finley, Nan Goldin, Elizabeth Hess, Tessa Hughes-Freeland, Carlo McCormick, and Kiki Smith—each contributed a personal memory, anecdotes, an analytical discussion…anything they wished in order to build a living profile of David Wojnarowicz. Aletti shares with us Wojnarowicz's lusty, dreamlike postcards; Cole (Wojnarowicz's attorney in his case against the censorious Reverend Donald Wildmon) recalls the artist's clear-headed and compelling self-representation during the trial. In an interview between Goldin and Wojnarowicz, made shortly before his death, the two artists discuss love, art, sex, and death. We are deeply grateful to all the contributors for their heartfelt and eloquent words and ideas, and for their generosity of spirit. They share with us a profound commitment to Wojnarowicz's work and to his beliefs. As stated earlier, Aperture is especially indebted to Tom Rauffenbart for forging ahead with us on this project.

In one of his texts, Wojnarowicz wrote about wishing he could give the people he loved a part of himself forever. It seems,

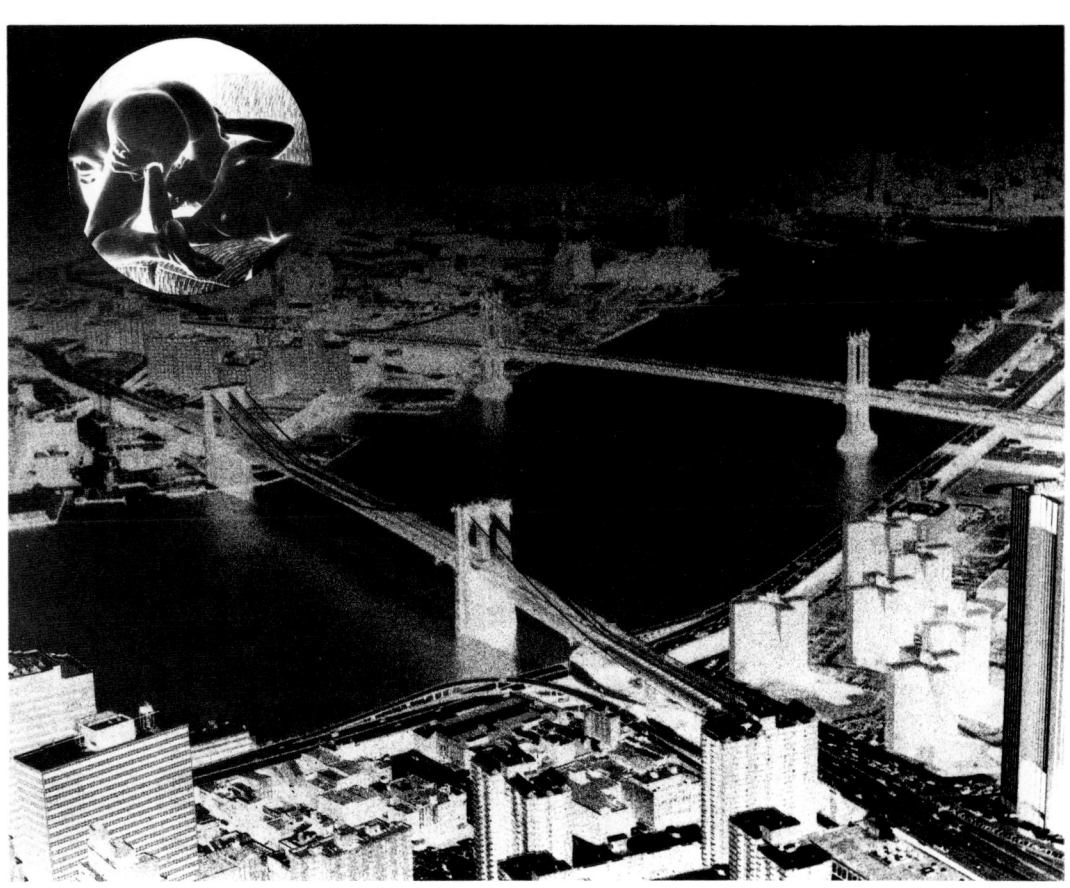

with his work, that this is exactly what he accomplished:

I wished for years and years that I could separate into ten different people: ten versions of myself in order to give each person I loved a part of myself forever, and also have some left over to drift across landscapes and maybe even go into death or areas which were dangerous, and have enough of me to survive the deaths of one or two or three of me…. now I'm in danger of losing the only one of me that is around. I'm in danger of losing my life and tell me exactly what gesture can convey or stop this possibility, what gesture of hands or mind can shut it down in its invisible tracks—nothing, and that saddens me…. Should I count backwards like the Mayans so that I never get older? Will the moon in the sky listen to my whispers as I count away?

THE EDITORS

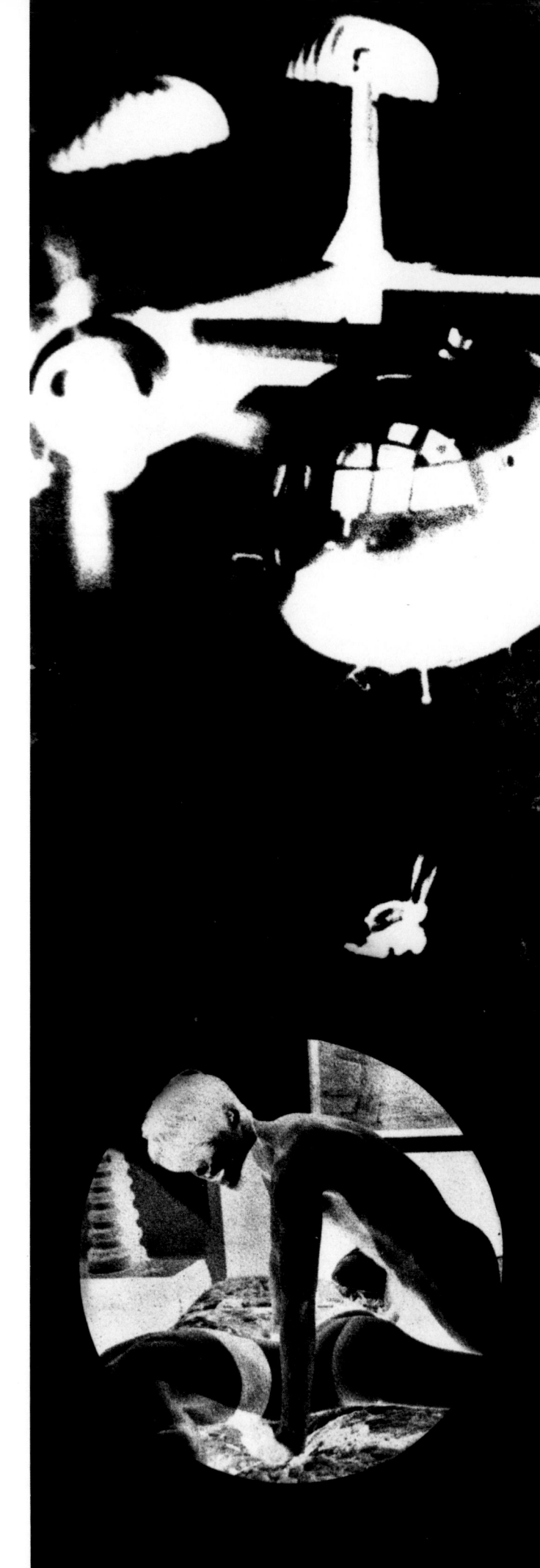

UNTITLED, *from the "Sex Series," 1988–89.*
Gelatin-silver print, 20 x 24"

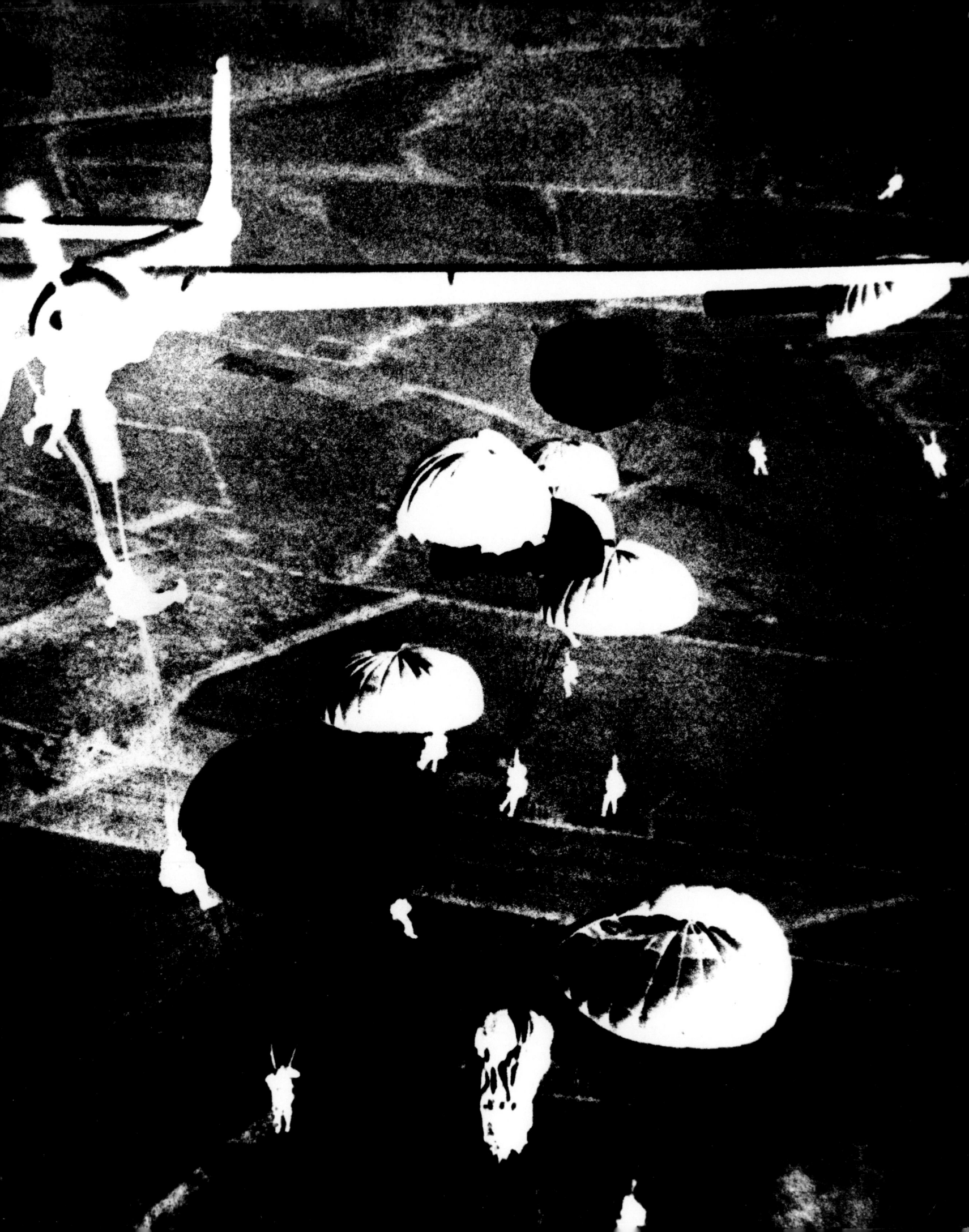

Passenger on the Shadows

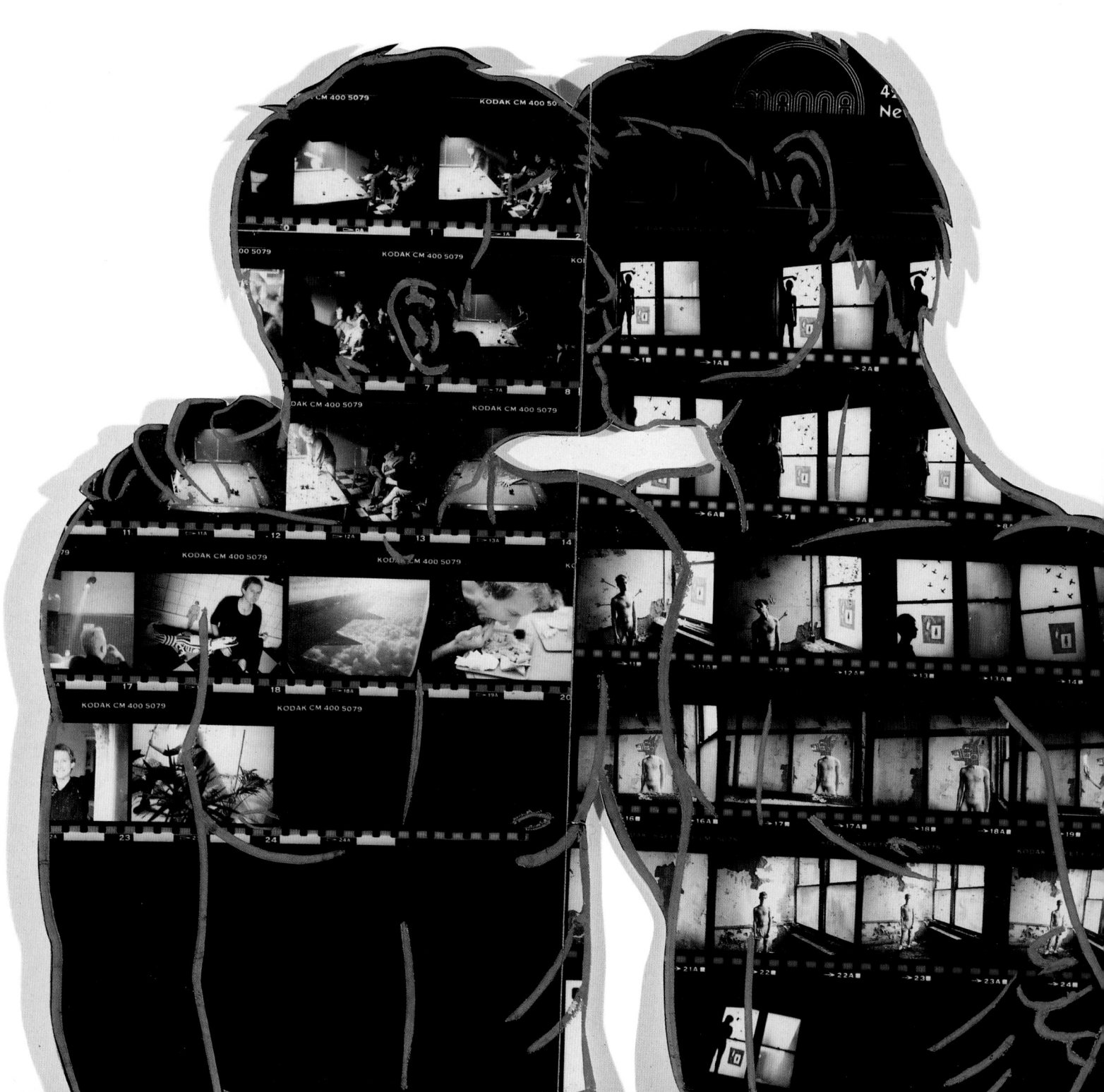

by Lucy R. Lippard

I have vivid memories of lightning through the glass windows of a darkened room.
                                                              —DAVID WOJNAROWICZ[1]

THE QUALITY OF LIGHT is a crucial feature in all of David Wojnarowicz's
art, and photography is the art of light and shadow, life and death. For a
sensitive child raised in a loveless darkness, light must always have played a
heightened role. Yet *lightning* is a better metaphor for what Wojnarowicz does
with the medium. He strikes with Olympian accuracy at the evil stupidities of an
American society beyond the fringes of which he often chose to live. The burning house or figure was his first artistic trademark, and he set some actual fires
in his long battle against greed and injustice. But if that were all he had done,
his art would not be as important as it is. The queer's X-ray vision reveals the
strata of love and desire, hatred and rage, that lie below the blowing dust of a
milennial culture.

   Wojnarowicz's photographs illuminate aspects of his ideas and creative
impulses that are neither as visible nor as available in his paintings, performances, film works, and actions. In their immediacy, their passion and lucidity,
their fierce authenticity, the photographs have more in common with his writings than with his paintings, for which they often provided raw material and
vignettes. The act of photography paralleled Wojnarowicz's compulsion, from an

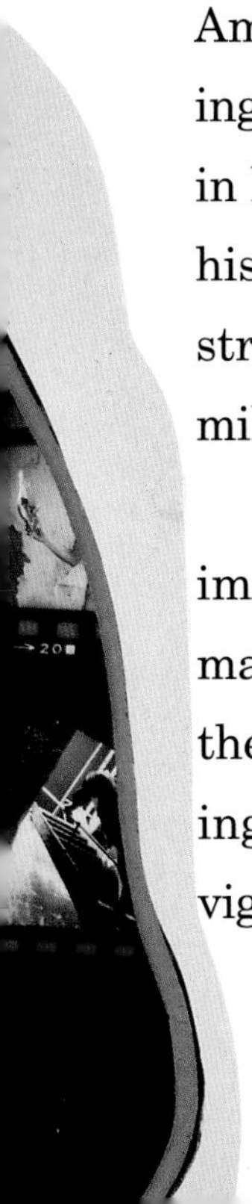

*All italicized passages
in this essay are by
David Wojnarowicz.*

Opposite: UNTITLED,
*1982. Acrylic on
color contact sheets,
11 x 12½"*

7

early age, to record an outlaw reality that is invisible in the dominant society. This need for total candor was a life force for the child of a violent family surrounded by neighbors who looked the other way and said nothing. *If you are a member of a minority it's a simple thing to be aware that laws are not meant as a reflection of the true society one lives in but rather as devices to control diversity and silence it.* In Wojnarowicz's photographs, the silence itself overwhelms the noise of a disintegrating civilization, the cries of pain, the crumbling of walls, the grinding of gears and screeching of brakes that are so prominent in many of his paintings. In the eight images of the "Sex Series," in particular, the nocturnal quiet of a sleeping monster is broken by views into other worlds. *I carry silence like a blood-filled egg, ready to drop it into someone's hands.*

In his writings as well as in his photographs, Wojnarowicz realized Christopher Isherwood's phrase, "I am a camera": *Someone once said that the ancients believed that light came from within the eyes and that you cast this light upon things in the world wherever you turned….When I move my eyes very slowly from left to right while sitting still, I can feel and hear a faint clicking sensation suggesting that vision is made up of millions of tiny stills as in transparencies. Since everything is generally in movement around us, then vision is made up of millions of "photographed" and recalled pieces of information.*

Wojnarowicz's first photographs, taken while he was in his teens, documented a daily life on the drug-sex-and-hunger-haunted streets that is almost unimaginable to those of us who have lived more prosaically: *A hustler nods out against a wall among the huge rush of people exiting from the three-dollar movie and he's squeezing his dick absentmindedly and I'm taking pictures which will never come out because of the light quality and the speed of the film but the visions are so intense that 'til the day I die I will always have these photographs in my brain.*

The camera he used was stolen and given to him by a friend, in around 1972; while he could liberate films from drugstores, there

was no money to print the hundreds of pictures. The films ended up first in bus-station lockers and then in some municipal lost and (never) found. So those first images remain illustrated only in the mind's eye as we read Wojnarowicz's writings. They were probably, like the later work, jolting illustrations of seeing–through.

He kept the camera and eventually shot more rolls; this time he was able to develop them. *For years ever since then, I've always taken pictures—wherever I go, I usually bring a camera. I would take rolls and rolls of film—mostly black and white—and get them developed as contact sheets.* By 1974 he was reading Jean Genet and William Burroughs. He recalled realizing then *what american society has been suppressing beneath its skin…. Realized this isn't nor has it ever been government for the people: felt more free with this acknowledgment.* The same year: *Came out to family and friends as a queer.*

These years of mobility and self-rehabilitation are indirectly chronicled in the extraordinarily poignant monologues that became *Sounds in the Distance*—conversations "photographically" recalled in great detail from the streets, the roads, the rooms, the coffee shops, the bars, the cars, the motels, and the beds Wojnarowicz had passed through in the seventies. By the end of the decade, he had traveled all over the United States, and in Mexico and France. Hitchhiking, freight hopping, biking, staying for some time in San Francisco, Paris, Normandy, farming on the Canadian border, Wojnarowicz sped through what was to be almost one third of his life: *I've always loved being anonymous and moving around traveling: In fact, that's the most powerful state for me to be in, away from any references. I love that moment. That's where my life makes sense…. I came to understand that to give up one's environment was to also give up biography and all the encoded daily movements: the false reassurances of the railing outside the door.* In the monologues recalled from the 1970s, the yearning, articulate voices of the unheard cry out for attention, as their lost images must also have punched their ways through the *dark veil.*

I never had access to a darkroom, but after Peter [Hujar's] *death, living in his place*

I've always loved being anonymous and moving around traveling: In fact, that's the most powerful state for me to be in….

Opposite: **UNTITLED**, *from the series "Arthur Rimbaud in New York," 1978–79. Gelatin-silver print, 10 x 8"*

I had access to his darkroom — that was the first time I was able to go back over years and years of negatives. That was in 1987–88. These negatives, and many slides, exist as an index to the artist's imagination. Wojnarowicz's own labels on the dozens of boxes, sheets, and envelopes of slides he left behind read like poetry, offering a synopsis of his iconography, and revealing the range of his vision. For example, one box: "sex images, frog (2 views), skeleton anatomy, skull, eyeball anatomy, maps Russia USA, Polaroid: target, rock surface, teepees, Navajo newspaper, corn and ruler, mummy, waterfall, electric chair drawing"; and another: "Rescue window man, men bridge drawing, bombed runway, Whirlpool, Pompeii dog, bridge, rib cage, roller coaster, leaf forest floor, clown head, lightning, snake head in jar, steelworks furnace, volcano cave earth crust, work stuff."

History is made and preserved by and for particular classes of people. A camera in some hands can preserve an alternative history. By 1979 Wojnarowicz had gotten hold of a broken super-8 camera, and he began making a film about heroin in an abandoned warehouse on the Hudson River (he flirted briefly with the drug himself, but made the film hoping to dissuade user friends). Like all of his work, it was informed by his sense of mortality. Technically a mess, and partially destroyed, the film has *beautiful sections of these very weird symbols. A person with a wrapped head, like an invisible man, would just sort of move into a room and through these endless door frames, like door frames on door frames on door frames, and all these beautiful elements of rust. So one figure's moving through the warehouse and another guy the same size, the same clothing, is moving in another direction and eventually they meet, on the roof, where you can see the Empire State Building, which is symbolic of the hypodermic. They collide on the rooftop. One holds out a gun and shoots the other in the head and all this ketchup flies out. He bends down and starts unwrapping the head and it turns out to be his own face that is revealed. Then it cuts into a hundred images of different people dead in their kitchens, on their rooftops, in their hallways, in the street.*

This was the first of some ten films Woj-narowicz shot but never edited or completed. One was about Hujar; another, called *Teaching a Frog to Dance (or Building a Patriotic Beast)* was two and a half minutes long and showed a disembodied pair of hands forcing a bullfrog to dance to patriotic music. *That's about making people go against their nature — the function of society.*

Also in 1979, with his old 35mm camera — now broken — Wojnarowicz began his first concentrated effort in photography: the series "Arthur Rimbaud in New York." In these thirty or so photographs of various friends wearing a sadly deadpan mask of the French poet (it has survived), he was *playing with ideas of compression of "historical time and activity" and fusing the french poet's identity with modern new york urban activities mostly illegal in nature.*

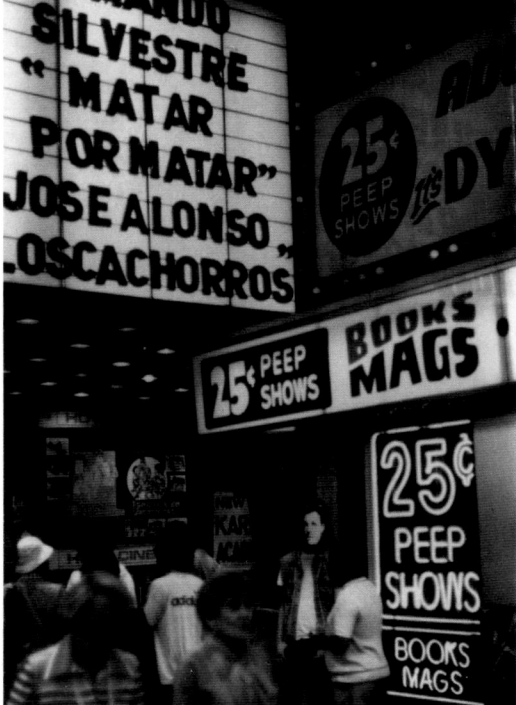

By this time, Wojnarowicz, though lacking in formal education, was highly literate, and identification with Rimbaud, the *poète maudit,* must have come naturally. A violently disruptive genius, author of *A Season in Hell,* he was homosexual, alcoholic, had lived on the streets and wandered Europe and North Africa; he died at thirty-seven (of carcinoma according to diagnosis, but it was likely syphilis), almost exactly a century before Woj-narowicz's own death from an equally painful and horrible disease. Described in his youth as a "lycanthropist" (lycanthropy was "the revolt of a maladjusted person against a society that he regards as shameful, and on which he piles every anathema he can think of"[2]), Rimbaud is the subject of essays with titles like "The Dialectics of Damnation," "The Poetics of Hallucination," and "The Aesthetics of Intoxication."[3]

Wojnarowicz's Rimbaud is always shown facing the camera, usually dressed conservatively in a dark turtleneck, white sweater, and suit jacket, or sleeveless with a vest. The mask photographs as almost real, its abnormal whiteness making the face the initial

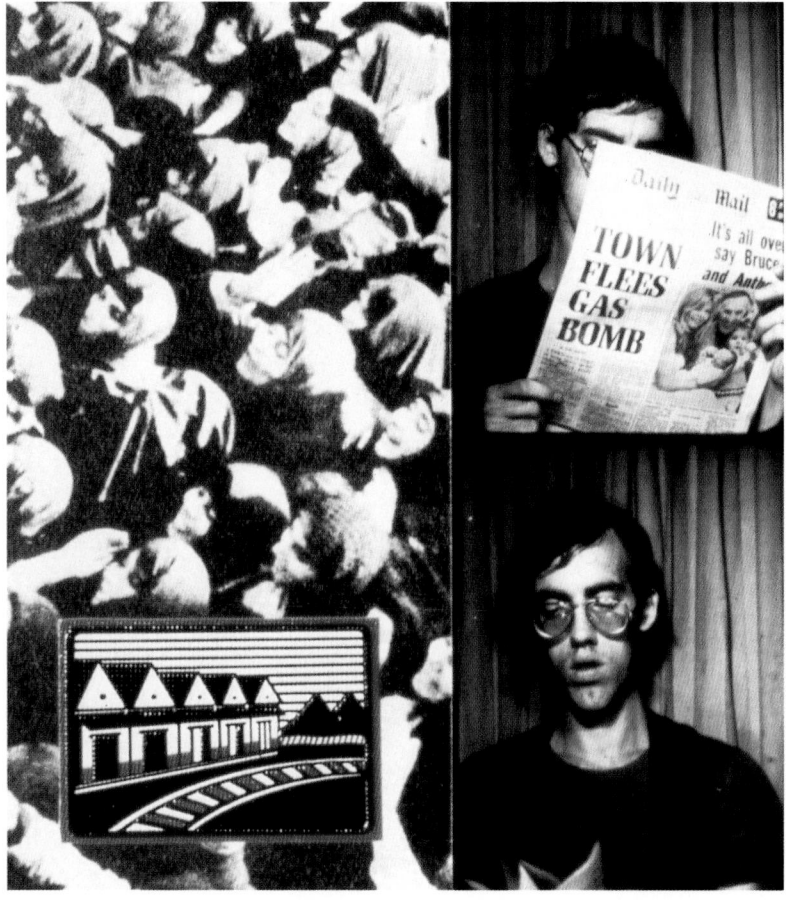

with other texts, such as Joseph Beuys's phrase "The Silence of Marcel Duchamp is Overrated." In one image, Rimbaud has sunk to the floor, a needle up his arm, a target behind his head like an off-center halo.

While this series is something of a one-liner compared to Wojnarowicz's later work, it is the first sustained visual artwork he made. (He didn't begin painting—off the walls—until 1982.) Even here, his photography is not "documentary" in any ordinary sense. The Rimbaud pictures reflect extremely personal emotions, *a particular frame of mind that only I can be sure of knowing, given that I have always felt alienated in this country, and thus have lived with the sensation of being an observer of my own life as it occurs.*

The Rimbaud images are, almost incidentally, beautifully composed and shot. Functioning as a *compression of historical time and activity*, they also constitute a kind of objective autobiography, permitting Wojnarowicz simultaneously to be himself and to step outside himself. The masked man records and perhaps exorcises a life his creator was gradually abandoning. Photographs, like writing, he said, could *strip the power from a memory or an event...cut the ropes of an experience.* At the same time, for viewers, those connections are not cut, but forged.

It would be impossible to write about Wojnarowicz's art, place him in art history, without retracing his tragically amazing biography. His work was made defiantly outside of contemporary art history, even as it helped form it. To ignore his life would be a betrayal of everything that he was trying to do: *Worked on a series of drawings that revealed everything people are pressured not to reveal.... All my life I've made things that are like fragmented mirrors of what I perceive to be the world.... Shifted my ideas of what making things could be. Started developing ideas of making and preserving an authentic version of history in the form of images/writings/objects that would contest state-supported forms of "history." Didn't really believe that it would survive time.*

Wojnarowicz was nine when he began hustling around Times Square, and he continued until he was seventeen, *looking for the*

focus of each image, before the surroundings are taken in. The series includes a tough Rimbaud in an undershirt, cigarette in closed mouth. Then he is on the Jersey shore; there's a working ship in the horizon (perhaps a reference to the artist's father). He appears in the bottom third of a photo under a sign that says simply "Entrance" on an industrial waterfront; next to a "primitively" painted palm-reader's sign and before another work of people's art (a Puerto Rican mural). He is in a subway headed for Flatbush Avenue; twice under a city bridge; four times hustling on Forty-second Street (with bar, peep show, bookstore). He is eating in a diner; in a meat-packing factory; lying on a bed with a beer, reading, then jerking off. Eight images were taken in the Hudson River warehouse that Wojnarowicz used as his studio/sketchbook/journal in those years. In scenes reminiscent of the heroin film, Rimbaud is seen holding a gun; standing before a passageway of door frames; next to some of Wojnarowicz's works, including Japanese ideographs and quotes from a book of American slang ("Junk, Nothing but Junk"), and

TOWN FLEES GAS BOMB,
SELF PORTRAIT, *1979.*
Black-and-white photographs
and collage on paper, 4⅛ x 3¾"

Opposite: UNTITLED, *1981.*
Black-and-white photograph
and spray paint on wood,
11 x 19"

weight of some man to lie across me to replace the nonexistent hugs and kisses from my mom and dad. On a secret visit to his mother in Manhattan, before he and his siblings moved in with her, they went to the Museum of Modern Art, where Pavel Tchelitchew's painting *Hide and Seek* made an impression on the child who sometimes hid in the trees. *I wanted to be an artist after that.* Ten years and an ordinary lifetime's worth of hair-raising experiences later, he says he *became a writer and took photographs.* It was almost another ten years later that he began paint-

circuit the sensory discs. I'm the robotic kid looking through digital eyes past the windshield into the pre-invented world.

The "pre-invented world" (which implies a certain fatalism) and the government-imposed illusion of a "one-tribe nation" (his aim was to break it all down into its diverse components) formed the armature of Wojnarowicz's inimical cosmography. In a double play, Carlo McCormick once called him "the outsider who refused to be taken in." If his paintings were the vehicles to a certain acceptance in the art world, the photographs

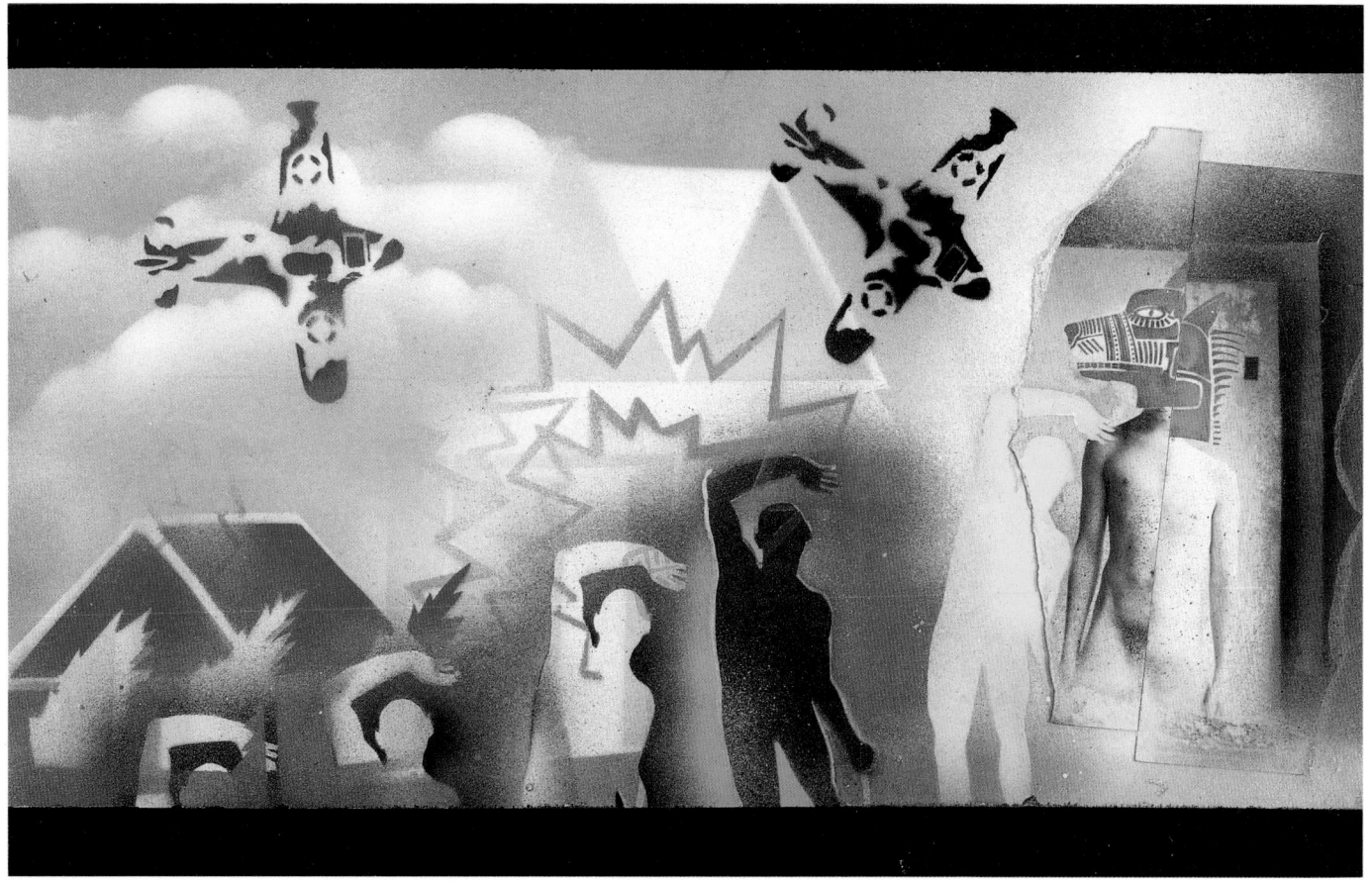

ing on canvas, so photography was his first visual art.

Wojnarowicz's autobiographical chronology in the catalog for the 1990 "Tongues of Flame" exhibition stops dead in 1982, the year he began to paint, marking, perhaps, the death of the total outsider: *Became more active in exploring art as a record of the times we live in as well as a vehicle of communication between members of certain social structures and minorities. I'm the robotic kid with caucasian kid programming trying to short-*

remained a source of trouble, even when they were copied or incorporated into a painting. It was, for instance, a selection of photographs and vignettes painted after photographs that the not-so-reverend Donald Wildmon of the American Family Association fallaciously extracted in 1990 for his virtually pornographic flyer to thousands of outraged Christians, informing them that "Your Tax Dollars Helped Pay for These Works of Art." *I think Wildmon should get himself a Gallery because he's a great appropriationist,* sug-

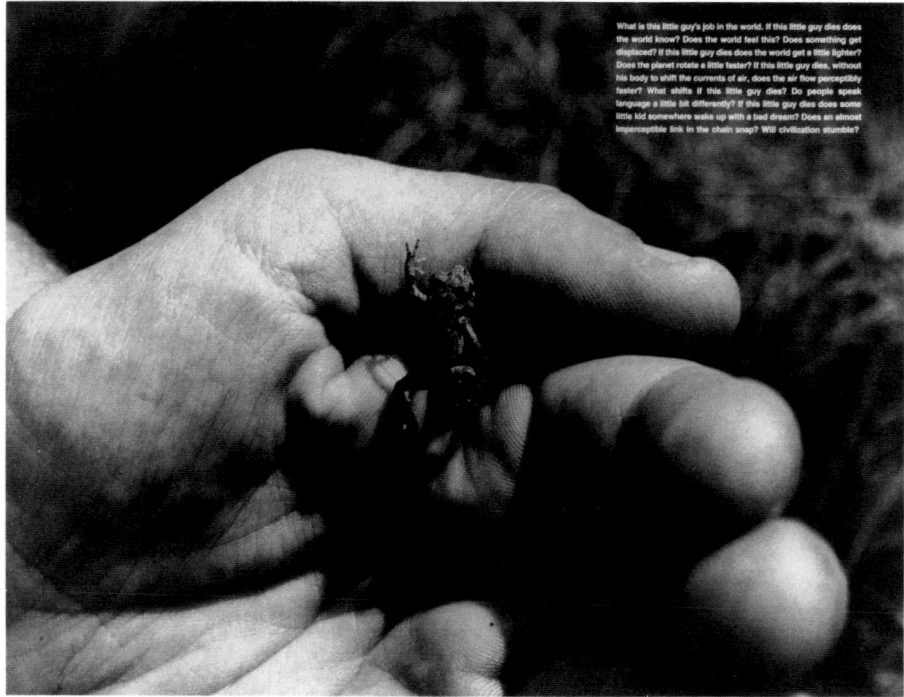

What is this little guy's job in the world. If this little guy dies does the world know? Does the world feel this? Does something get displaced? If this little guy dies does the world get a little lighter? Does the planet rotate a little faster? If this little guy, without his body to shift the currents of air, does the air flow perceptibly faster? What shifts if this little guy dies? Do people speak language a little bit differently? If this little guy dies does some little kid somewhere wake up with a bad dream? Does an almost imperceptible link in the chain snap? Will civilization stumble?

WHAT'S THIS LITTLE GUY'S JOB IN THE WORLD, *from an untitled series, 1990. Gelatin-silver print, 13½ x 19"*

Opposite: **ANATOMY & ARCHITECTURE OF DESIRE,** *1988–89. Gelatin-silver prints and acrylic on wood, triptych, 70½ x 34" overall*

gested Wojnarowicz, who litigated with the Center for Constitutional Rights as a freedom of expression issue. (In a token victory, he was awarded only one dollar by the court.)

Despite the need to maintain "digital eyes" and a necessary armor for his own vulnerability (*I have always experienced fear living in the world…. Maybe it was daddy, maybe it was mommy, maybe it was the American dream*), Wojnarowicz was also capable of extreme compassion for others' pain. Regarding a writer whose unrequited and unwelcome advances to him constituted harassment and finally psychological violence, Wojnarowicz wrote (in the *East Village Eye,* 1986): *His gestures toward love were set up with a built-in rejection. And if anyone deserves some sense of love it is this guy.* While he had every reason to be a sociophobe, Wojnarowicz always had close friends—those to whom he dedicated *Close to the Knives:* …*all the guys and girls future and past who give chaos reason and delight* [among them] *the drag queens along the Hudson River and their truly revolutionary states…for their beautiful brush fires in the social landscape.* Perhaps some of Wojnarowicz's "luck" in surviving the roughest trade out there can be attributed to the tenderness he seems to have brought with him to even the most sordid encounters. Similarly his "luck" in the art world

was augmented (or countered) by the extraordinary honesty and responsible humanity (is it too corny to call it love?) that was inseparable from the work, and from the rage.

This same tenderness and compassion—the antidote to outrage, just as the peaceful, ordered photographs might be seen as antidotes to the furious chaos of many of the paintings—is evident in the photograph of a hand holding a frog, very gently. Another picture shows a beetle crawling across a palm, and a third—of a much smaller frog in a hand—bears a text that begins "What is this little guy's job in the world?" Wojnarowicz's identification with the vulnerability of animals parallels that found in much early feminist art. Citing the way "most artists" use human figures to convey emotion, he decided early on to *take that power away from people and give it back to "nature" by using animals as metaphors.* (Ignatz the mouse from the comic "Krazy Kat" is the artist's revolutionary stand-in in early work.)

A powerful image of battered, bandaged hands holding an empty nest suggests either desolation or the healing power of "nature." (The wounded hands also appear in a painting and in *Close to the Knives,* pushed between prison bars, reaching out for falling snowflakes. *I was thinking of human society's rejection of nature. That came from thinking about the word "nature," which we immediately distanced ourselves from the moment we invented the word for it, even though we're part of it. It completely surrounds us. We ingest it in order to survive, we breathe because of it.*

In the unrelenting flow of rage and misery that emerges from Wojnarowicz's narratives, however, what passes for "nature" in our culture does play a major role—benign and at times terrifyingly transformative. Wojnarowicz remarked on recurring dreams about tornadoes and tidal waves that continued for years. In real life, escaping evil, he often fled into the woods: *I think of these trees and how they look like the winter forests of my childhood and how they were always places of refuge: endless hours spent among them creating small myths of myself alone or living in hollowed-out trees or sleeping in nests twenty times larger than crows' nests made of sticks instead of twigs. I realized then how I always*

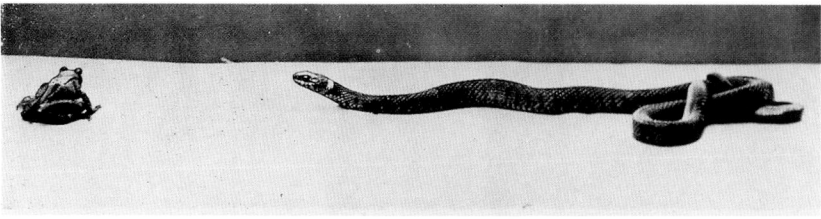

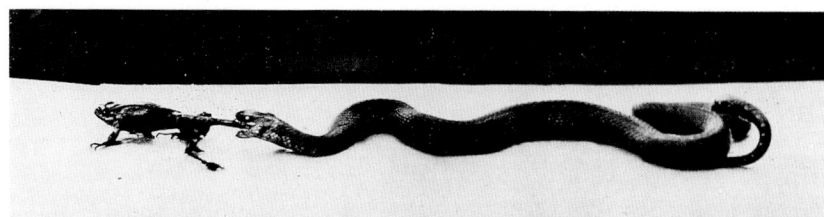

tend to mythologize the people, things, landscapes I love, always wanting them to somehow extend forever through time and motion.... Once I discovered the universe of the forests and lakes, I went there whenever possible to forget the irrational brutality and violence experienced in the tiny version of hell called the suburbs...the Universe of the Neatly Clipped Lawn. On the other hand, Wojnarowicz knew what it was like to be in the "jungle" of the inner city, to be hunted, and to hunt for survival. (A five-part photo narrative that he used in several works shows a large snake approaching a frog, catching it, and swallowing it, in stages.)

In another recurring dream, which he first experienced in 1963, he was...*walking a dirt road and finding a pond and diving in and swimming to the bottom and entering a cave and swimming til I'd run out of air and at the last moment surfacing inside a cave filled with beautiful stalactites and stalagmites that were iridescent, I'd wake up peaceful.* Wojnarowicz followed up on this one, taking buses into the country, finding a lake or pond, wading in fully dressed, then hitchhiking back to the city. The images of water in his art similarly imply a kind of purification or comforting oblivion. In another dream, he heard the line "This is life—let's swim in it." Dirt seems to have played the same role. (Both could be seen as a return to origins.) He made several photographs of objects buried in or lying on crumbling dirt, the most haunting of which is his own face, partially buried, eyes closed. Most easily read as an image of death, it can also be seen as an emergence myth. The eyes are tightly closed, as though they are about to open, while the artist creates, or gives birth to himself from *prima materia*: *the face beneath the sands of the desert still breathing.* In *Dust Track I* and *II*, he concentrated, rather atypically, on the patterns made in a silvery sand by tires under a parking garage in Paris—not coincidentally Duchampian turf—which formally recall Max Ernst's frottages.

If Wojnarowicz must be "placed" in the art world, he belongs less with his East Village contemporaries than in the company of older mavericks like Dan Graham (the New Jersey photographs of the late 1960s), and especially Robert Smithson, with whom the

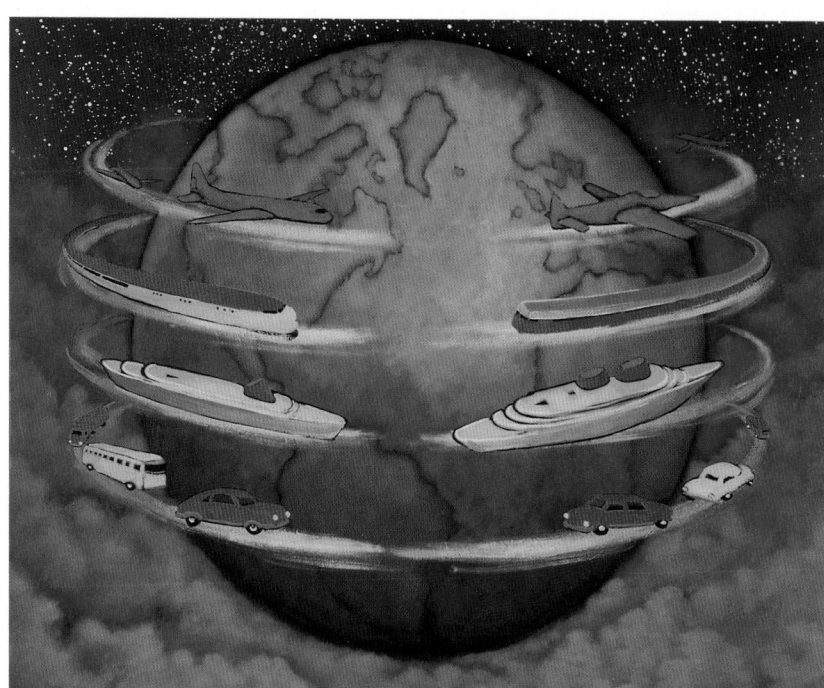

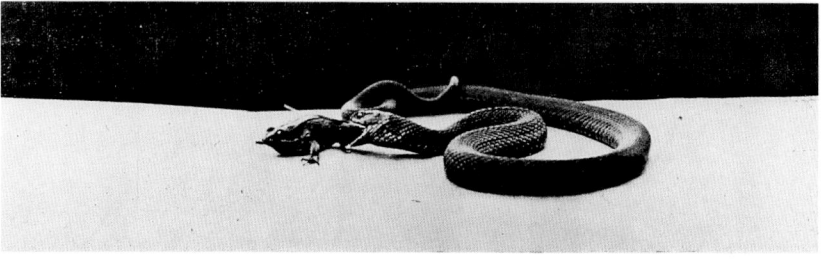

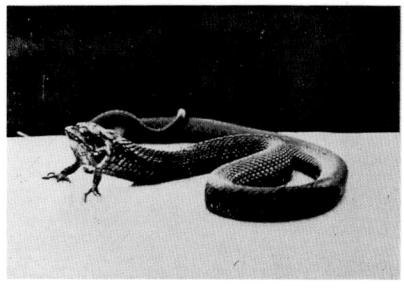

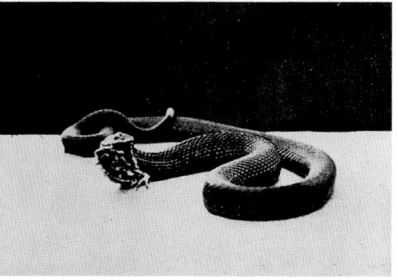

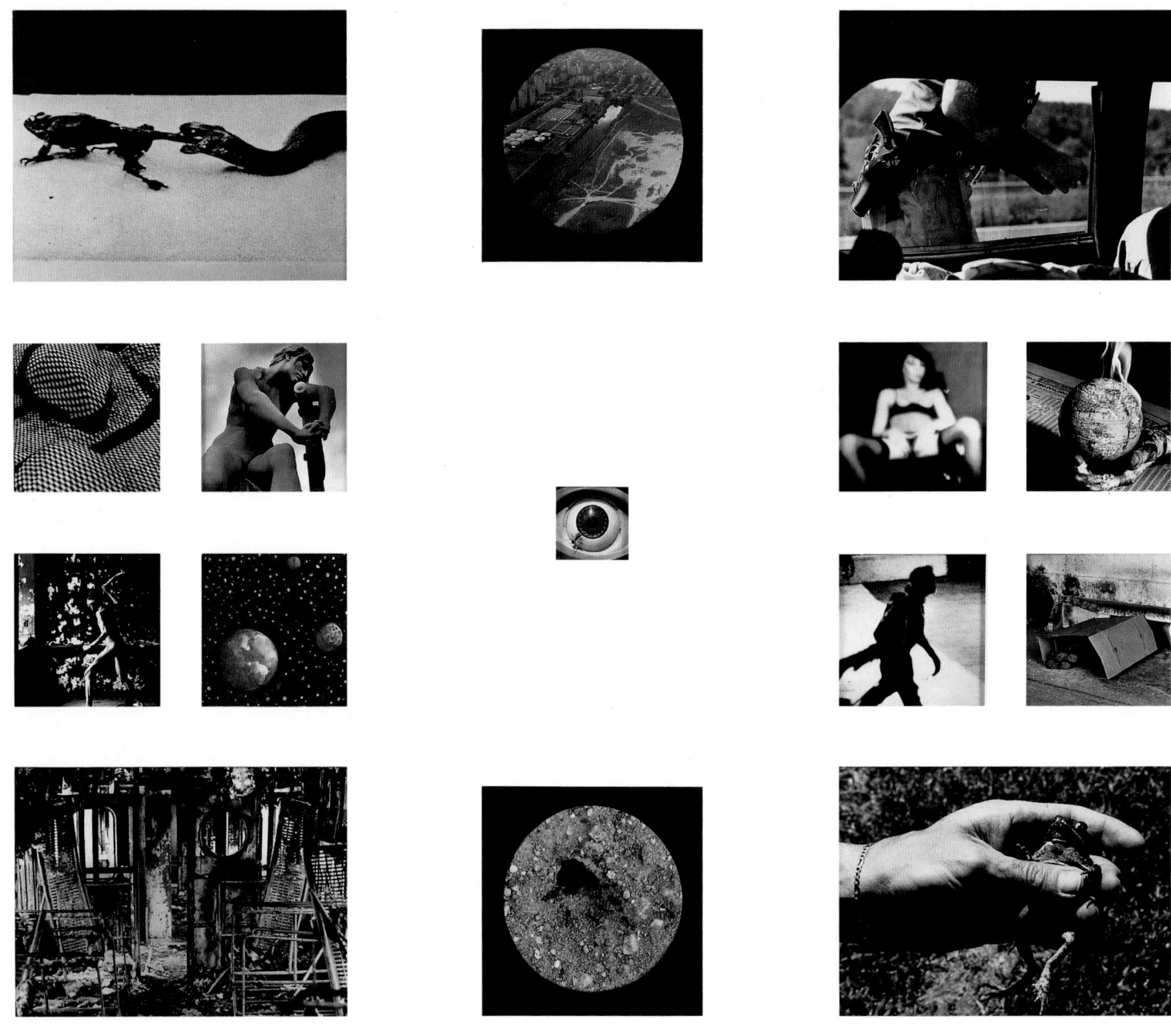

**WEIGHT OF THE EARTH
PART II**, *1988– 89.*
Gelatin-silver prints and
watercolor on museum
board, 39 x 41½" overall

parallels are less historical than uncanny. It
seems unlikely that Wojnarowicz was greatly
interested in Smithson's work. He was not a
"gallery-goer," and for all Smithson's interdisciplinary wanderings, he was deeply involved in the art world that Wojnarowicz
warily rejected. Smithson was killed in a
plane accident in 1973, while the younger
man was still on the road. Yet both were
artists whose writings were "literary" rather
than "critical"; both used photography to
great effect, and neither considered himself
a photographer. Above all, they shared a per-
verse and similar sensibility.[4] Even Smith-

son's early collages look like awkward studies
for Wojnarowicz's later and fully realized
paintings. There are many distinct elements
common to both artists' work: New Jersey,
science fiction (especially by J. G. Ballard),
maps, reptiles, dirt, dinosaurs, geological
time, and a fascination with the industrial
landscape and architectural decay. A little-
known series of Smithson's images reverses
landscape from positive to negative as Wojnarowicz did in the "Sex Series." And of
course both died in their thirties. In Smithson's text "Incidents of Mirror-Travel in the
Yucatan," the god Tezcatlipoca — "demiurge

of the 'smoking mirror'"—tells the artist: "That camera is a portable tomb, you must remember that."[5]

As Victor Masayesva writes:

Photography is a philosophical sketching that makes it possible to define and then to understand our ignorance. Photography reveals to me how it is that life and death can be so indissolubly one; it reveals the falseness of maintaining these opposites as separate. Photography is an affirmation of opposites. The negative contains the positive.[6]

It has become a cliché to call photography the art of memory, yet it is impossible to avoid the way it played that role in Wojnarowicz's life and work. *There's a constant associative quality to everything that can spark a memory from a year ago or something that I witnessed ten years ago....It's breaking the barriers of time.* After leaving the streets, his *restless walks* took him back there—*slight traces that cut me with the wounding nature of deja vu, filled with old senses of desire. Each desire, each memory, so small a thing, becomes a small river tracing the outlines and the drift of your arms and bare legs, dark mouth and the spoken words of strangers.*

In 1990 Wojnarowicz was asked by the University of the Arts in Philadelphia to be a "visiting photographer"—which was exactly how he saw himself in relation to the medium: *I don't even know how to operate a camera on anything other than automatic.... I woke up one night with the thought that the people in this society we call America who can read the instruction manuals from front to back and then follow them to the letter are people in positions of power.* He used the talk as an educational polemic on the role of the media in American life, the "dangerousness of the 12-inch-tall politician" (the one seen only on TV, never in real life); the ordinary citizen's lack of access to the media (*As a person who owns a camera I am in direct competition with the owners of television stations and newspapers....*); and the lethal censorship of AIDS information. In passing, he observed that in the art world, *photography is one of the most misunderstood mediums because no one can really explain in a rational*

way what makes a good or bad photograph other than the artist's intent.... The nature of the camera's mechanisms makes it possible to never take a 'bad' photograph. You can always get something on film and if it is blurry and out of focus 'badly' lit you only have to claim intent and the art world will consider it.

His stills were often from movies, printed from super-8 film. In one series of photos (a cockfight, a breaking wave, the legs of burlesque dancers, the mummy of a child), the film reference is made clear by the inclusion, in merged bands, of parts of the upper and lower frames, so that each image is literally framed by the partial repetition that characterizes photography as a medium and also characterizes Wojnarowicz's use of certain images. *I used to wonder where the urge to photograph came from. I mean, there are literally billions of photographs of the Eiffel Tower spread all over the world by tourists with cameras. I imagine people sleep better at night having those daily proofs of the existence of the Eiffel Tower in boxes underneath their beds.*

Scorn for the art world's permissiveness, and insecurity about the quality of his own obsessive, almost casual photographic activity may have kept Wojnarowicz from taking photography "seriously" in an aesthetic sense until after Peter Hujar's death (which may also have been a factor; it was, after all, his mentor's medium). Until then, despite the major role of photography in his creative life, Wojnarowicz used it primarily as a source, collaged or imitated, usually in miniature scale, in his paintings.

Wojnarowicz was twenty-six in 1980 when he met Hujar—surrogate father, brother, briefly lover—the strongest and most positive influence of his life: *My experiences with Peter were in a great way responsible for everything that I've done. He encouraged me in a way that I had never gotten. It was like finding a member of one's own tribe, such a similar frame of reference, only*

> I woke up one night with the thought that the people in this society we call America who can read the instruction manuals from front to back and then follow them to the letter are people in positions of power.

a 20-year age difference....He really demanded that you bring it all right up to the front and not deny things.

Hujar is best known for his book *Portraits in Life and Death* (1976), which combined images of mummies in the Palermo catacombs (taken in 1963) with portraits (taken in 1974–75) of his friends — a motley and fascinating crew, including Susan Sontag, William S. Burroughs, Edwin Denby, Divine, Fran Lebowitz, Anne Wilson, Vince Aletti, Paul Thek, Charles Ludlam, Anne Waldman, and John Ashbery, among others. His later portrait of Wojnarowicz is one of the most beautiful, and sexiest, reflections of that lean and intense figure. Hujar confirmed many of Wojnarowicz's own suspicions about being an "artist." *Peter always told me the art world is not about art. He managed to keep the art world at a distance. He was always aggressive about it, alienating people. The anger he carried alarmed people. He had a flurry of attention in the 70s and successfully shoved it all away. I could see it in myself — this sort of self destructive streak in terms of the formalities of the art world. He looked at it as self protection. It protects the source of what you do.*

Perhaps in respect for Hujar's earlier work, Wojnarowicz never incorporated into his art the extraordinary series of photographs — actually film stills — that he took of mummies in Guadalajara in 1986. In grainy, blurry outline, he captured the circle of life/death with the mummies of children aged by decay and adults returned by the same process to a fetal innocence. The figures of the dead — usually fully dressed — become dolls, idols, babies, crones. The "expressions" on their faces range from poignant to ecstatic to ferocious, a full panoply of human emotion in stop time. (Only one appears in Wojnarowicz's formal œuvre; it is not, oddly, one of the most powerful, although the choice of a screaming child was understandable.) A social component is added by the fact that these were bodies exhumed and exposed because there was no money to maintain their graves.

Hujar had given him some printing pointers, but Wojnarowicz recalled developing *an eye for printing and the possibilities in the print more than my physical experience*

UNTITLED, *1989.*
Black-and-white photographs,
acrylic, spray paint, and
collage on Masonite, 48 x 96"

in printing would let me catch up to. That creates a lot of tension in the photograph itself....
I just try to follow intuitively what properties of the print attract me — the luminous edges, or whatever. Only a small percentage of these prints "became art," but had Wojnarowicz

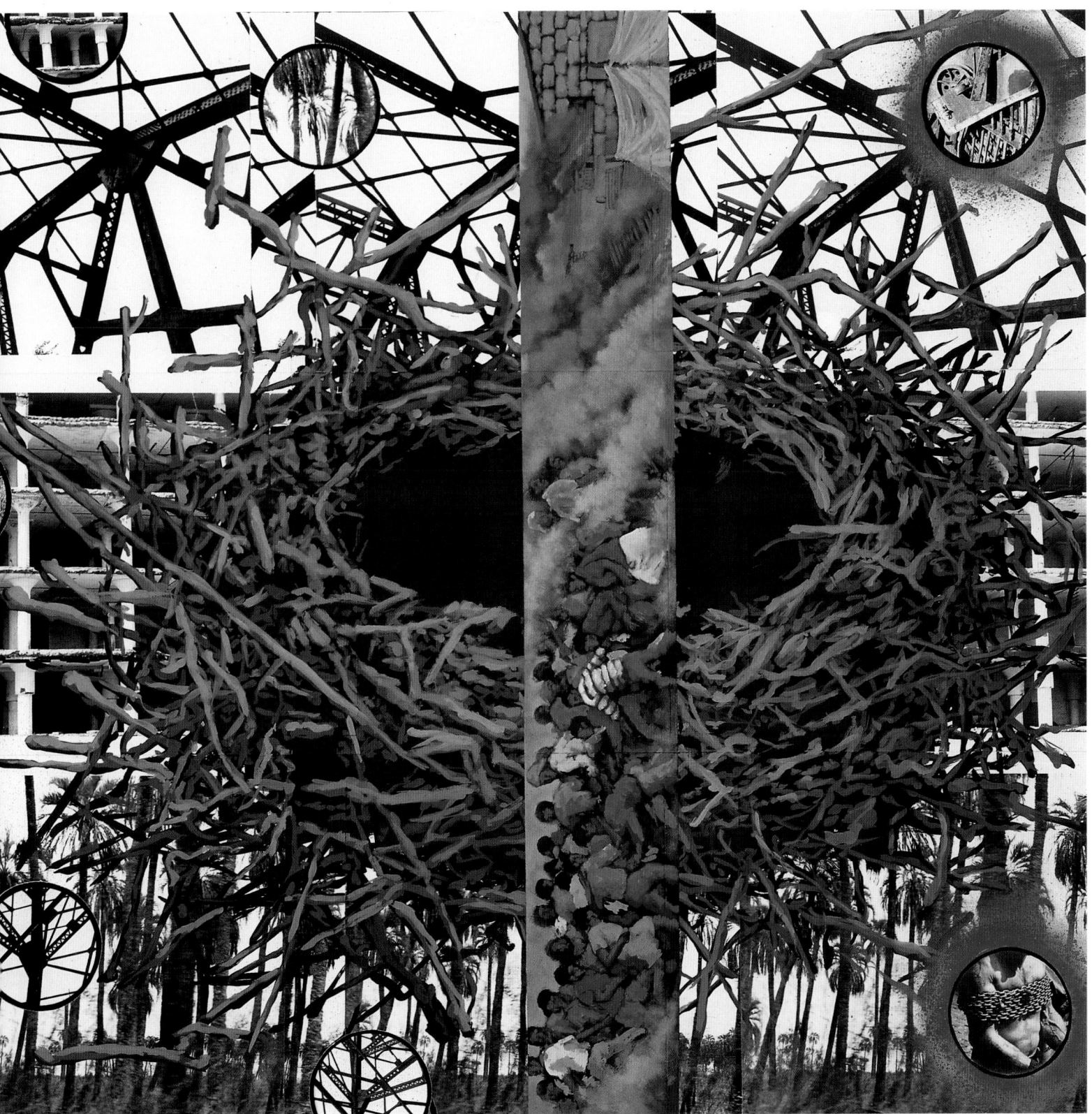

concentrated on photography rather than on painting, certainly many more of them would be perceived as his Art.

Any medium Wojnarowicz touched became clearly his. His visionary genius transformed whatever he took up. It was more than a question of style. In 1989 he performed *ITSOFOMO* with Ben Neill at The Kitchen. His videotape was reportedly the most striking element of the performance piece. He described it as *beluga whales and black water... these images slowly came out of darkness, appeared and disappeared, then as the performance went on started accelerating and by the end it was like the monitor had exploded with information and images…. The Cardinal O'Connor image was the scariest in the show. I projected it as a slide on the wall and used a strobe camera to start from way back so it was just a point of light then it twisted and curved and suddenly this frantic face came right up into the frame and on the other three monitors were rats decomposing at an accelerated pace like those Disney flowers that open up. And images of Christ's head blowing up with firecrackers, images of workers breaking apart a church in Mexico.*

The apocalyptic tone of Wojnarowicz's work is not surprising. From an early age, the artist took risks; this was simply part of a life that could never be taken for granted. At six he was almost swept away by a flood, and a childish "game" might have been a proto–Chris Burden performance: *Me and another kid would lie down on the long sloping highway outside our doors to make the enormous trucks that came barreling over the hill hit their brakes. At the last second, we'd jump up and run into the woods.* He was six or seven when he was homosexually initiated — by a teenage neighbor, and by his own mad and violent father, who also made a habit of shooting his pets, shooting guns in the living room, and putting a gun to the heads of his wives and children, whom he beat with dog chains and two-by-fours. At ten, Wojnarowicz *developed a habit of hanging off the roof ledge by my fingertips, dangling over 8th avenue at night as a test of strength.* Later in life he would close his eyes for a quarter of a mile at a time while driving fast through the Southwest—as if life itself had not offered him enough cliff-hangers.

Reading the autobiographical chronology in the "Tongues of Flame" exhibition catalog, it seems incredible that Wojnarowicz was neither killed nor jailed. Despite the extraordinary pain from a childhood he never could shake, in some ways he led a charmed life. When he was four, his grandmother told him often and at length that she saw angels around him. At seven he was told by the Mother Superior at his Catholic school that

he was "in the devil's wings and would go to hell." Death was always at his side and at one point he began to think he was indestructible. *Hell is a place on earth. Heaven is a place in your head.* Then came AIDS, so often touted as a biblical plague, and Peter Hujar's death, and his own diagnosis, which changed everything.

When I found out I felt this abstract sensation, something like pulling off your skin and turning it inside out and then rearranging it so that when you pull it back on it feels like what it felt like before, only it isn't and only you know it…the first minute after being diagnosed you are forever separated from what you had come to view as your life or living, the world outside the eyes. The calendar tracings of biographical continuity get kind of screwed up….the entire landscape and horizon is pulling away from you in reverse order to spell out a psychic separation.

From this period came the most emotionally successful painting-with-photographs Wojnarowicz did. *Untitled* (1988) combines the most outraged text about AIDS that he wrote (beginning "*If I had a dollar to spend for health care*" and ending "*…all I can feel is the pressure and the need for release*") and three of the most beautiful photographs — taken moments after Peter Hujar's death, of his face, his hand, his feet. If Wojnarowicz's photographic reputation were based on these pictures alone he would go down in posterity, but the small painting with a border of photos, money, place-names (AIDS is everywhere) and collaged sperm-shapes (invading the White House on a twenty-dollar bill) cut into geometric ideographs — is a masterful summing-up of his talents. It has become a talisman for the growing body of art about AIDS.

The "Sex Series" also comes from this anguished, but fertile, period. He said it was about surveillance and sexual diversity. At an early age Wojnarowicz was told that God sees and knows all. The idea for the inset circles came from an experience in Mexico City, when he stood on a cliff over a very poor barrio and looked down through the zoom-lens of a super-8 camera at a one-legged man and a child playing on a headless rocking horse. In a passage that also reflects on the scale changes he used so well in his paintings and photography, Wojnarowicz remarked on the

Hell is a place
on earth.
Heaven is a place
in your head.

Opposite: FUCK YOU
FAGGOT FUCKER, *1984.*
*Black-and-white photographs,
acrylic, and collage on
Masonite, 48 x 48"*

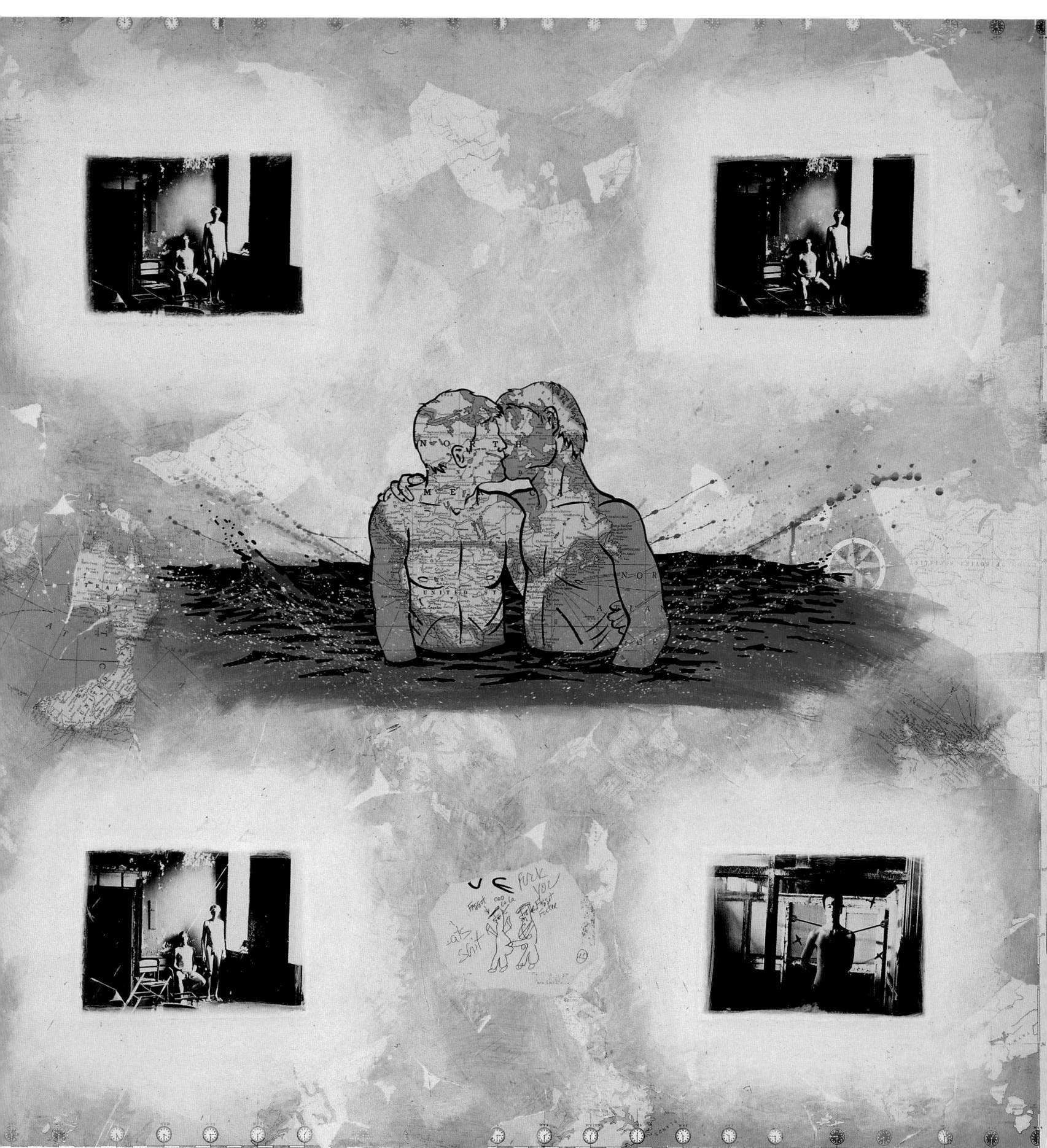

parallels between photography itself and *the act of surveillance; or the searching for evidence whether through the circular portal of a telescope as in looking into outer space, or the circular portal of a microscope as in examining matter for evidence of disease or foreign life.* He said the circle also represented a cell (presumably a reference to the AIDS virus as well); those round apertures, portholes, peepholes (as in Forty-second Street porn shows) also suggest orifices. The camera is not only eye but body part. The eye as target, the target as eye, looking the murderers in the eye, the lens. *To make the private into something public is an action that has terrific repercussions in the pre-invented world.*

Although he was using more photographs in his paintings at the same time, the first fully photographic pieces, in 1988, were surprisingly austere, and a few images were allowed to stand on their own, such as the marvelous untitled picture of buffalo plunging over a cliff, taken from a diorama in the Museum of Natural History in Washington, D.C. This dramatic image of the cruel destruction of useful nature—disturbing in its fusion of natural and unnatural—became one of his best-known works (it was used as an album cover by the rock band U2). For the most part, however, the photos he used over the years were arranged in balanced rows, or else framing a single, often smaller image (as if vanishing), such as the grinning dog with large, superimposed teeth in *The Weight of the Earth Part I*, or the false eyeball with an ant crawling on it in *The Weight of the Earth Part II*. The surrounding vignettes in these and related works are the components of the vocabulary gathered in his travels—sometimes enigmatic, sometimes polemic (as in the ones centered on the American flag and on the blue/red screaming head).

The "Sex Series" was sparked by an accident in the darkroom, which showed Wojnarowicz how to overlay images by blocking

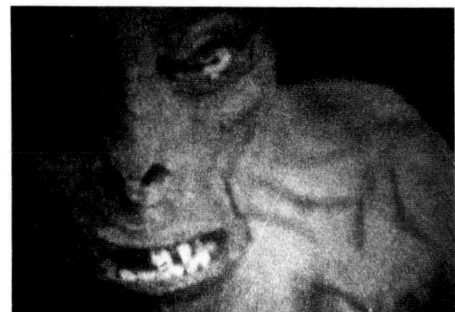

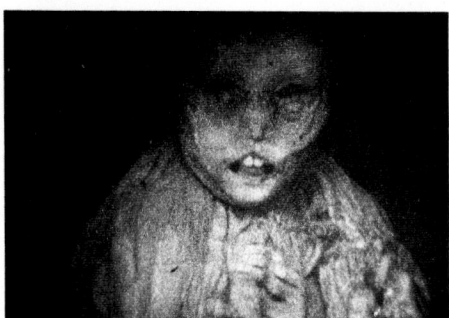

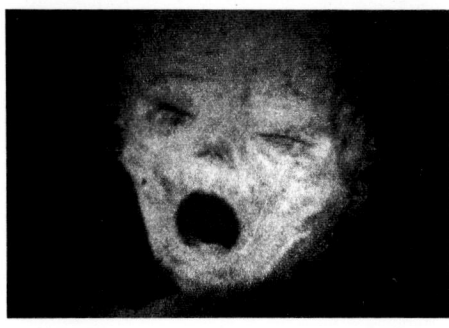

MEXICAN MUMMIES, *1986–87.*
Three black-and-white photographs made from super-8 film stills

Opposite: UNTITLED, *1989.*
Black-and-white and color photographs on museum board, 22¼ x 30½" overall

out areas and reprinting. The images in this case came *out of the writing and they worked their way into photography.* They were also fueled by an experience in Paris, where a homoerotic piece of Wojnarowicz's was censored from a show that was purportedly about sex, but was actually, he realized, about *straight white male fantasies.* The photomontages (not collages) were enlarged from color slides and printed on black-and-white paper, and the effect is even eerier than a simple negative reversal. Three of the pictures include texts. The strongest ones are the simpler ones—those in which each of the five striking "landscapes" (aerial views of two bridges into Manhattan; ship at sea; plane spewing parachutists; house and water tower; and dead trees in swamp water) is pierced by a single "hole" into the private realm of sexual experience—all the basic gender couplings, literally a series, or serial sexuality. The disks of erotic imagery (appropriated from Hujar's porn collection) hover over the quotidian landscapes like huge moons, other planets, invading spaceships, or parallel realities. Everything is dark and silent. The reversal of light and dark generates new sources of light and energy, haloing mouths, genitals, hands. *These days I see the edge of mortality. The edge of death and dying is around everything like a warm halo of light sometimes dim sometimes irradiated.*

Perhaps the most haunting of these five is the anonymous white house and water tower. The circular and angular forms evoke UFOs and "ordinary" people as well as Truman Capote's *In Cold Blood* and other rural/suburban nightmares—partly because of a reference in Wojnarowicz's writings to the water tower as a sniper's nest.

The three remaining images in the "Sex Series" are: a serpentine train in a western landscape with text and four "holes"; the Manhattan bridges again, with two text blocks, five circles, and a chaotic montage that is difficult to decipher; and a tornado flanked by six disks and overwritten with three texts. Despite the texts, these three are harder to "read" than the other five, whose oneiric simplicity remains open to any number of subtle and sinister interpretations. The tornado piece is the most overtly ominous, its cameos revealing blood cells, a radio

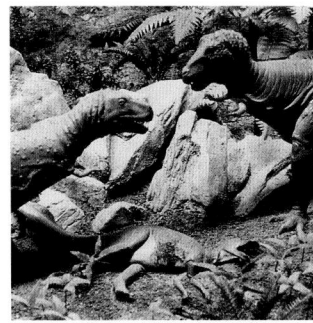

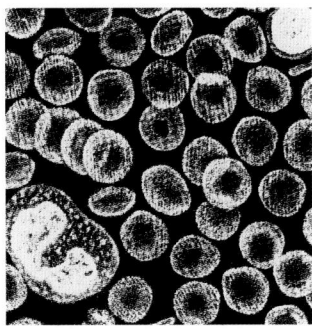

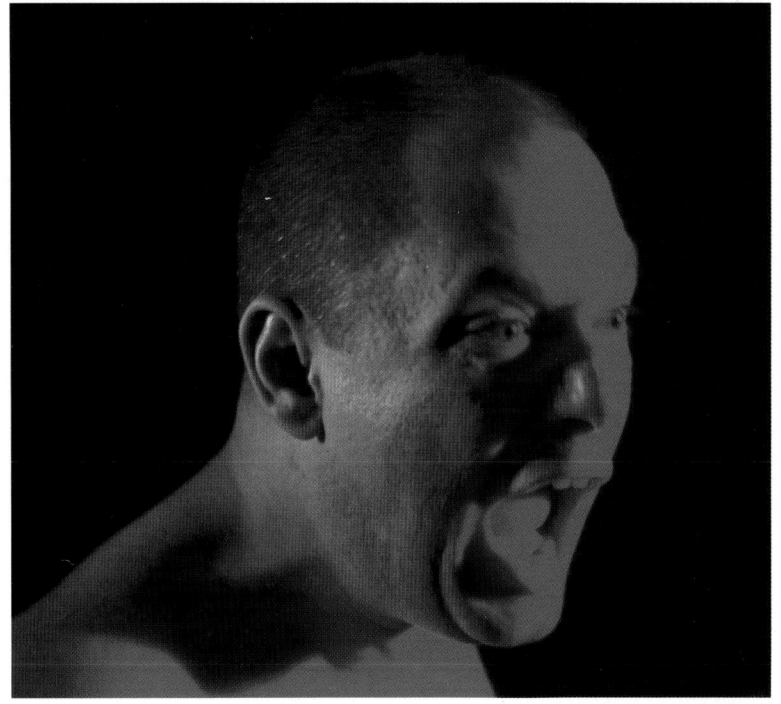

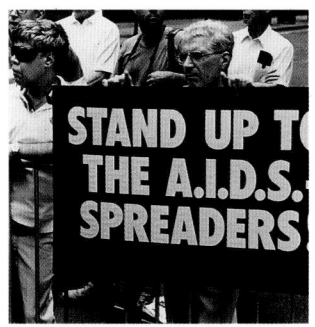

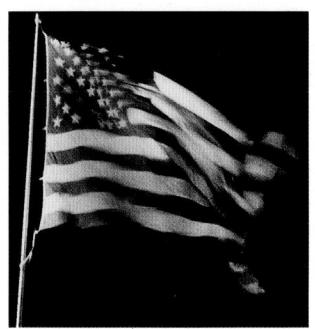

transmitter, money, a baby skeleton, and Saint Sebastian; its texts lead inexorably from a satisfying subway pickup to violence against gay men to the use of AIDS as a weapon against ignorance.

The role of photography in Wojnarowicz's paintings, and his photographs' relationship to the paintings, are issues that are complicated by the fact that he crossed the barriers of medium with such ease (so photography's role is just that of any other element in the complex whole that is his life's work); they are simplified by the fact that the content is the same as in other media. The painstaking reproduction in paint of found and original photographs in the "Elements" series — the four impressive paintings that brought Wojnarowicz serious attention in the art world when shown at Gracie Mansion's gallery in 1986 — may have been in the interest of a unified surface.

Collage, with or without the glue, has been the stylistic/emotive armature for Wojnarowicz's art since the beginning. It was stimulated by the jolt from juxtaposing photography and painting/drawing. For instance, contact sheets resemble windows, and he sometimes collaged or painted over contact sheets, altering the view. He identified the source of his collages:...*it's my experience — I have thousands of these little films or slide transparencies inside my brain: one thing is superimposed on top of another.... Collage is the art of making a new whole out of discarded and often disparaged parts*. As a kid, Wojnarowicz cut out "Archie" comics and reassembled them to reflect his sexual desires. Later, on the street, he worked with an ex-con on tape-recording experiments: *We'd tape street sounds in cut-up fashion and replay the tapes simultaneously sitting inside a refrigerator box on twelfth avenue*; in the early eighties, the tape recorder became his musical instrument in the band 3 Teens Kill 4 — No Motive.

Like collage-master Max Ernst (whose photo-collages and frottages are echoed, perhaps coincidentally, in Wojnarowicz's early work), he frequently experienced hypnagogic visions — those singular, crystal-clear images that insert themselves between waking and sleeping. *For years I've taken pictures of things because they were psychologically loaded.... I realized that the photographs were like words in a sentence and that what I try to do is to construct paragraphs out of the multiple images*. And for all the brutal contemporaneity of Wojnarowicz's art, he balanced, like Ernst, between the raucous and iconoclastic humor of Dada and the anarchic poetry of Surrealism.

The formal/geometric simplicity of most

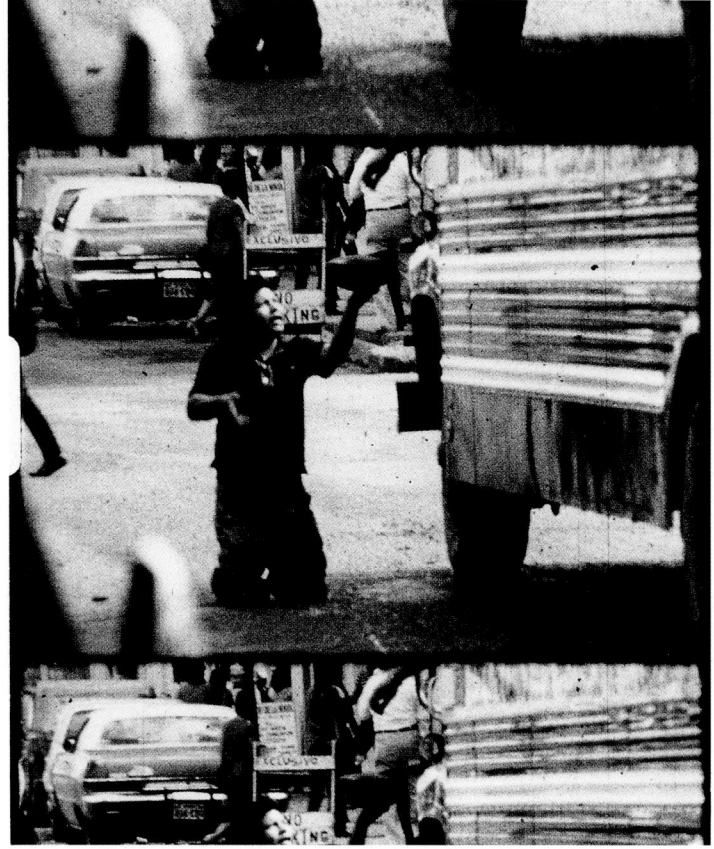

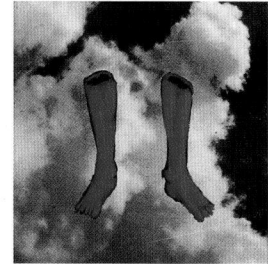

of Wojnarowicz's photographic representations was paralleled in a group of poetic 1989 paintings, several of which were painted and collaged over a "photo-collage" background of money, bills of various denominations. These include the striking *Fear of Evolution* and *Bad Moon Rising,* in which the wounded Saint Sebastian's headless body becomes the cross-cultural myth (Frida Kahlo is only one among many contemporary artists who made use of it) of a tree growing from a martyred body, struck down by love or politics, that is also thrusting roots into the earth. With its central image and symmetrically placed square photo-vignettes, it was predicted by the same composition in the deceptively lyrical *Fuck You Faggot Fucker* of 1984, in which two men, standing in water up to their waists, kiss over a background of maps. (Wojnarowicz used maps as a metaphor for government, and tore them up to destroy boundaries—national and moral.)

He had three ways of using photographs in his paintings: as sources, backgrounds, and vignettes. The first is exemplified by the "Elements" series, with the recurring images drawn from photographs (some of which were seen in later pieces as photographic works—such as the snake head in the bottle, the neon gun sign, coupling males, nebulalike cells, rubble landscapes).

In several major paintings from the late eighties, the painted images float on photo backgrounds. In *Something From Sleep,* his "self-portrait as dinosaur" drawn from a dream, a green bough in its mouth like a proffered olive branch, lumbers across a chaotic photographic field of mostly circular devices suggesting the temporal and transtemporal. In *Where I'll Go After I'm Gone,* the "allover" field is again composed of mostly circular photographic images (wheels, shells, cells, and a self-portrait) careening across a grid that evokes great depth. Flat on the surface are more circular photographic vignettes, some emerging in auras of golden light: moons, eyes, three kinds of trees, Hermes's winged foot, an indigenous shaman figure, a fetus, two men, a white mule.

In *Untitled* (1989), all three formal uses are evident. The image is highly and almost geometrically structured. Three black-and-white photographic horizontal bands (from bottom up: palm trees, building frame, iron scaffolding) form the background. Fourteen circular vignettes, some haloed in red, accompany a huge painted nest and a vertical band that is a multicolored painting in itself, taken from a news photograph of Haitians escaping from a fire. The vignettes are architectural (sometimes details drawn from the backdrop), natural, and "political" (a bound torso, an aerial shot of a crowd), and these three elements might be seen as the subject of the work. Oppressed people of color (too often perceived by the dominant culture as closer to "nature" than to "culture") make their escape; the great comforting nest waits; natural and cultural shelters provide the context.

Nature and culture, life and death, peace and war, internal and external also formed the grid against which a 1991 exhibition at P·P·O·W was presented. Large, lusciously seductive, colorful paintings of flowers (drawn from photographs in an old botany book) — provide fields for the fragments of private reality that Wojnarowicz intended as *a magnet that can attract others with a similar frame of reference: thus each public disclosure of a fragment of private reality serves as a dismantling tool against the illusion of ONE-TRIBE NATION: it lifts the curtains for a brief peek and reveals the possible existence of literally millions of tribes.* Hujar loved flowers, and Wojnarowicz, mourning him, recalled the house being filled with flowers during his illness, *some so big and wild that they didn't even look like flowers: more like beings from some lunar slopes.*

In these most unabashedly beautiful of Wojnarowicz's paintings, the message is very quiet, very lethal, and the prime vehicle for that message is photography. Three of the 1990 paintings — *We are born into a pre-invented existence*; *He kept following me*; and *Americans can't deal with death* — are titled after the beginnings of the lengthy texts almost illegibly superimposed on their surfaces in light-on-dark type. Several square photo vignettes are lined up across the picture planes, demanding attention by pushing their way past the beauty of the flowers, overwhelming those powerfully exotic and sexually suggestive forms (each contains a phallic element) with a deadly black-and-white reminder of another reality. Nature represents life, sex, color; the colorless vignettes of a blowing American flag, skeleton, viral cells, fanged serpent head, all represent a culture of danger and death. But then again, the flowers are also rather ominous *fleurs du mal*, and an orgasm is a "little death." *I am a bundle of contradictions that shift constantly. This is a comfort to me because to contradict myself dismantles the mental / physical chains of the verbal code. I abstract the disease I have in the same way you abstract death.*

A rare equal pairing of photography and painting, *Untitled* (1988–89) — a painted film still — shows a legless Mexican boy begging for money from a passing bus; the second frame is a painting of his lost legs below the knee, in red, against a cloud, in some sort of dismemberment heaven. This and many of the other images could be mythological references to all the various gods, who, like Osiris, have been dismembered and then re-membered: *I love mythology... America's nearly spiritually dead, but at least we still deal with a few mythic images — especially in the form of animals. We give animals stature in our cartoons or in our toys...we deal with evil and good as mythic images in children's toys....popular culture still carries the most spiritual reverberation.*

The nature of Wojnarowicz's juxtapositions is always meaningful, even when the meaning is elusive. A fourth painting in this show departs from the subtlety of the "flowers of evil" group; perched on a skeletal black leaf, with an unnaturally glowing orange-and-blue bloom behind him, is a spider with Jesse Helms's grinning face and a swastika on his back. *I've been vocal about taboo subjects like my desires, my hatred, my rage. I've been investigating my rage and making works out of it, and boy, it feels good! It feels good to put words to it, it feels good to name the very things that send people running if that's how little they can deal with themselves and their own impulses....people*

> ...each public disclosure of a fragment of private reality serves as a dismantling tool against the illusion of ONE-TRIBE NATION: it lifts the curtains for a brief peek and reveals the possible existence of literally millions of tribes.

have found it necessary to define their sexuality in images, in photographs and drawings and movies in order not to disappear.... I'm beginning to believe that one of the last frontiers left for radical gestures is the imagination.

Clues to the complexity of Wojnarowicz's symbolism are found throughout his writings. All his life, he saw through and into what surrounded him and acted on what he saw. These acts ranged from shoplifting captive animals to filling the stairwell outside the Leo Castelli Gallery with bloody cow bones, contextualized by wall stencils of knife, fork, empty plate, and burning house (this action/installation was a collaboration with Julie Hair), to calling Cardinal O'Connor a *fat cannibal from that house of walking swastikas up on fifth avenue* and fantasizing his and other political enemies' gory deaths in print, to laying his body and his "career" on the line in the AIDS battles.

I know I'm not going to die merely be-

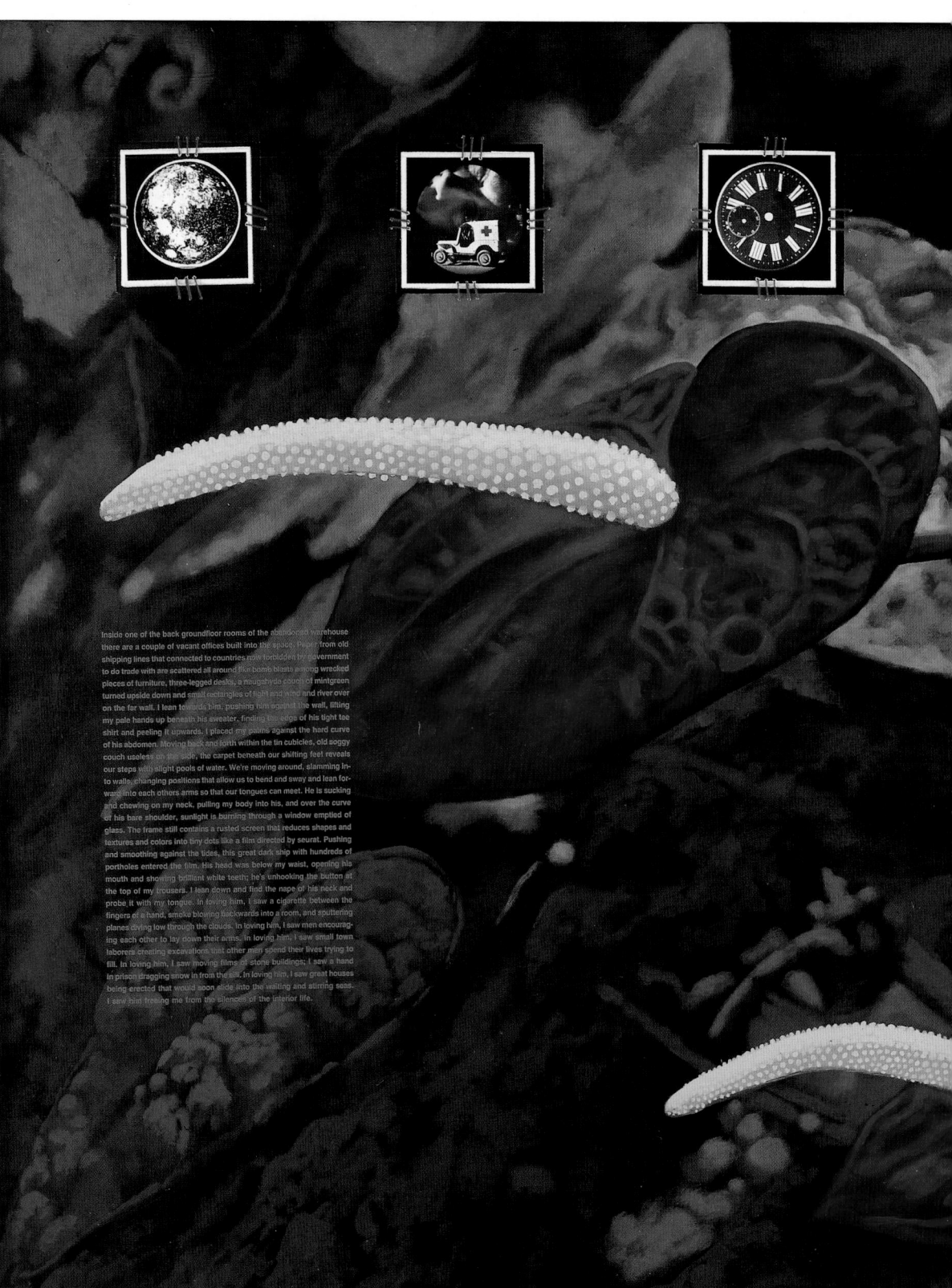

HE KEPT FOLLOWING ME,
1990. Black-and-white photographs, acrylic, string, and text on board, 48 x 60"

24

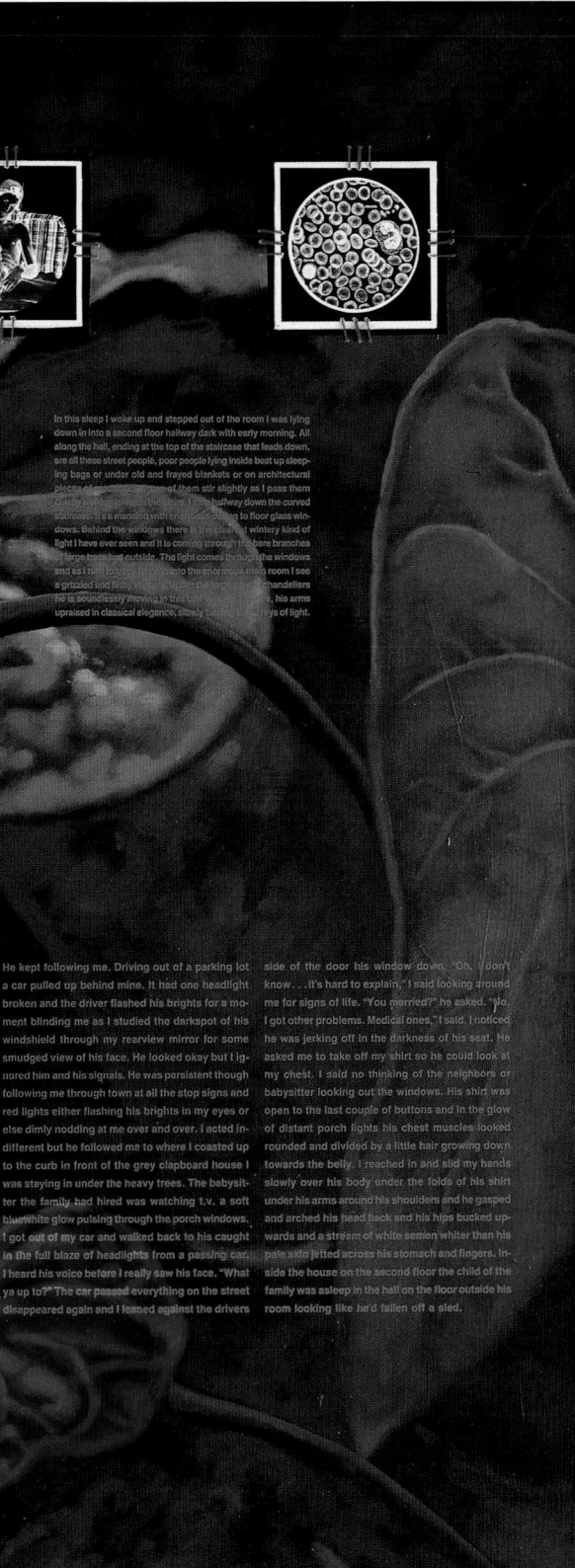

cause I got fucked in the ass without a condom or because I swallowed a stranger's semen. If I die it is because a handful of people in power, in organized religions and political institutions, believe that I am expendable. Open skies, or "heavens," figure in many of Wojnarowicz's lyrical, mystical paintings. The image of wind, of curtains blowing at an open window, is associated with a spirit world, with both life and death. Sometimes a surface, covered with dollar bills standing in for a greedy civilization, is torn to reveal the light, the sky beyond. Approaching his own death, he wrote: *I'm a blank spot in a hectic civilization. I'm a dark smudge in the air that dissipates without notice. I feel like a window, maybe a broken window. I am a glass human. I am a glass human disappearing in rain. I am standing among all of you waving my invisible words. I am getting so weary. I am growing tired. I am waving to you from here. I am crawling around looking for the aperture of complete and final emptiness. I am vibrating in isolation among you. I am screaming but it comes out like pieces of clear ice. I am signaling that the volume of all this is too high. I am waving. I am waving my hands. I am disappearing. I am disappearing but not fast enough.*

Earlier, talking to a dying friend who may or may not have been able to hear him, he said: *I don't know what you're seeing but if there's light move towards it.* 🐾

1. All passages in italics are quotations from Wojnarowicz himself, taken from interviews with the author and from the books *Tongues of Flame*, ed. Barry Blinderman (exhibition catalog, Normal, Ill.: University Galleries of Illinois State University, 1990); *Close to the Knives: A Memoir of Disintegration* (New York: Vintage Books, 1991); and *Memories That Smell Like Gasoline* (San Francisco, Artspace Books, 1992).

2. See George Zyed's description of "lycanthropy" in Pierre Petitfils, *Rimbaud* (Charlottesville: University Press of Virginia, 1987), p. 104.

3. All from Harold Bloom, ed., *Arthur Rimbaud*, New York: Chelsea House Publishers, 1988.

4. See Robert Sobieszek, *Robert Smithson: Photo Works* (Albuquerque: University of New Mexico Press, 1993).

5. Robert Smithson, "Incidents of Mirror-Travel in the Yucatan," *Artforum*, vol. VIII, no. 1 (September 1969), p. 28.

6. Victor Masayesva, *Hopi Photographers/Hopi Images*, (Tucson: Sun Tracks and University of Arizona Press, 1983), p. 90.

How was it that we began discussing cameras on that particular day? I mean the day that David's feet swelled to twice their normal size. He was staring at the awful things when I got to his room. There were cracks in the skin, and he could feel things breaking inside. I remember the doctor's arrival, the way he crossed his arms and looked baffled, then prescribed a diuretic. This would turn out to be David's last stay in the hospital, and each day seemed to bring some horrible new medical surprise.

Once medicated, though, David insisted on a trip to the smoking lounge for a cigarette. Naturally, a wheelchair was out of the question. He would hobble on the feet that were "breaking," one white-knuckled hand around the I.V. stand. He'd been connected to that I.V. for something like five solid months, refusing to allow the doctor to insert a Hickman catheter. The Hickman was "too brutal," he complained, and I think he thought it too final. And for that reason, he now had track marks, which he began to show me as we sat down in the lounge.

I remember these medical details clearly, but not how we turned to the topic of cameras there in the cheerless nicotine den. I know that at some point David talked about Peter Hujar, his mentor and dear friend, who'd died of AIDS in 1987. Peter had repeatedly tried to show David how to use his Leica, his street-shooting camera, and David was telling me he just couldn't get the hang of that stuff about F-stops. That's why he'd always used an automatic, though any camera of Peter's would certainly be the best camera. I told him I used to have a Nikon F, but lost it years ago when my apartment was robbed, and I'd never found another camera I liked as well. "Really?" he said. "I'll give you that camera of Peter's." I can't remember how I replied. I know I was surprised—and very moved. Everything that had once been Peter's was precious to David. But I also expected him to forget this conversation. David was beginning to lose his memory.

As soon as certain infections cleared up,

he was going to have his spleen and gall bladder removed. I know we started discussing this because the other person in the lounge—a geezer in a wheelchair—decided to butt in to inform us that he'd just had his gall bladder removed by laser. Easy. And he had this fantastic incredible doctor. David got up to go to the bathroom and as he winced and tottered toward the door, the geezer mentioned the doctor's name. David turned and said angrily, "That guy nearly killed a friend." Peter had seen "that guy" and been advised to inject himself with his own shit. As soon as David left the room, though, the geezer assured me that under the care of this particular quack, his own T-cell count had risen miraculously. From zero to seven.

About two weeks later, David had someone call me from the hospital to make sure I was coming that afternoon. He was about four days out of surgery, still very weak. "I have something for you," he announced when I arrived. He pulled Peter's camera out from under the bedclothes. It was wrapped in two plastic baggies.

I'm supposed to be one who finds words for such moments. "When you told me before that you were going to give me this camera…" I began. David looked up blankly. He had forgotten the entire earlier conversation. He thought the idea had just come to him: that I must be given this camera, and must have it that very day. Tom Rauffenbart, David's boyfriend, had been forced to go search the loft, where he finally turned the thing up at the bottom of a file drawer. But I don't quite remember the order of events. Maybe I learned all that later. Maybe the minute he handed me the camera I began with my stumbling thanks, my clichés. Honored. So grateful. So speechless. Overwhelmed. "I figured you could do some stories where you did both the words and the pictures," David said. That was all. He didn't have time to hear the stumbling things, as he prepared to go out of the world. I would just have to move forward, my work cut out for me. 🐾

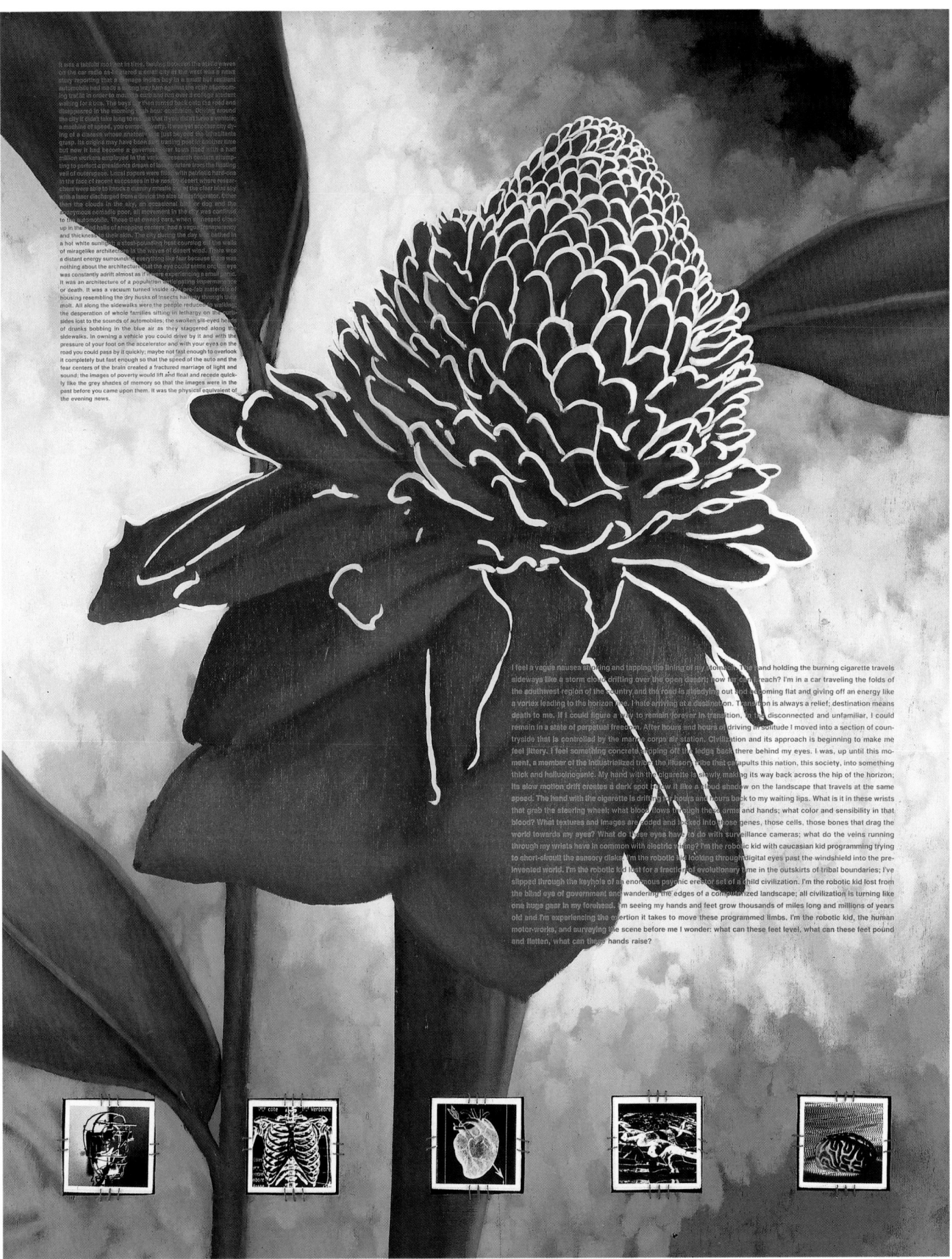

It was a twilight foot-print in time, bowing between the static waves on the car radio as I stared a small city at the west was a news story reporting that a teenage indian boy in a small but resilient automobile had used a swing key-bar against the rush of (uncertain) in order to make this earth and run over another student waiting for a bus. The boys were then turned back onto the road and disappeared in the morning with hour confusion. Driving around the city it didn't take long to realize that I could turn a vehicle, a machine of speed, your owner, poverty. It was yet and casually dying of a classes whose another ship just beyond the inhabitants grasp. Its origins may have been as a trading post to another time but now it had become a government over town filled with a half million workers employed in the various research centers, attempting to perfect a presidence dream of loss nowhere from the floating veil of outerspace. Local papers were filled with patriotic hard-ons in the face of recent successes in the nearby desert where researchers were able to knock a dummy missile out of the clear blue sky with a laser discharged from a device the size of a refrigerator. Other than the clouds in the sky, an occasional bird or dog and the occasious nomadic poor, all movement in the city was confined to the automobile. Those that owned cars, when witnessed close up in the cool halls of shopping centers, had a vague transparency and thickness to their skin. The city during the day was bathed in a hot white sunlight a stash-sounding heat coursing all the walls of miragelike architecture in the waves of desert wind. There was a distant energy surrounding everything like fear because there was nothing about the architecture that the eye could settle on; the eye was constantly adrift almost as if it were experiencing a small panic. It was an architecture of a population anticipating impermanence or death. It was a vacuum turned inside out; pre-fab materials of housing resembling the dry husks of insects halfway through their molt. All along the sidewalks were the people reduced to walking; the desperation of whole families sitting in lethargy on the curbsides lost to the sounds of automobiles; the swollen slit-eyed heat of drunks bobbing in the blue air as they staggered along the sidewalks. In owning a vehicle you could drive by it and with the pressure of your foot on the accelerator and with your eyes on the road you could pass by it quickly; maybe not fast enough to overlook it completely but fast enough so that the speed of the auto and the fear centers of the brain created a fractured marriage of light and sound; the images of poverty would lift and float and recede quickly like the grey shades of memory so that the images were in the past before you came upon them. It was the physical equivalent of the evening news.

I feel a vague nausea stirring and tapping the lining of my stomach. The hand holding the burning cigarette travels sideways like a storm cloud drifting over the open desert; how far can it reach? I'm in a car traveling the folds of the southwest region of the country and the road is straightening out and becoming flat and giving off an energy like a vortex leading to the horizon line. I hate arriving at a destination. Transition is always a relief; destination means death to me. If I could figure a way to remain forever in transition, in the disconnected and unfamiliar, I could remain in a state of perpetual freedom. After hours and hours of driving in solitude I moved into a section of countryside that is controlled by the marine corps air station. Civilization and its approach is beginning to make me feel jittery. I feel something concrete sloping off the ledge back there behind my eyes. I was, up until this moment, a member of the industrialized tribe the illusory tribe that catapults this nation, this society, into something thick and hallucinogenic. My hand with the cigarette is slowly making its way back across the hip of the horizon; its slow motion drift creates a dark spot I view it like a cloud shadow on the landscape that travels at the same speed. The hand with the cigarette is drifting for hours and hours back to my waiting lips. What is it in these wrists that grab the steering wheel; what blood flows through these arms and hands; what color and sensibility in that blood? What textures and images are coded and locked into those genes, those cells, those bones that drag the world towards my eyes? What do these eyes have to do with surveillance cameras; what do the veins running through my wrists have in common with electric wiring? I'm the robotic kid with caucasian kid programming trying to short-circuit the sensory disks. I'm the robotic kid looking through digital eyes past the windshield into the pre-invented world. I'm the robotic kid lost for a fraction of evolutionary time in the outskirts of tribal boundaries; I've slipped through the keyhole of an enormous psychic erector set of a child civilization. I'm the robotic kid lost from the blind eye of government and wandering the edges of a computerized landscape; all civilization is turning like one huge gear in my forehead. I'm seeing my hands and feet grow thousands of miles long and millions of years old and I'm experiencing the exertion it takes to move these programmed limbs. I'm the robotic kid, the human motor-works, and surveying the scene before me I wonder: what can these feet level, what can these feet pound and flatten, what can these hands raise?

When I put my hands on your body, on your flesh, I feel the history of that body. Not just the beginning of its forming in that distant lake but all the way beyond its ending. I feel the warmth and texture and simultaneously I see the flesh unwrap from the layers of fat and disappear. I see the fat disappear from the muscle. I see the muscle disappearing from around the organs and detaching itself from the bones. I see the organs gradually fade into transparency leaving a gleaming skeleton gleaming like ivory that slowly revolves until it becomes dust. I am consumed in the sense of your weight the way your flesh occupies momentary space the fullness of it beneath my palms. I am amazed at how perfectly your body fits to the curves of my hands. If I could attach our blood vessels so we could become each other I would. If I could attach our blood vessels in order to anchor you to the earth to this present time to me I would. If I could open up your body and slip up inside your skin and look out your eyes and forever have my lips fused with yours I would. It makes me weep to feel the history of you of your flesh beneath my hands in a time of so much loss. It makes me weep to feel the movement of your flesh beneath my palms as you twist and turn over to one side to create a series of gestures to reach up around my neck to draw me nearer. All these moments will be lost in time like dust in the wind.

WHEN I PUT MY HANDS ON YOUR BODY,
1990. Gelatin-silver print and silk-screened
text on museum board, 26 x 38"

Opposite: UNTITLED, *1993. Gelatin-silver*
print, 28½ x 28½"

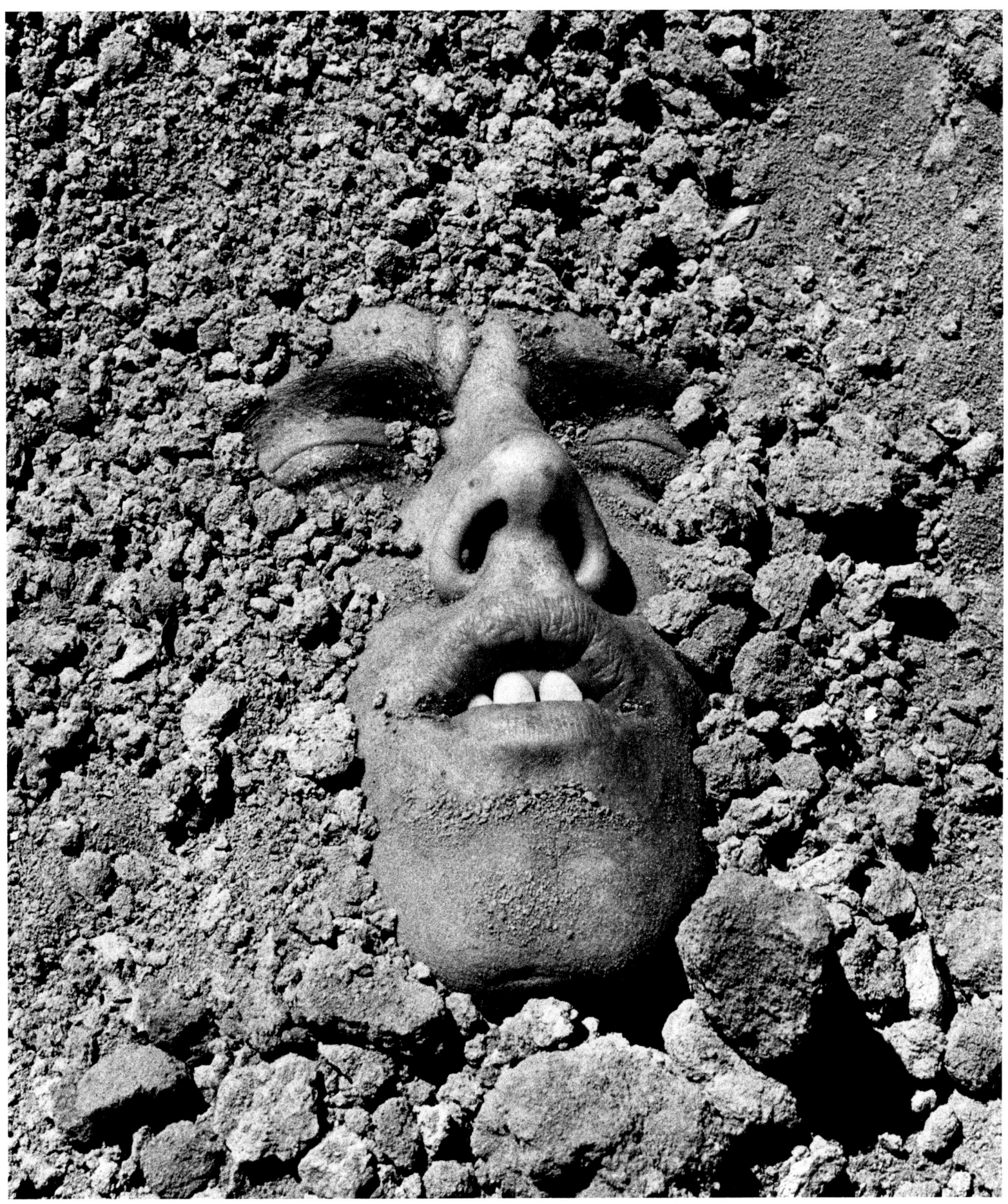

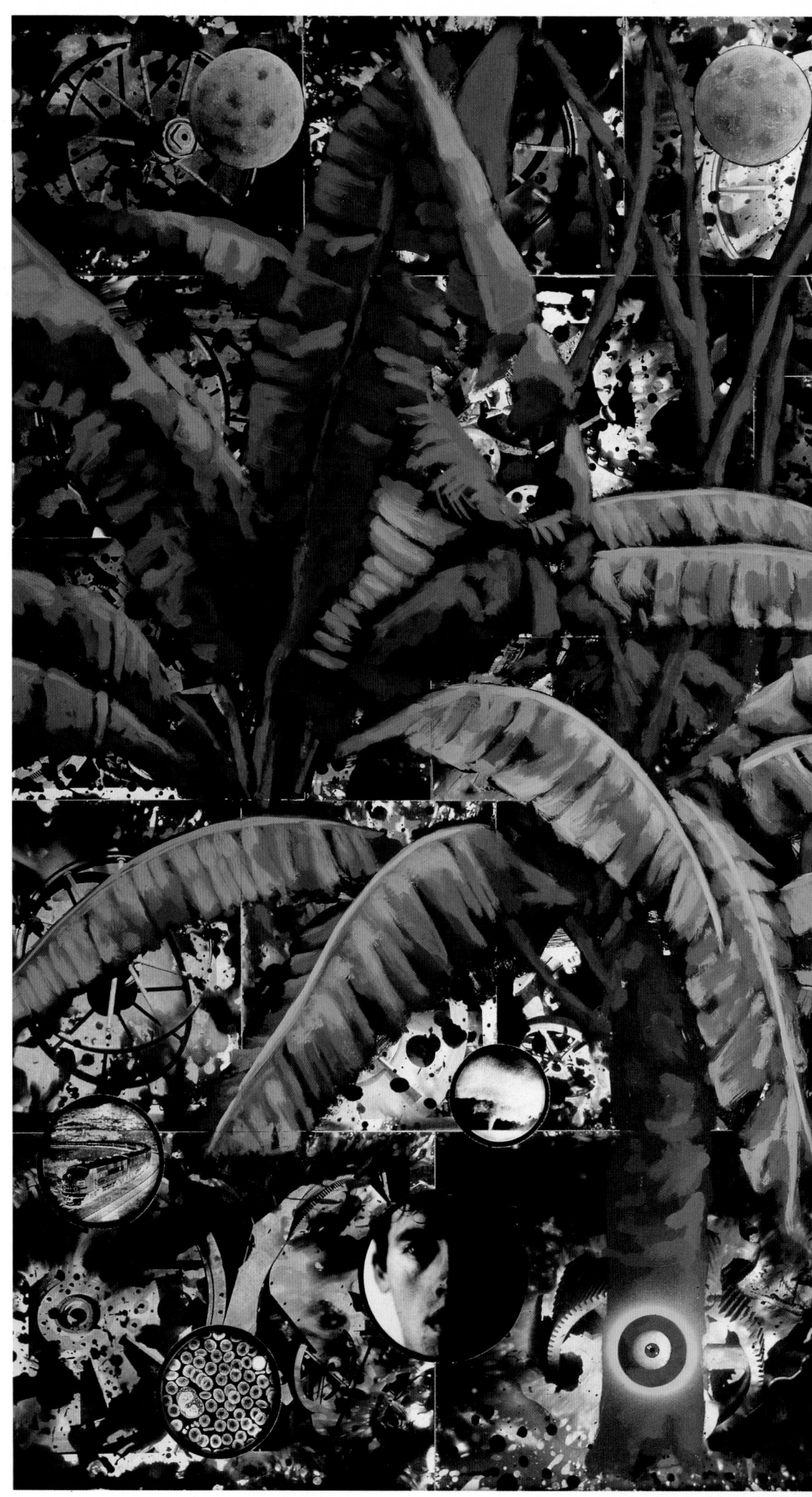

WHERE I'LL GO IF AFTER I'M GONE,
1988–89. Black-and-white photographs,
acrylic, spray paint, and collage on
Masonite, 45 x 64"

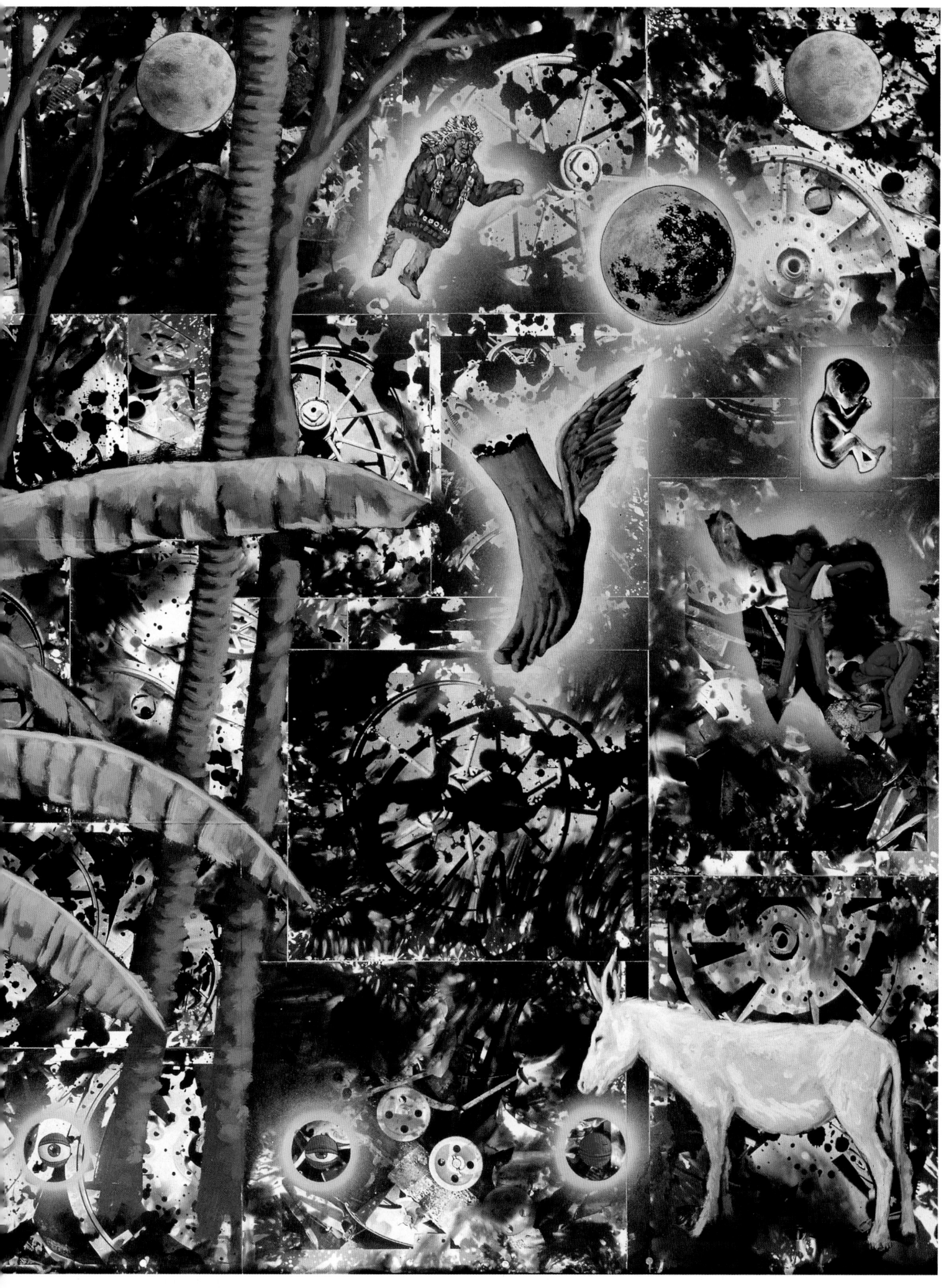

DAVID WOJNAROWICZ did not grow up dreaming that some day he would become an artist. A famous artist. He was born with more than his share of talent, not a particularly rare abundance, but a significant one. Talent is easy, especially when it's innate. Becoming an artist is hard. To be a great artist, you must be willing to give yourself to your work. Not entirely, of course, but you must understand your own talent, develop it, protect it, let it run free. A difficult life frequently destroys this possibility, but life is the purest source material. David understood the complexity of this simple notion. He had the wisdom to transform his life into art.

And what a life. Read his books. Lots of people write about David's personal life, but his own writings tell the story best. We are a country that wants artists to do only one thing well, otherwise they are labeled dilettantes. The art world has had difficulty accepting that David was a brilliant writer, photographer, and painter. Should we just call him an artist? If we diminish the range of his achievement will his art be more palatable?

But calling someone an artist won't help. Not in America. Here, artists are widely considered to be ignorant, infantile, unprofessional, and unsocialized. Just ask the tobacco man, Senator Jesse Helms, or David's personal friend, the Reverend Donald Wildmon of the American Family Association. They'll tell you that artists are second-class citizens, so when you slap the gay label or the feminist label onto that package, you can bet it won't go through the mail without some special handling. David is the one artist who brought the Reverend to court — to his knees — in New York, no less. Where we are all sinners. We are all Salman Rushdie. We are all Karen Finley.

David had little interest in playing the part of the Great Artist. He had nothing but disdain for the Great Art-World Establishment. Perhaps he might have changed his tune had he lived long enough to bask in the radiance of its attentions. But I doubt it.

When invited to dine at the Upper East Side home of one of his most prominent collectors he became sick upon arrival, and left before dinner. He once started to have a similar attack while we were wandering around SoHo one afternoon looking at art. I remember him explaining to me that he didn't want to make any image — ever — that could be plunked down in a gallery and removed from its ideological intentions. "That's impossible," I told him. "It's not," he said.

David's life had nothing to do with the art world, and his work was inseparable from his life. There's a bit of Andy Warhol here, but there's a political gap as wide as the Grand Canyon between these two queer, working-class artists. Andy went to parties and David went to demonstrations. Both artists shaped the future, but David, unlike Andy, wasn't afraid of people; David wasn't afraid of being queer.

Until this book, no one has really considered how consequential photography was to David Wojnarowicz's overall body of work. His traveling companions understood because they watched him work. It must have been like watching an artist in his or her own studio. David was a travelin' man, and the

AMERICA: HEADS OF
FAMILY/HEADS OF STATE,
*1989–90. Installation view,
from "The Decade Show," New
Museum of Contemporary Art,
New York City*

Opposite: WATER, *1987.
Black-and-white photograph,
acrylic, ink, and collage on
Masonite, 72 x 96"*

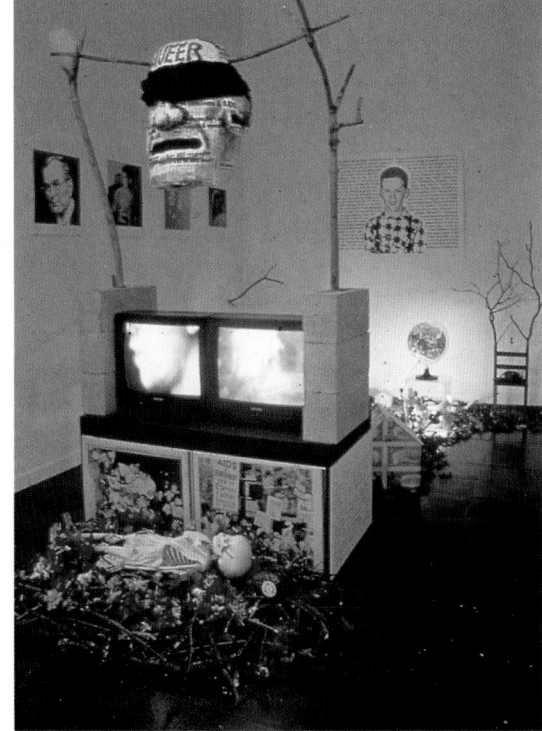

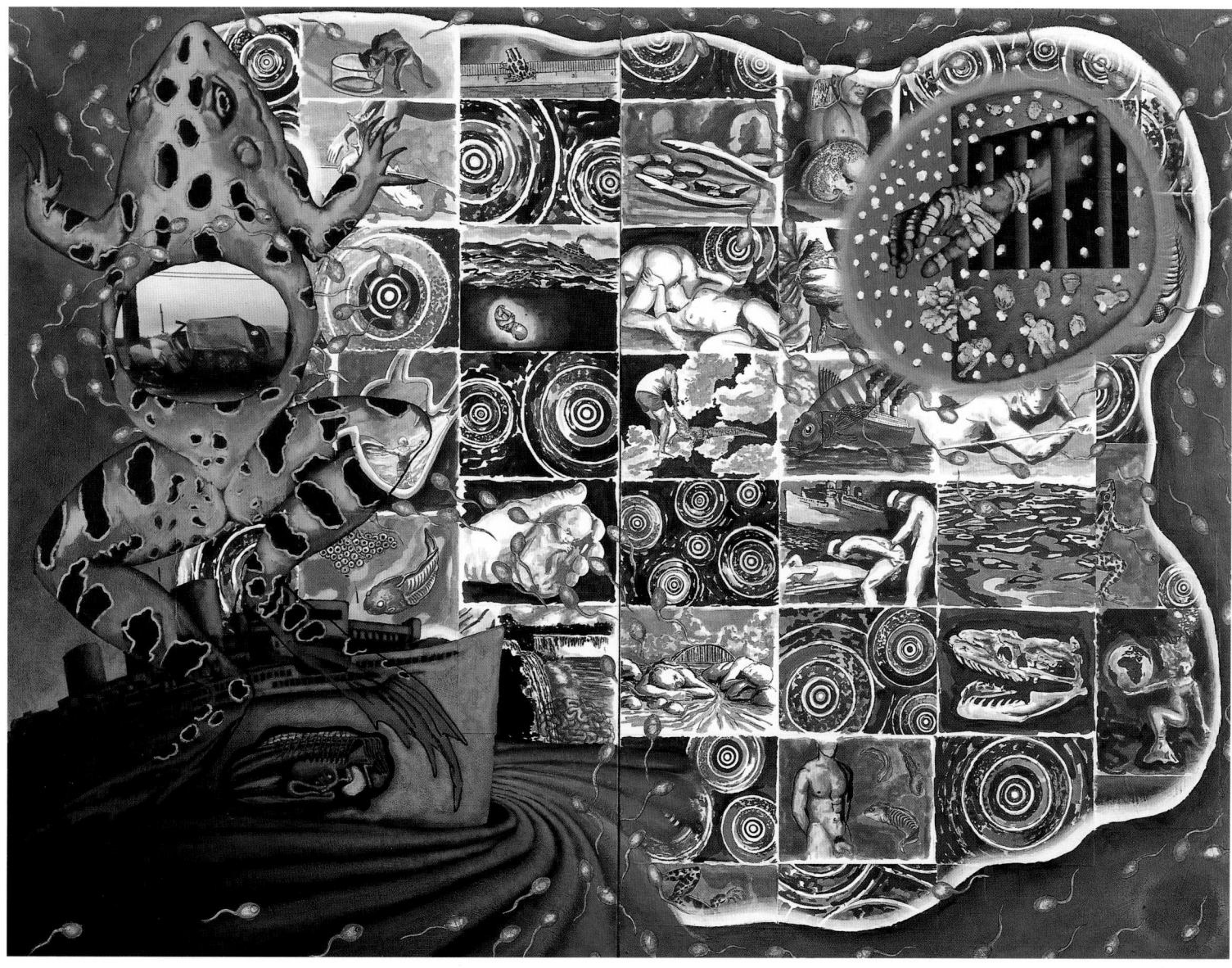

camera allowed him to turn the road into a landscape, every new city into a canvas. The camera recorded his insights like a sketch pad, or diary. But the pictures weren't personal, like snapshots. They weren't primarily about personality or feelings. The photographs depict the artist's visions, as works of art must.

David worked in the world, not just in New York, not just in the East Village, not just in the one room (once Peter Hujar's room) where he did everything, including die. His art — like his photographs, and his photo-based paintings — is broad, filled with texts and images inspired by his aspirations for us all.

David had the most subversive imagina-tion; he was able to reinvent the world while watching its demise. While watching his own demise. He understood that his real compe-tition was the television set, not his artist peers. He wanted to communicate with the same authority as the tube. That's why his work can play in galleries, on record albums, in comic books. It's the same work in each context; unlike other eighties artists, he did not make one kind of work for the art world and another for the masses. The scope of his art was ambitious enough to leapfrog (he loved frogs) over the art world with a single hop. Equally important, David's voice, throughout his work, in all media, is clear, singular, monumental. When David screamed we listened and the enemy shuddered. 🐸

IN 1979 I STARTED MAKING WORK USING human-body images. My father died, and for several years after that, my work was primarily about death—until about 1983 or '84, when Maggie Smith and I went to Mexico for the Day of the Dead. I was so impressed by the vitality of the Mexican people that I decided to start making work about being *here*

in the body. For me, it was the beginning of my work.

My first project was a lino print—sixteen feet by eleven inches—called *How I know I'm here.* I asked David to come over and take photos of me doing different activities—from which I could make the drawings for the print—like eating pomegranates, putting my foot in my mouth, pretending to pick nits from my niece's hair.

This photo was from songs I'd written for the Cardboard Air Band about being locked below the floorboards and people walking around on top. I asked him to take a picture of me with my tongue in the floorboards, which I used in the print.

David took this photo for me about ten years ago and now it still resonates for me and makes me think of his laughter. ⌂

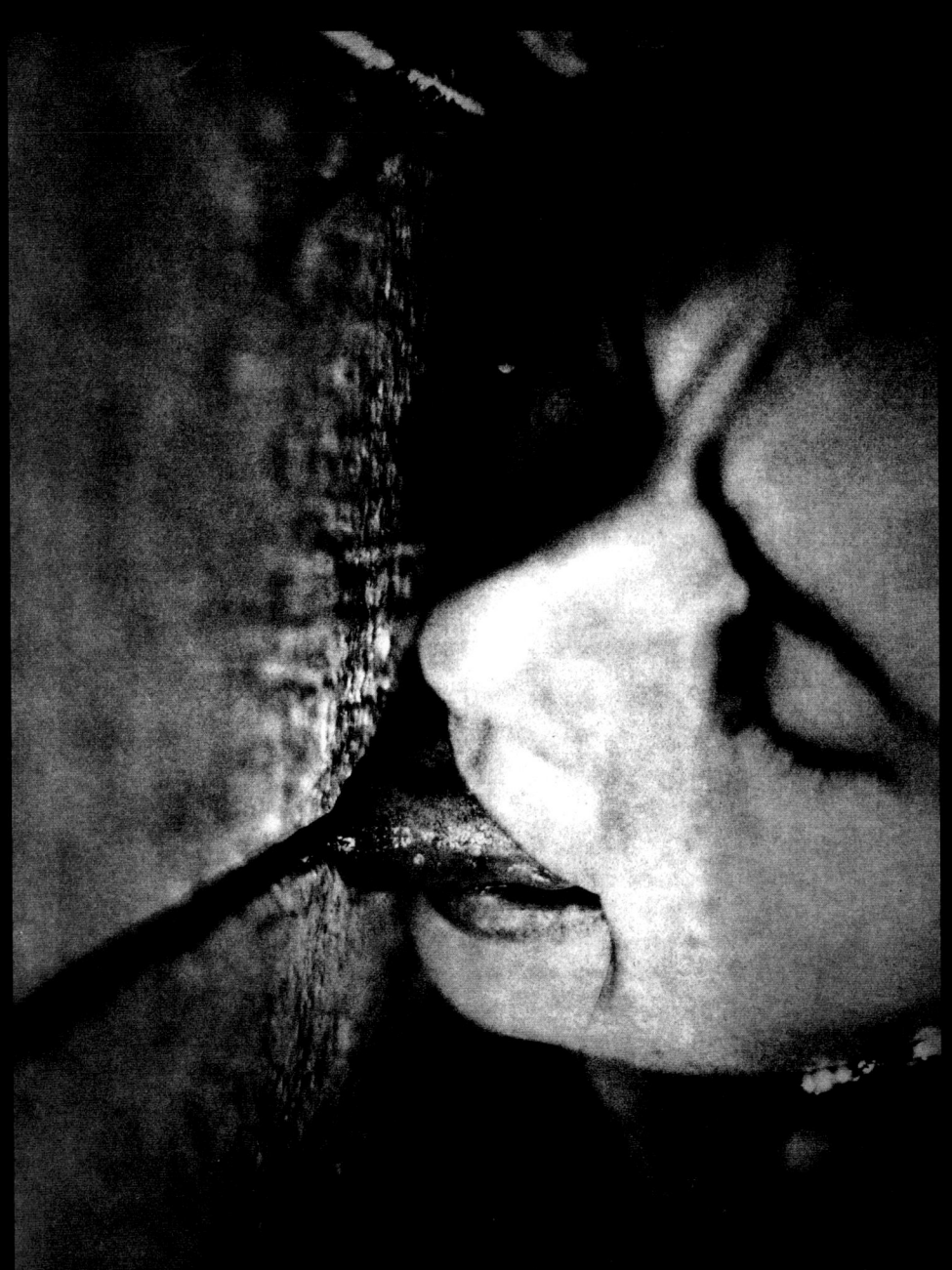

Kiki Smith, MY SECRET BUSINESS, *1993. Gelatin-silver print, 10 x 8"*

Opposite: "YOU KILLED ME FIRST," *1986. Installation view, Ground Zero Gallery, New York City*

IT EVIDENTLY IS TIME NOW for David Wojnarowicz to be entered in some way into the realm of history—where art exists to deny and defy that cultural nullification of death with the delusion of cultural immortality. I cannot, however, seem to separate my recollections of David from the stream of events and people surrounding our lives then. I don't have a good memory. When I try to conjure him back to mind, his voice is always intermingled with those of others lost to time. How shall Wojnarowicz be remembered?

For me, I can think of this: the first article I ever wrote was about David, in a way. It was about this abandoned West Side pier where he began doing these guerrilla painting installations. There was this other painter working there with David then, a beautiful soul, an elegant and kind Argentinian named Luis Frangella. I met Luis through David and the second article I wrote was on an exhibition of Luis's work. They were so different from one another, yet somehow through their friendship and collaboration they attained a manner of creative symbiosis that added vast new dimensions to the work of both artists. David no doubt jolted Luis's refined sensibilities into a kind of spontaneity, rawness, and primal, urgent energy that was at odds with the grace and grandeur of Luis's classicism. But from Luis David learned how to really paint.

I think they each enjoyed and learned a great deal from the very particular perspective, or point of view, of the other. They took a number of extended trips together. (One I remember was a trip to Richmond they took with Christof Kohlhofer, Marguerite Van Cook, James Romberger, Tessa Hughes-Freeland, David West, and myself. They all took acid and proceeded to brilliantly trash this beautiful gallery space with a collaborative mural of the epic grotesque. But that's another story.)

After one trip David took with Luis to Argentina, they came back somewhat estranged; from that point, while they always remained friends, they never seemed as close as they had been. Eventually one day I got from Luis a clue as to how their ties had been strained. David had this hyperactive metabolism. He would eat and eat many meals in the course of a day and remain perpetually skinny and undernourished. He just seemed to burn through food at a phenomenal rate. David needed to eat every few hours, he *really* needed to, he was *hungry*. Now, if David didn't get enough to eat, he could sometimes get into a mood. The amazing balance he fought to keep between his extremely dark side and his profound sense of hope would slip out of

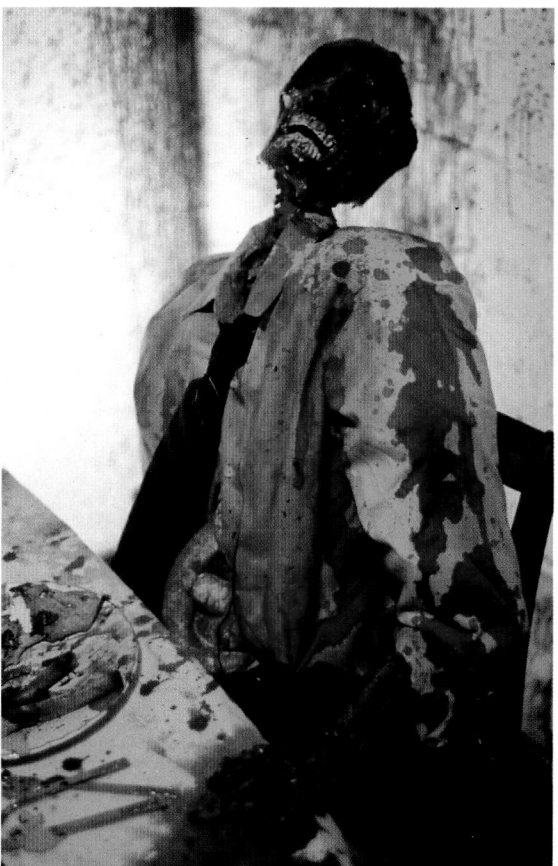

whack. It seems that David and Luis were deep in the jungle in Argentina and David got hungry.

So that's it. When I tried to remember something about David I heard Luis's voice (also silenced by AIDS) in my ear telling me, as he did so many years ago, "Please don't tell David this, but...."

That was David: hungry. He was the hunger artist, his whole quest for nourishment and enlightenment was right out of Hamson's *Hunger*. I guess when I think back on my relationship to David, it seems that I was perpetually sitting across from him in some restaurant, over breakfast, lunch, or dinner. Hunger is a craving, an uneasy sensation, a weakened condition, an urgent need. It is above all a very strong desire. It is that hunger that made Wojnarowicz such a great artist. 🐾

BEING A LAWYER FOR David Wojnarowicz put me in a curious position. David spent most of his life outside the law. As a child, he ran away from home, lived on the streets, dropped out of high school, stole, used drugs, and hustled. In a Lower East Side version of Horatio Alger's American dream, he somehow managed to pull himself up out of all that and become an enormously talented and succesful artist and writer. Yet even then he remained outside the law. He was, after all, a gay man, and as such the laws of most states made him a criminal solely because of his sexual orientation.

David angrily criticized the law in its many forms, from those proposed by Senator Jesse Helms and passed by Congress, to those pronounced by Cardinal John O'Connor under the authority of the Catholic Church, to that silently followed by major art museums across America, which David denounced for failing to exhibit "any kind of sexual imaging other than white straight male erotic fantasies."

What could a lawyer do for a man who lived his life in spite of and in defiance of the law? One thing a lawyer often does is speak for his of her clients, giving voice to complaints and concerns that might otherwise go unarticulated. But David hardly needed representation in that sense; representation was what he did best. His life's work reflects a remarkable ability to represent himself in a wide variety of media, and at the same time to represent the perspectives of those with whom he shared the streets, the piers, and the Silver Dollar coffee shop of New York City. The power of his work is precisely its ability to bring us face-to-face with worlds long shunted aside.

So David had little use for the law, and certainly didn't need me to speak for him. Rather than represent him, I like to think that I acted as editor and guide, helping him use the legal system to continue his work. In a sense, the law was another medium through which to communicate: he'd done performance art, videos, graffiti, photogra-phy, painting, sculpture, essays, and music. Now he'd use the law.

I worked with David in his lawsuit against Donald Wildmon and the American Family Association. Wildmon had taken the catalog from David's retrospective "Tongues of Flame," rephotographed small "pornographic" images cropped from large multi-image collages, and created a pamphlet filled with those isolated images as part of Wildmon's attack on the National Endowment for the Arts. David's show had been supported with an NEA grant, so Wildmon sent the pamphlet out to every member of Congress, every major media outlet, and thousands of so-called "Christian leaders," characterizing the pamphlet's images as David Wojnarowicz's art, funded by tax dollars. This was a lie: the images were in fact Wildmon's own pornography, funded by the devotees of the American Family Association.

The NEA debate had been fueled, as are most debates about sexuality and its representation, by paranoia, exaggeration, fearmongering, and outright lies. David decided to call Wildmon on the lie he had propagated about David's work. He sued Wildmon, arguing that by misrepresenting his work, Wildmon had violated, among other things, the New York Artists' Authorship Rights Act.

Our success depended on demonstrating that Wildmon's pamphlet had distorted the meaning of David's work. In one sense, this could not have been a simpler task: the documents, as lawyers like to say, spoke for themselves. Yet in another sense, our success depended on David's ability to explain the meaning of his works to a federal judge from a very different walk of life. He explained his life and work with such matter-of-fact clarity and insight that no one could have been unaffected (except perhaps Wildmon himself, who sat waiting to be called to the witness stand).

One of the images in question — seized on not only by Wildmon but also by several others in the attack on the NEA — was a portrait of Christ shooting up. Surely this was nothing other than the purest blasphemy. Yet David calmly and movingly explained the genesis and meaning of this image:

I lived for a short time in a small primitive village in the south of France, and I lived with a family of which there were three generations living in a single house. One day outside the bedroom window of the grandfather on the ground outside I saw a pile of hypodermic needles, and I asked the family what they were doing there, and they said he was diabetic and that he self-administered insulin and then tossed the needles out of the window for lack of a better place to dispose of them.

I came back to New York and returned to living on the Lower East Side, and saw that there was a great deal of drug addiction in the streets, and I also saw a few friends who had succumbed to that illness, and I was thinking about medicine in terms of how it's used as a benevolent treatment of an illness, or else it's used by sensitive people in order to nullify their sense of life or what their lives feel like living in this social structure.

So I thought about my upbringing, I thought about what I had been taught about Jesus Christ when I was young, and how he took on the suffering of all people in the world, and I wanted to create a modern image that, if he were alive physically before me in the streets of the Lower East Side, I wanted to make a symbol that would show that he would take on the suffering of the vast amounts of addiction that I saw on the streets. And I did this because I saw very little treatment available for people who had this illness.

Ruling for David, the judge prohibited Wildmon from distributing any more copies of the pamphlet, and ordered him to send a corrective mailing to all of the thousands of individuals who had already received it.

We also sought damages for harm to David's reputation, but the judge, finding no hard evidence that the value of David's work had declined, awarded only a single dollar in nominal damages. David's suit, of course, was not ultimately about money; it was about calling Wildmon to task for using distortions and lies in his effort to stop the NEA from supporting artists, like David, who communicated perspectives the fundamentalist right would rather did not exist.

David did not fit easily into the form of a lawsuit. He blanched at having to wear a jacket and tie to court. In his pre-trial depositon, he repeatedly frustrated Wildmon's attorney, who asked open-ended questions about the meaning of art criticism and of David's work and then objected when David gave long, thoughtful answers rather than the simplistic responses the lawyer expected. At one point during the trial, as the lawyers argued over an objection to a question put to David by Wildmon's attorney, David asked if he could get into the argument; the judge declined.

But most of all, David was a private person, and the lawsuit was a very public dispute. He testified in deposition and at trial that he lived an isolated life, seeing friends rarely. He communicated with the world through his art, and he preferred it that way. He was willing to be astoundingly candid about himself—in his art. In person, he was surprisingly shy. In a way, the lawsuit was about protecting that means of communication from the distortions of the fundamentalist right.

When the suit ended, David insisted on receiving his payment in a one-dollar check signed by Wildmon. He planned to use the check in his art — back on his own turf. I saw David only a few times after that, and most of our conversations were about his health. I never did find out whether Wildmon's check made it into a Wojnarowicz. 🐾

> I wanted to create a modern image that, if he [Jesus Christ] were alive physically before me in the streets of the Lower East Side... would show that he would take on the suffering of the vast amounts of addiction....

I'M TRYING TO WRITE something that makes sense but nothing makes sense. I'm trying to tell you how much I miss him. But you'll never know.

In the courtroom—that asshole creep Wildmon is pretending he doesn't know what a collage is—how he raped David's work. That evening and evenings more we would just talk with anger and humor, all the politics, the crap, the art world, the shenanigans. David so much wanted justice.

I wish he could meet my daughter, Violet.

The day after David died I saw him in a tree in my front yard. It was a twisted tree all knotted up with pine turns and twists. He was perched in the tree waving at me.

Later that day, a window slammed shut on my pinky and broke my little finger. I love that broken finger 'cause it reminds me of David. Reminds me of David in the tree.

Sometimes we'd drive in his broken-down station wagon. But to us it seemed a lifeboat, a dream boat, a ferryboat, a steamship. We are on vacation. Get my white boxer Harriet in the wagon and set off. Somewhere yonder; Field, maybe.

Opposite: **BAD MOON RISING**, *1989. Black-and-white photographs, acrylic, string, and collage on Masonite, 37 x 36½"*

SCIENCE LESSON, *1981–82. Black-and-white photograph, spray paint, and stencil on Masonite, 96" x 13' 8"*

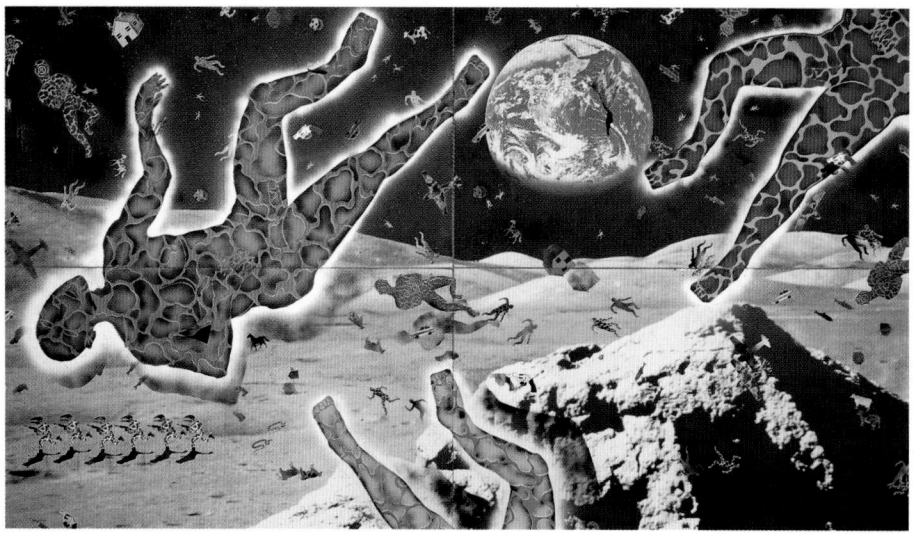

Both of our fathers were murderers. Suicide.

Conversations. Justice always a must. Turn pain into compassion, sometimes. Anger. Censorship. Politics. NEA.

That warm summer night walking on Second Avenue with you and Peter Hujar after I performed at the Boy Bar. A champagne douche. We were just kids, we were just kids.

Right now, I'm staring at the baby elephant skeleton you gave me. It's not everyone who has a baby elephant.

Charms, amulets, talismans.

Toadies, creepers, crawlies. And you only got a dollar from that bastard Wildmon for misrepresenting your work.

You had beautiful hands.

Limbo, Gracie Mansion, Pyramid, Civilian Warfare, Life Café before it was hip—David was there.

Intense.

Let me tell you a story.

Once I dropped by. I just thought I'd drop by to see David.

David: "I'd like to know why you are coming by."

Me: "I just felt like seeing you."

David: "I want to know why."

Me: "Sorry, DAVE—it's nothing heavy—I just came by."

David: "Look, I want to know why you want to see me."

Me: "Will you relax, pour me a cup of coffee?"

Everything became intense.

We'd see what was wrong.

What was right.

It's seven A.M. and you are sitting at my kitchen table. Today, it is a beautiful autumn day. On this day, we both had a life ahead, dreams, and art, love. Outside in the East Village, there is another world—In this room we were waiting for the bone shop to open.

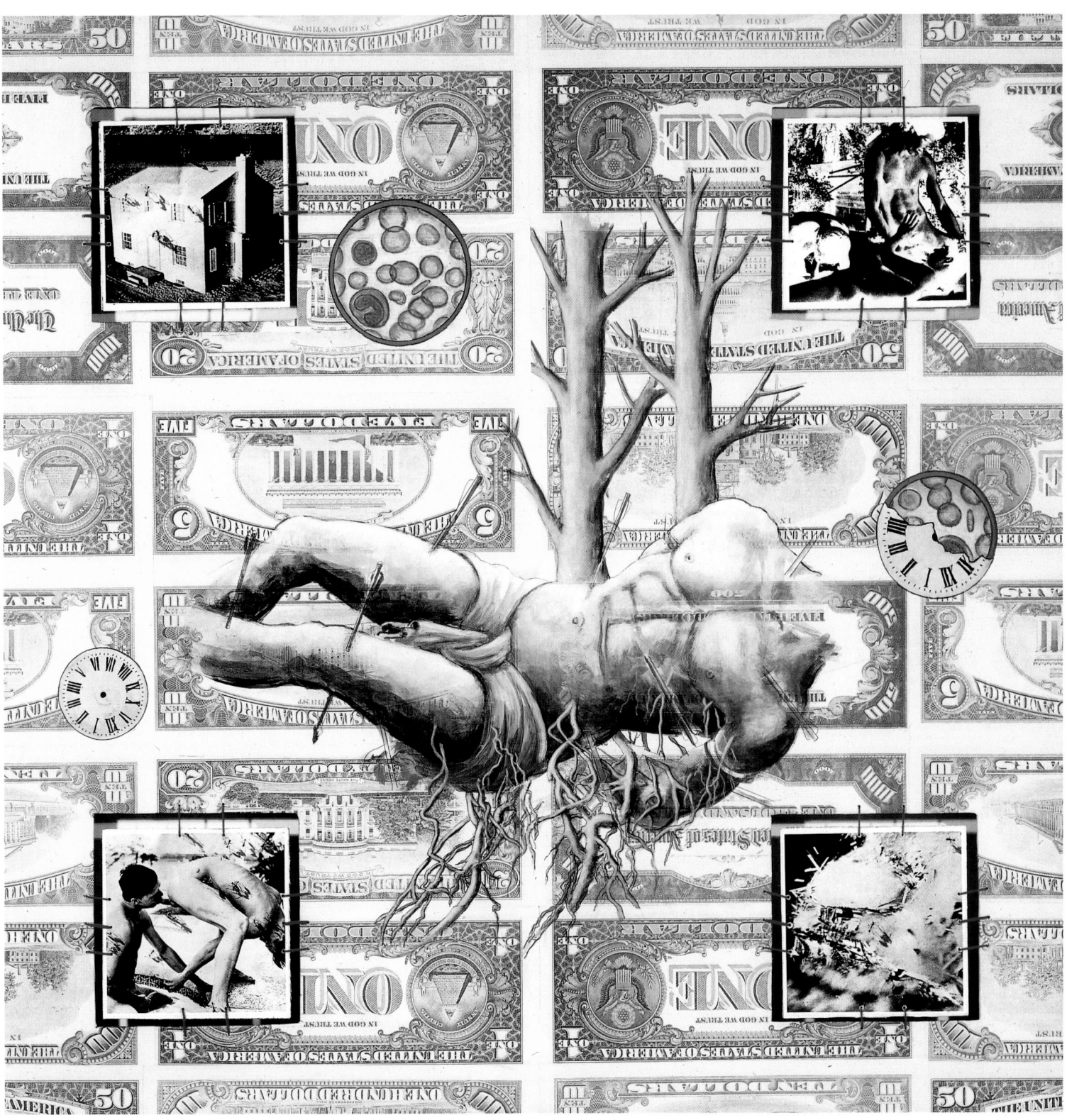

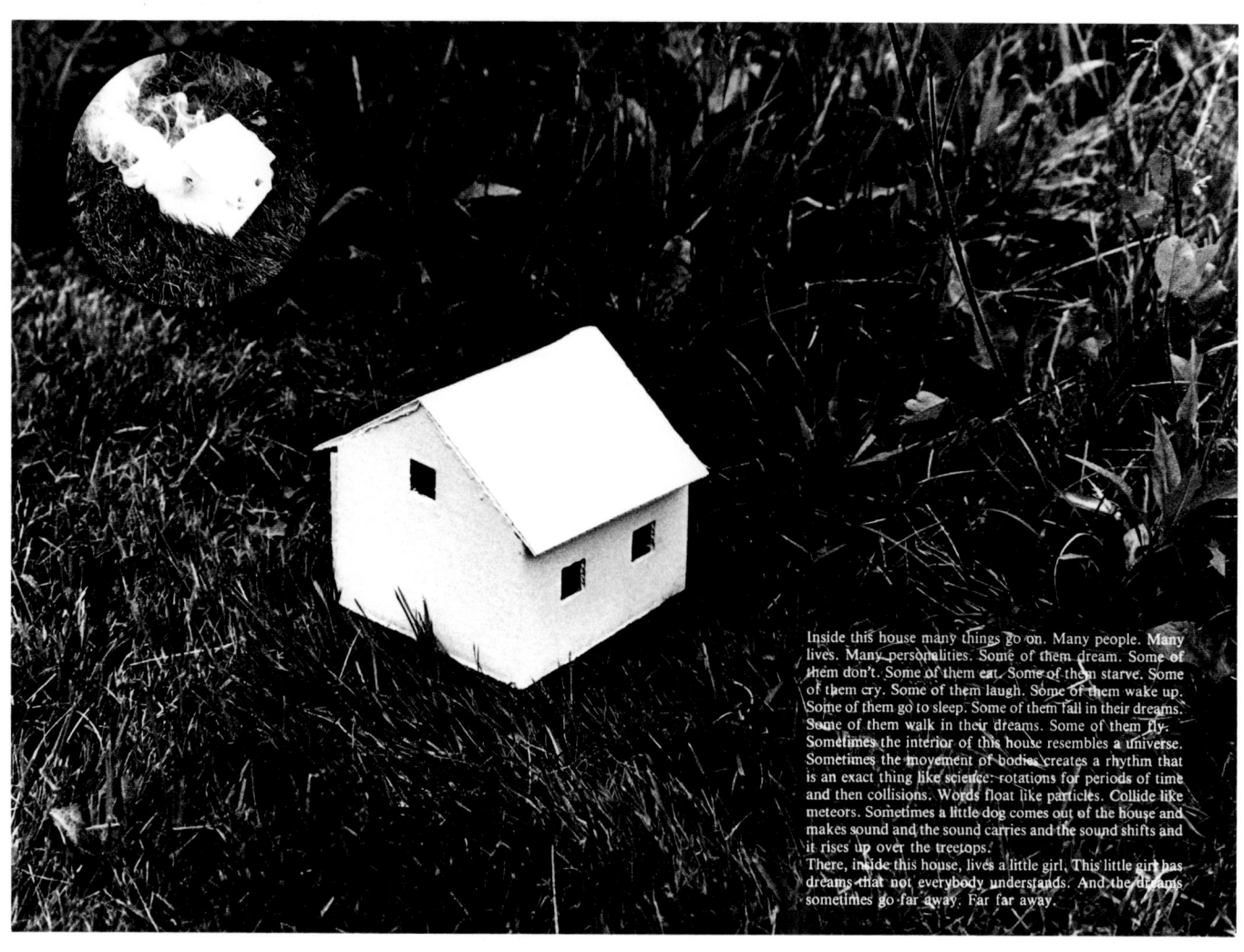

Inside this house many things go on. Many people. Many lives. Many personalities. Some of them dream. Some of them don't. Some of them eat. Some of them starve. Some of them cry. Some of them laugh. Some of them wake up. Some of them go to sleep. Some of them fall in their dreams. Some of them walk in their dreams. Some of them fly. Sometimes the interior of this house resembles a universe. Sometimes the movement of bodies creates a rhythm that is an exact thing like science: rotations for periods of time and then collisions. Words float like particles. Collide like meteors. Sometimes a little dog comes out of the house and makes sound and the sound carries and the sound shifts and it rises up over the treetops.
There, inside this house, lives a little girl. This little girl has dreams that not everybody understands. And the dreams sometimes go far away. Far far away.

INSIDE THIS HOUSE, *from an untitled series of unique prints, 1990. Gelatin-silver print, 13½ x 19"*

Opposite: **FEAR OF EVOLUTION,** *1988–89. Black-and-white photographs, acrylic, string, and collage on Masonite, 42½ x 36½"*

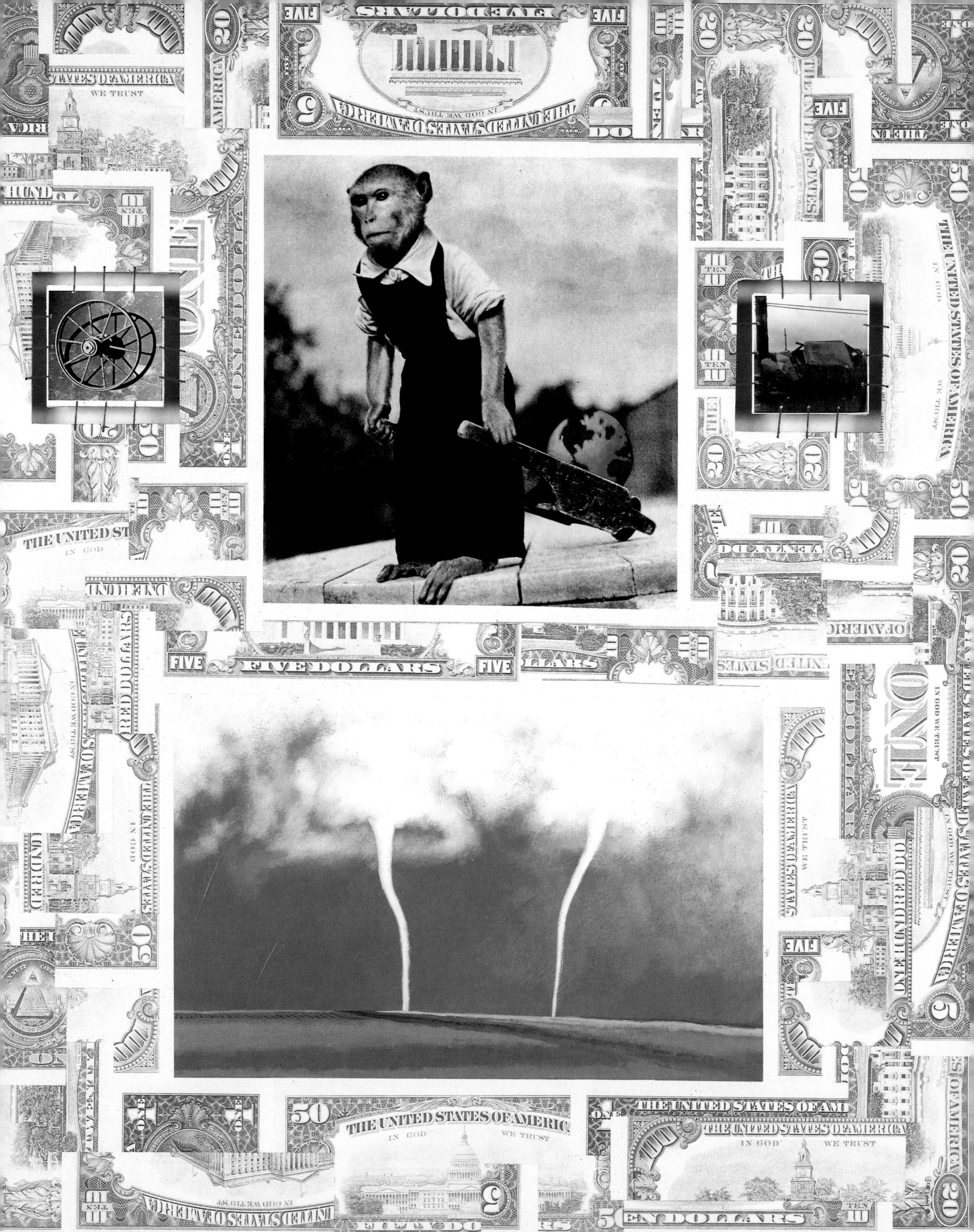

Death Valley, May 1991

Hey Vince,

Just what the doctor ordered. Lots of rest and silence and beautiful landscapes. Am on a ranch but no horses. A motorcycle cowboy walked by with no shirt army tatoos unbelievable body and sexy bowl legs and I was standing in a field and dropped to my knees and quickly made the sign of the cross. Sigh. Hope yer doing fine.

Love David

IT'S WITH NO LITTLE EMBARRASSMENT that I remember offering to be David Wojnarowicz's editor. It seems foolish, pathetically presumptuous now, but I thought I could save David from his mistakes — polish up that raw word spew before it hit the public eye. It's not like David was unpublished when I met him; though this was long before *Close to the Knives*, his hallucinatory, diaristic shards had been showing up all over. Trouble was, I was reading them like a prim copy-editor. David's writing was visceral, like hooking into some direct current from his brain and gut, but it was way too smart to be mistaken for neobeat primitivism. So misspellings—like the "tatoos" and "bowl legs" in his postcard above—and the occasional awkward or self-conscious phrase alarmed me. How could he be so careless? I thought. How could I have been so dumb? David's brilliance in any art form had nothing to do with rules or boundaries.

2/27
Albequerque, New Mexico

Hey Vince,

Having traded skyscrapers for dusty rose colored buttes and ochre valley I take long rides thru all that solitude—otherwise I ride or walk around this strange city full of gov't. war employees or run down violent drunks or in the better moments in the late afternoon + early evening before the cool night

descends seeing shirtless Chicano men lying on their beds through the propped open doors of their motel rooms rubbing their bellies—oh, or the near naked metal boys building the new pool outside the window in a blaze of sunlight + shadow.

Adios — L. David

Maybe it's just that after Peter Hujar (who had introduced me to David) died, I felt somehow protective of David. It's not like he was easily bruised or otherwise unprotected; clearly, he was tough and independent and shrewder at fending for himself than most of us. But he had a boyish earnestness and vulnerability (the unexpected flip side of his very public, pointedly theatrical rage) that invited concern — and returned it. Since I was hardly among his close circle of friends, I was surprised to get postcards from David when he was off on one of his trips. They were like little films, queer road movies, abruptly jump-cut but vividly atmospheric. No matter how casual the tone, David sketched in the scenery, snapped a portrait, and established the mood as carefully as any auteur. Sex was always in the air, just out of reach; its possibility lit up the landscape like a match dropped into a pool of gasoline.

From Mexico:

Vince—

Lovely boys shirtless + hip playing pool in pale green halls with lazy ceiling fans. 15 year old boxers with broken teeth sitting on the sea wall in Progresso looking for love. You would go crazy here. Anteaters + lizards. Beautiful Indians + tiny street kids with 40 year old eyes blowing fire. Mex. City was more intense got attacked by 5 guys but got away. Hope yer fine.

L. David W.

Montage, collage, patchwork, megamix. David's theme was often solitude (the underside of independence), but nothing exists in isolation here. He flashed pictures like

Opposite: **SEEDS OF INDUSTRY II,** *1988–89. Black-and-white photographs, acrylic, and collage on Masonite, 24 x 30"*

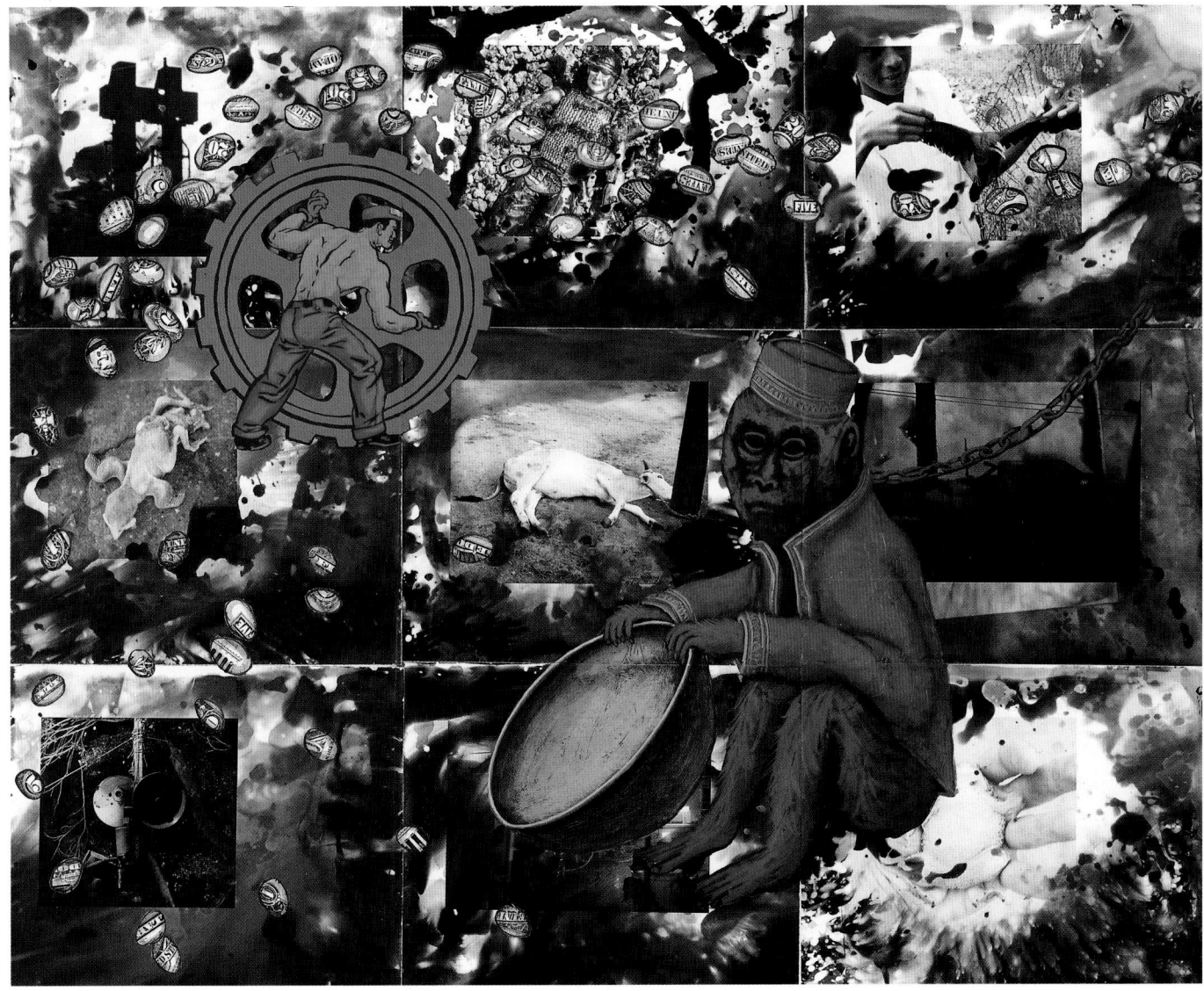

strobes, piled them up, overlapped and gridded them. His postcards were dense with images, just like his paintings where photos were stitched right into the canvas (sutured bodies of work) or the many photographs within his photographs. Each image opened up to another, world without end. Life was a monkey with a wheelbarrow holding the earth, a snake devouring a frog, ants crawling over a wooden eye, buffalo tumbling over a cliff, men fucking, and Peter Hujar dead white in his hospital bed. Life, like art, was full and dense, terrible but too vital to miss. Always alert to the great confusion of the world—its sex, garbage, throwaway beauty— David left nothing out except self-pity.

A card of Gila Bend, Arizona, postmarked Bakersfield, California, June 8, 1983:

Hi Vince,

Drove from Tucson to here yesterday an hour or two before dusk stopped at the crest of some mountain watching the light fade over the curve of the earth with silhouettes of goofy cactus and desert scrub and occasional cars or trucks slicing thru the silence and a bunch of honey bees trying to drink from the steel rim of the water fountain a 16 wheel rig pulled in just as it got dark and a young guy with no shirt + cowboy boots covered in dirt + sweat jumped out "What's up?" and kicked each tire on the truck while I held my breath and climbed back in and drove away and I wondered what it'd be like if it were a perfect world.
     Adios, L. David 🏠

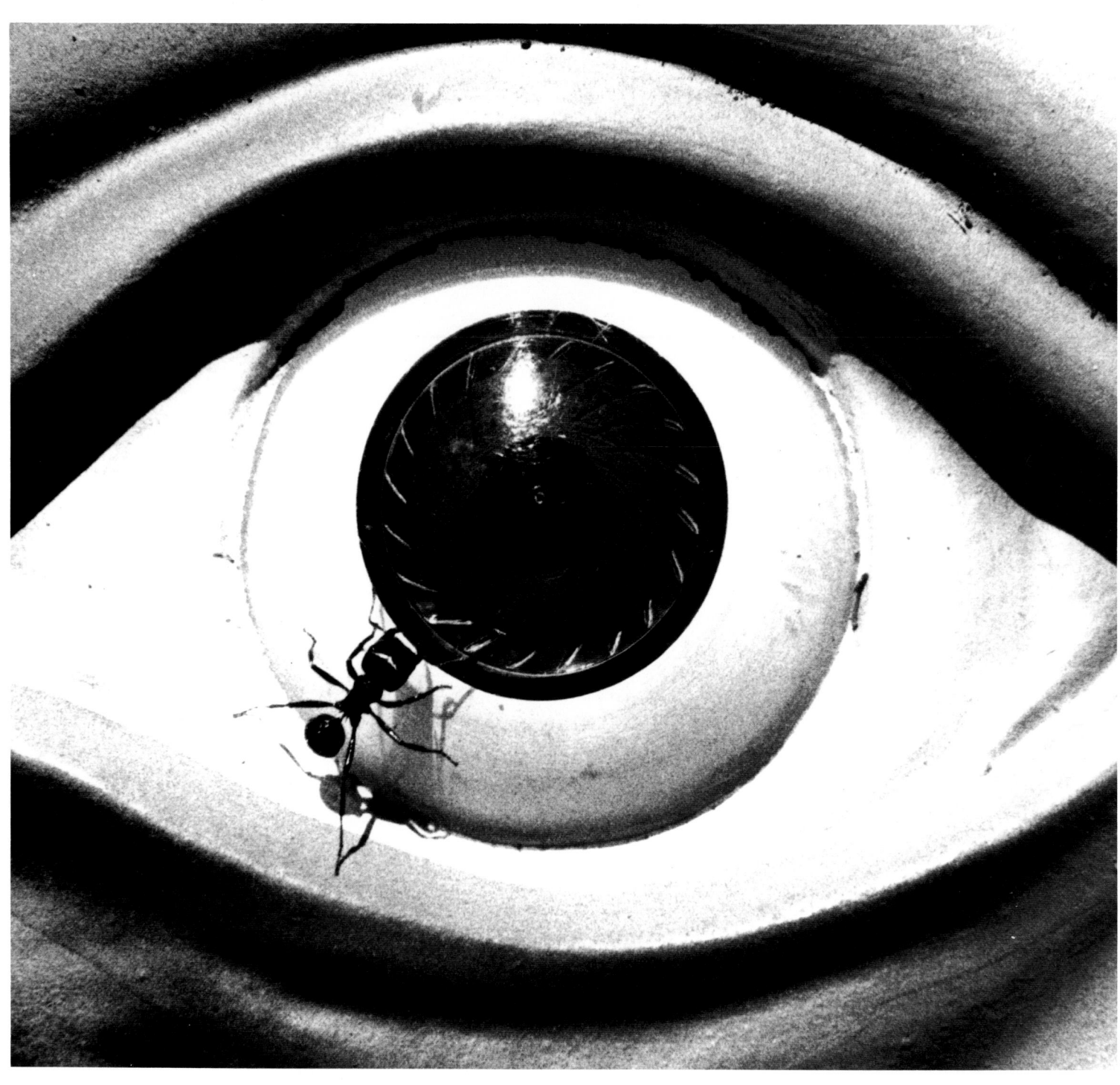

UNTITLED, *from the "Ant Series," 1988–89.*
Gelatin-silver print, 16 x 20"

Opposite: UNTITLED, *from the "Ant Series,"*
1988–89. Gelatin-silver print, 27½ x 34"

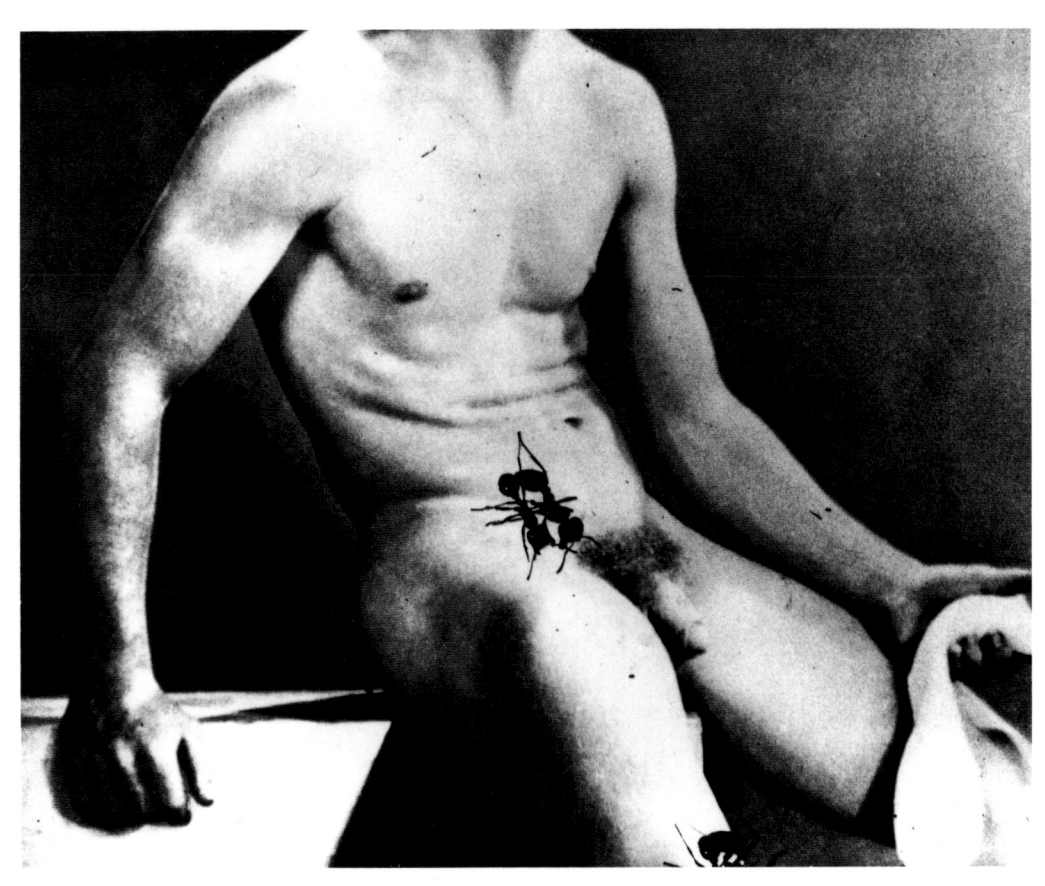

DAVID HELPED ME BUY A CAMERA and encouraged me to keep shooting. The first moving images of his I saw were in the form of a short super-8 film called *Fire in My Belly*, made during a trip to Mexico. It included haphazard images from the bus mixed with bullfighting shots from the TV, a pendant globe turning, human lips sewn together, nude torsos dancing in stroboscopic lights, ants crawling in microscopic detail, and a little red rubber devil.

We were going to shoot dolphins leaping over the film he shot of Peter. It was around this time that David was making the large photographs. 🐾

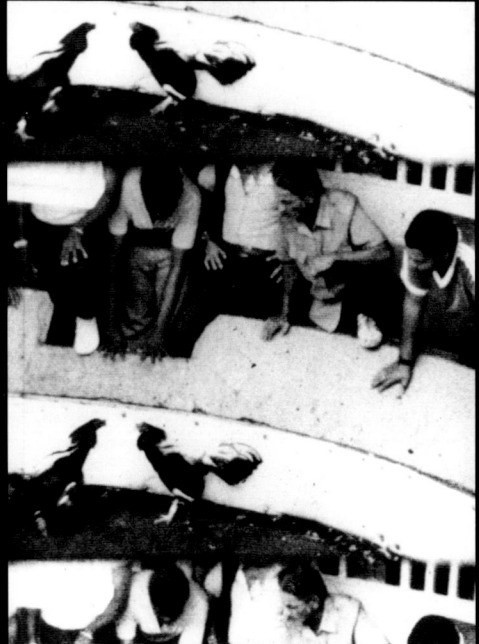

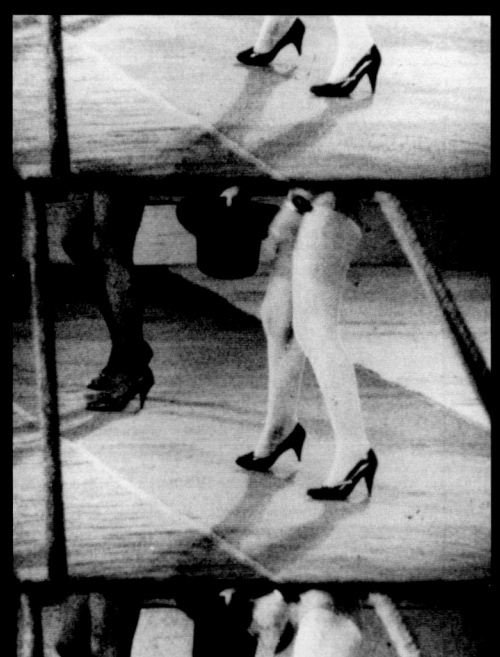

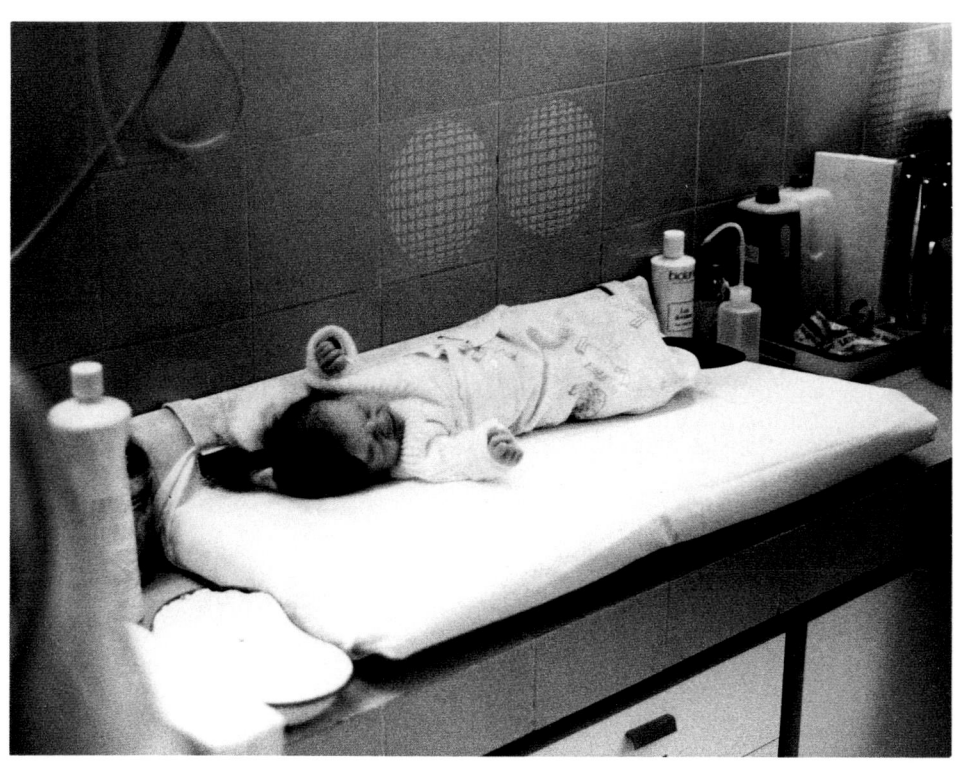

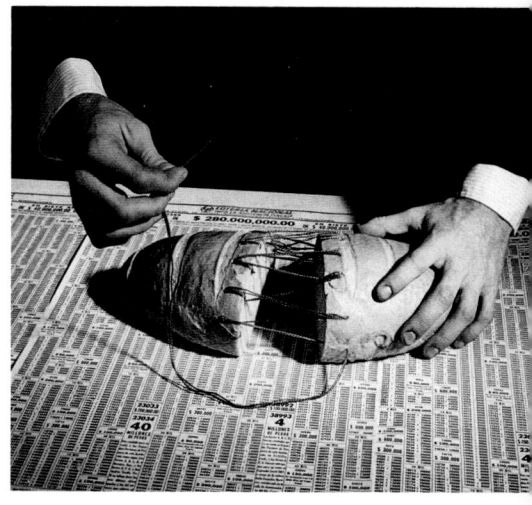

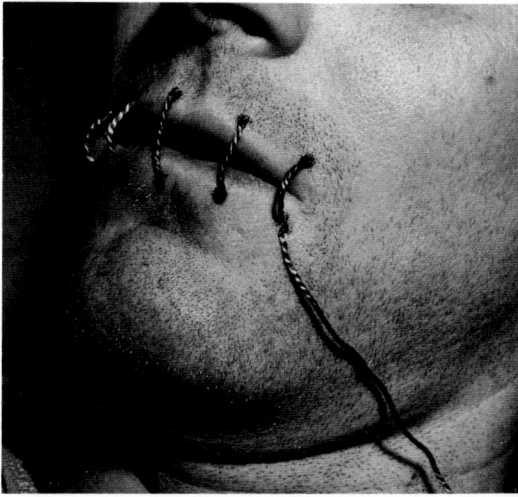

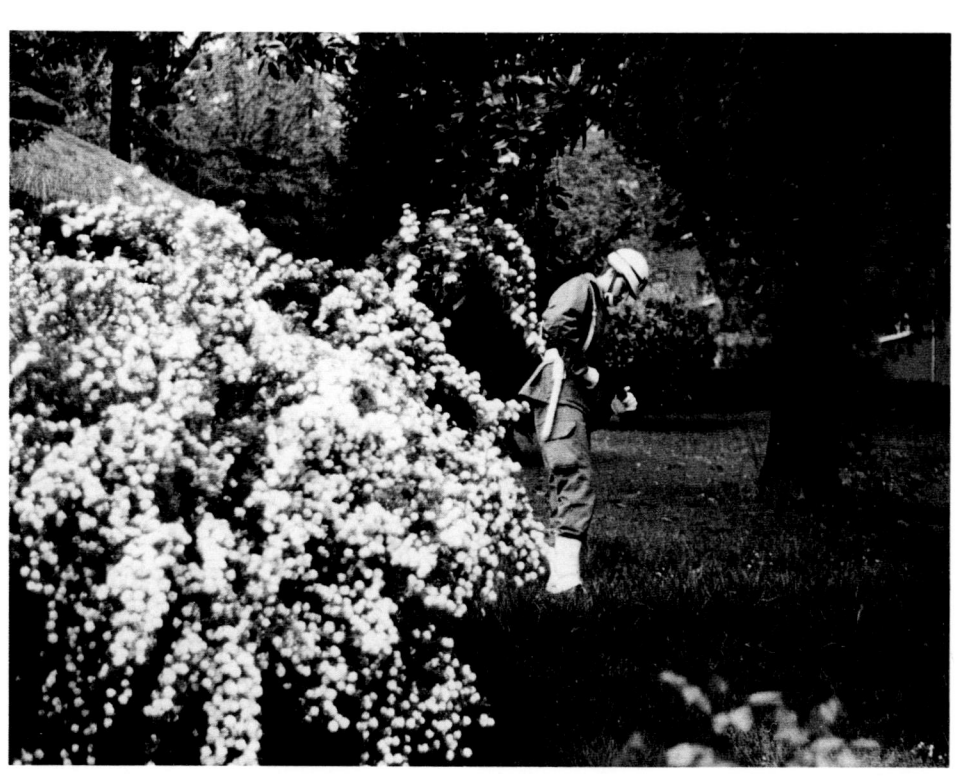

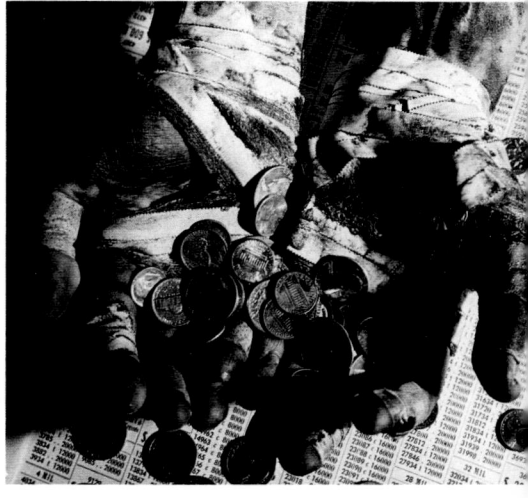

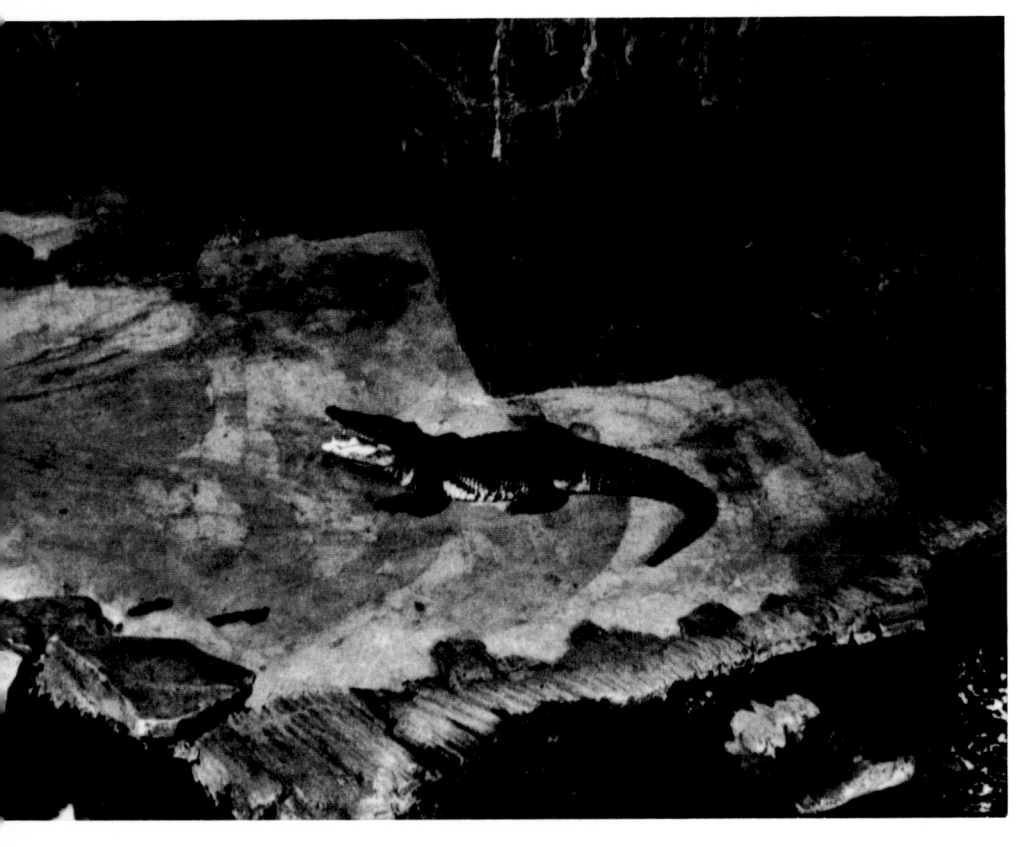
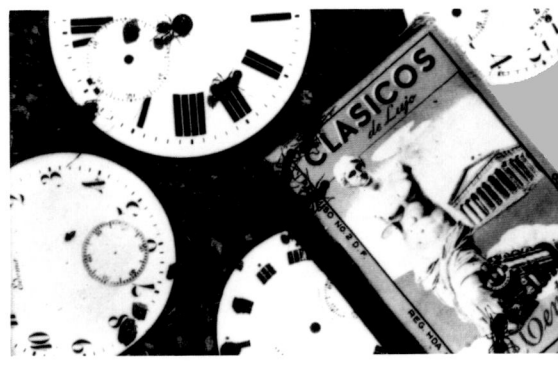
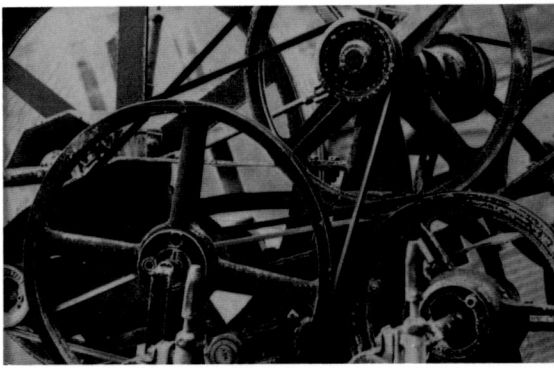
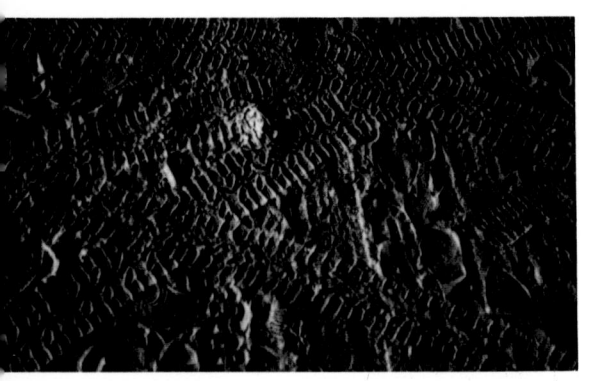
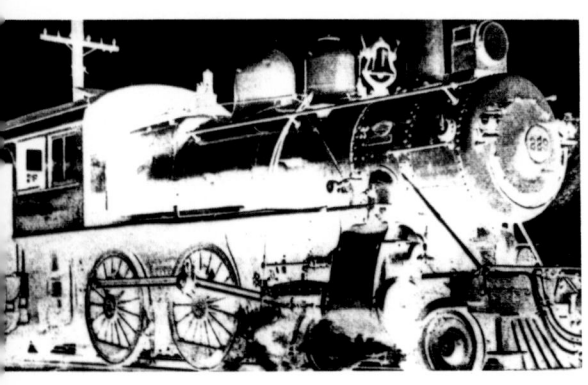
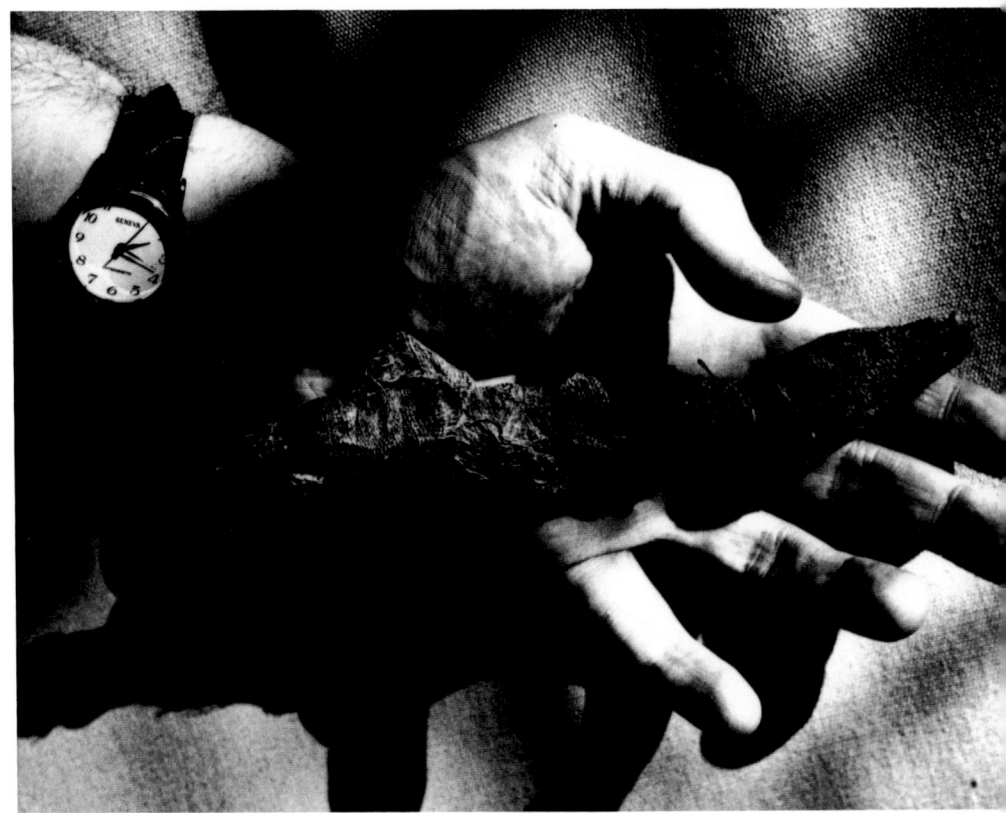

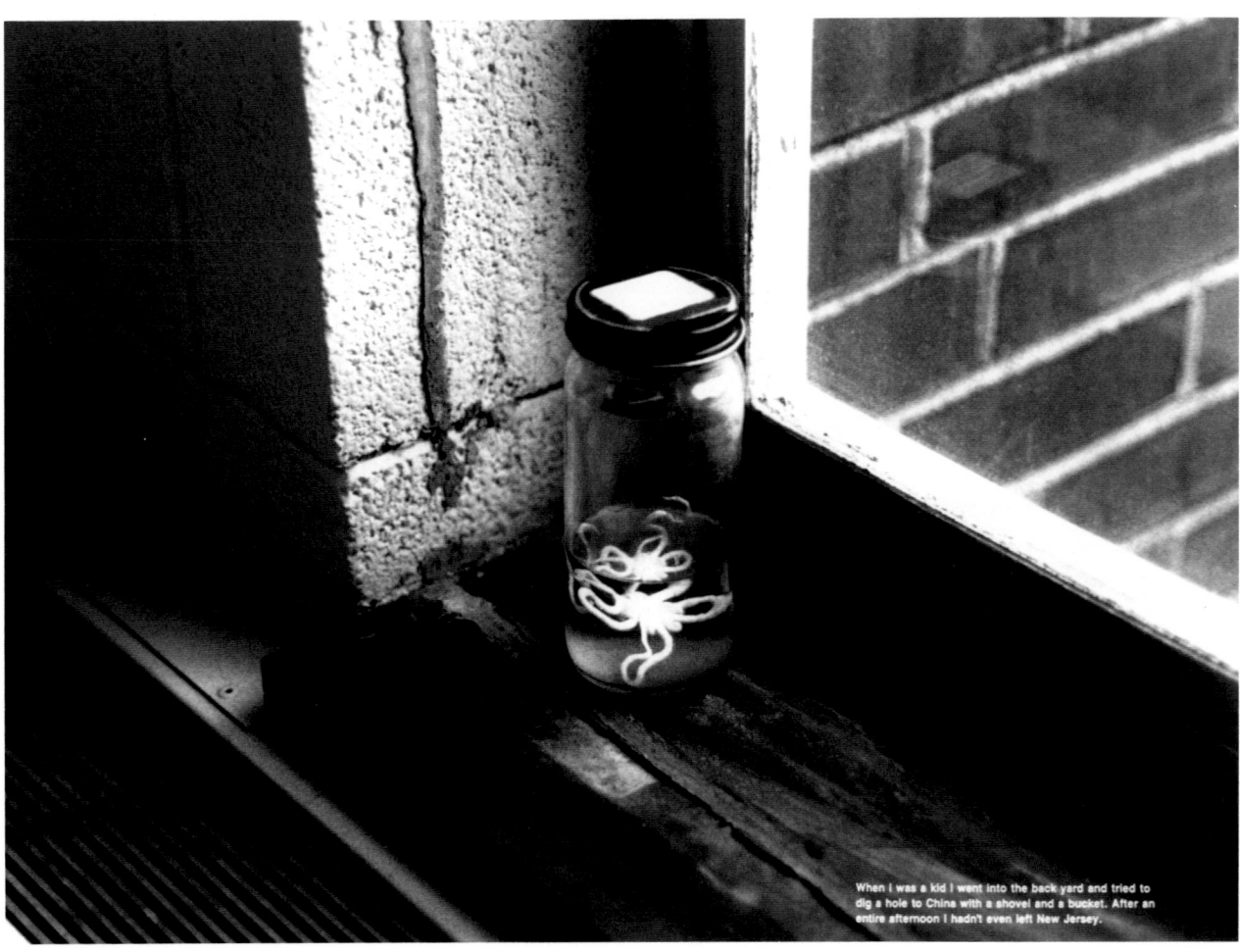

When I was a kid I went into the back yard and tried to dig a hole to China with a shovel and a bucket. After an entire afternoon I hadn't even left New Jersey.

WHEN I WAS A KID, *from an untitled series, 1990. Gelatin-silver print, 13½ x 19"*

Opposite: **TIME,** *1988–89. Gelatin-silver prints on museum board, 32 x 33" overall*

CAMERAS WERE DAVID'S constant companions. On our first date, we went to the beach on a cold January evening and photographed each other photographing each other at sunset. Riding around in a car, David would snap photos through the windshield or from a camera held outside the window in one hand while steering with the other. (And sometimes, it seemed, with a coffee container and cigarette in the third.) He would spend hours in front of the TV, fiddling with the color controls, shooting Polaroids of the images on the screen.

He used any number of cameras, both still and 8mm film, but his favorite was a simple Pentax SLR set for semiautomatic exposures, equipped with a close-up lens.

He liked to photograph industrial sites for reference images, and was always in search of factory yards where he hoped to find massive discarded gears, abandoned rusted cars, and remnants of broken machinery. He'd explore deserted buildings and town dumps as thoroughly as an archaeologist searching for signs of a lost culture.

In Mexico, at a garbage dump near Mérida in the Yucatán, David climbed atop a huge mountain of trash and decaying garbage in order to photograph packs of wild dogs and small groups of people, their noses and mouths covered with dirty bandanas, competing for scraps of food. In the meantime, I hid in the car with the windows tightly closed, cowering at what seemed like millions of parakeet-sized flies swarming in the air outside.

As interested as he was in all of these sights, nothing fascinated him so much as searching out and photographing live animals or insects. (I should also include dead ones, as the appearance of road kill was often

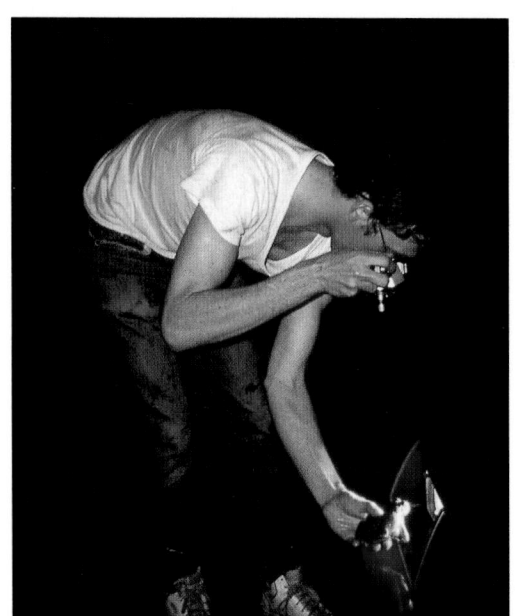

David Wojnarowicz, 1986.
Photograph by Tom Rauffenbart

Opposite: HELL IS A PLACE ON EARTH, *from an untitled series, 1990. Gelatin-silver print, 13½ x 19"*

the primary reason for a rest stop along the side of a busy highway.) Sometimes this search would lead us to visit local attractions in our travels: in Puerto Rico we attended many cockfights; in New Orleans it was a dilapidated "snake farm" located on a once busy, but now largely ignored highway; on another visit to New Orleans we discovered an alligator farm on the northern shore of Lake Pontchartrain, where we watched as bull alligators gobbled up stripped skulls of nutria, a giant rodent accidentally introduced to the Louisiana bayous and now multiplying rapidly (incidentally, they make great road kill); in Florida, during a car and boat trip through the Everglades we watched Seminole men wrestle weary alligators; and in Mérida, we attended a second-rate bullfight during which one of the bulls broke its own front leg while making a sharp turn, an event David wrote about in his first book *Close to the Knives*:

There is a gasp and cry from the crowd. The bull in all its twists and turns before the various assaults from the banderillero has broken its front leg. When the bull is confronted with the matador's cape, it drops its head low and paws at the ground, its leg goes floppy and obscenely doubles back on itself. After a wobbly charge, in trying to come to a stop, the bull's leg bends backwards and throws it into the dust. The crowd is caught in shocked identification. After surveying the situation, the matador shakes his head in sympathy and disgust. He arches his feet and points his sword at the bull in an affected graceful, arched motion. He takes aim with his X-ray eyes on that invisible point between the rolling curves of the bull's shoulders; the true point where the entrance of the steel blade will still the heart. Smell the flowers while you can.

As enticing as any of these places or events was, the first priority of any excursion trip was the search for a pond, lake, forest, swamp, or jungle where he might find critters — the creepier the better.

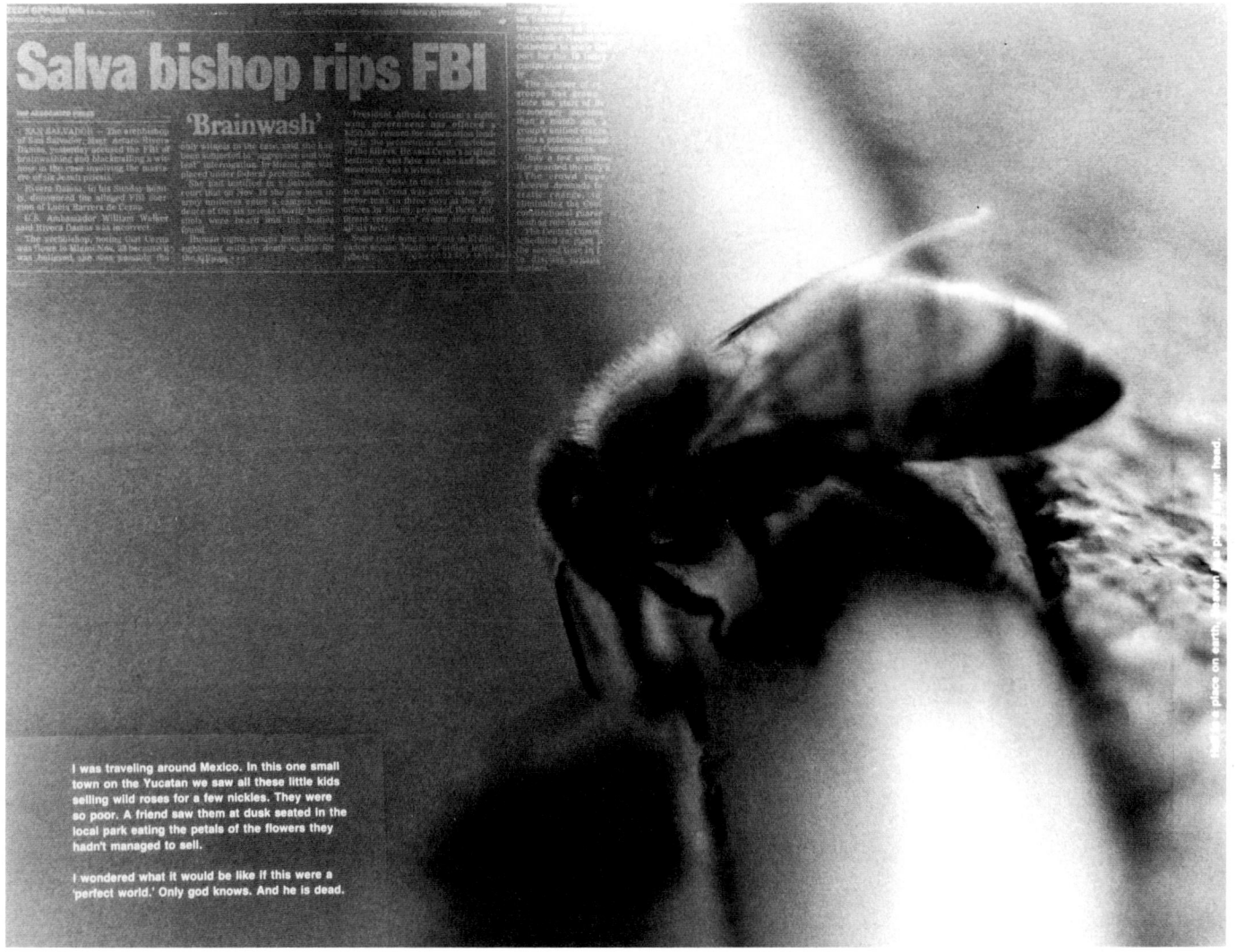

I was traveling around Mexico. In this one small town on the Yucatan we saw all these little kids selling wild roses for a few nickles. They were so poor. A friend saw them at dusk seated in the local park eating the petals of the flowers they hadn't managed to sell.

I wondered what it would be like if this were a 'perfect world.' Only god knows. And he is dead.

On one trip to Louisiana, we left New Orleans at dawn and drove several hours to meet Greg Guirard, a photographer and author, who has published several beautiful photo-essay books on the Atchafalaya Basin. In a small boat we spent a magical day exploring the severely drought-reduced waters of the bayous near his home. Giant egrets, snow-white against the dark background of ancient cypress trees, glided through the humid air of the swamp like ghostly visions, while a pair of Woody Woodpecker lookalikes pounded away at a nearby tree. At the first chance, David hopped on shore and began turning over rocks and dead tree branches until he found a small nest of unidentifiable, eyeless, slimy creatures squirming underneath. Gently he picked one up in his fingers, held it in front of his camera, snapped a few shots, and just as gently returned it unharmed. When we returned to Greg's home, we spent several hours searching out snakes in a nearby pond.

In the Yucatán, at the Mayan ruins of Chichén Itzá, he spent hours filming an endless column of leaf-cutter ants, each ant carrying a green cutout piece of leaf back to its nest. At the Great Swamp of New Jersey he focused on a water snake slowly swallowing a huge bullfrog.

While on our first trip to Puerto Rico, we went on a midnight excursion to a deserted road in a palm forest near the town of Loaiza and discovered hundreds of huge toads and giant land crabs hopping and scurrying along the surface of the dirt road. Under the glare of our rental car's headlights, he photographed whatever he could catch, holding each specimen at arm's length, turning it every which way to get just the right angle for the shot. I don't think I've ever seen him as happy as he was at that moment.

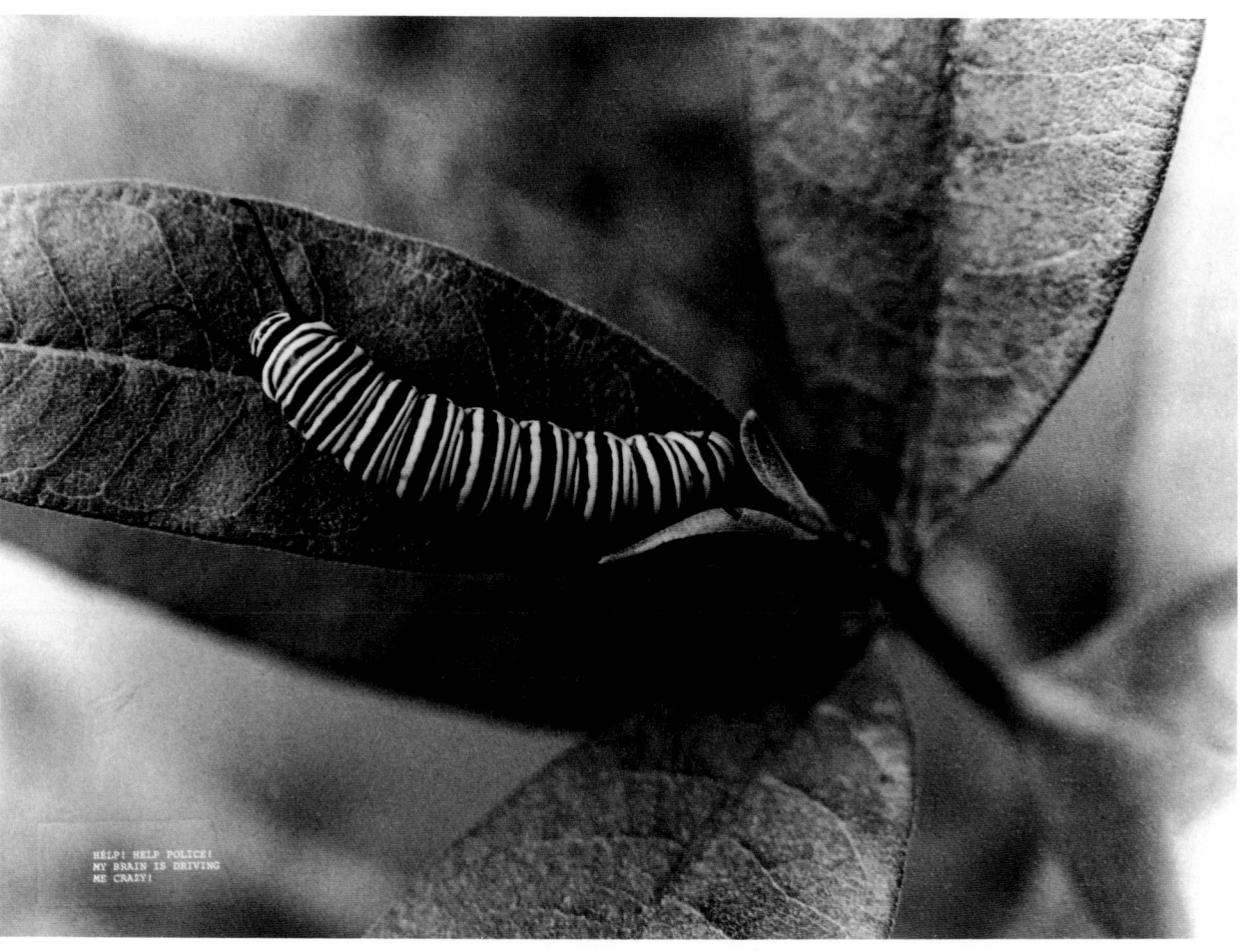

HELP! HELP POLICE!
MY BRAIN IS DRIVING
ME CRAZY!

MY BRAIN IS DRIVING ME CRAZY, *from an untitled series, 1990. Gelatin-silver print, 13½ x 19"*

Opposite: **FEVER**, *1988–89. Gelatin-silver prints on museum board, 31 x 25" overall*

David's interest in animals started during his childhood when, in an attempt to escape from his harrowing home life, he'd explore ponds and streams near his home in New Jersey.

His respect for life was so strong that he thought nothing of putting us in danger in order to avoid squashing some creature appearing out of nowhere in front of us when we drove. Once in Mexico, he, our friend Anita, and I were on our way to visit the ruins at Coba. On one long stretch of road he insisted that I drive at a snail's pace so as not to smash into any of the thousands of butterflies swirling through the air around our car. I tried, but no matter how slowly I drove, there were casualties, and as each body hit the windshield he would groan and flinch in sympathy.

But the incident that I remember most vividly took place on the last day of one of our many trips to New Orleans. During a visit several months before, he had found a pet shop outside of the city that specialized in selling different kinds of tarantulas. He had waited for months for this trip so that he could bring back some red-legged specimens. On the way to the airport for our return flight we stopped there to buy them.

Before he could make his purchase, he noticed two box turtles for sale, one of which was clearly sick. He knew which kind they were and the fact that they were an endangered species and illegal to sell. He immediately bought them both and insisted that we return to New Orleans so that he could take them to the Audubon zoo for treatment.

Already late for our flight, we raced back to the zoo, where the staff confirmed that the turtles were in very bad shape and, moved by David's concern, agreed to try to save them. Furious at the treatment given the turtles at the pet shop, he abandoned his goal of buying the tarantulas. We never knew if the turtles survived, but we returned to the zoo on later trips and were sure that we recognized them living contentedly in the Louisiana Bayou exhibit. 🐾

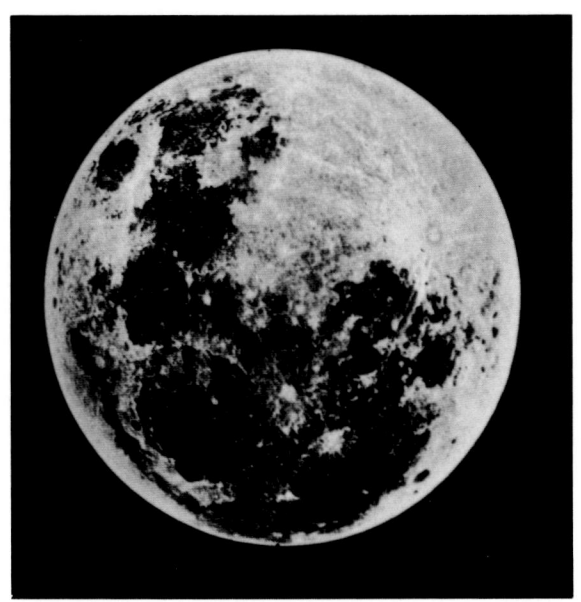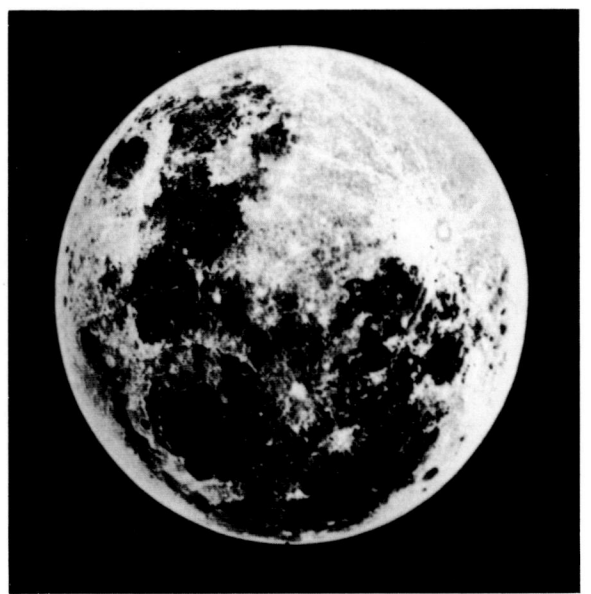

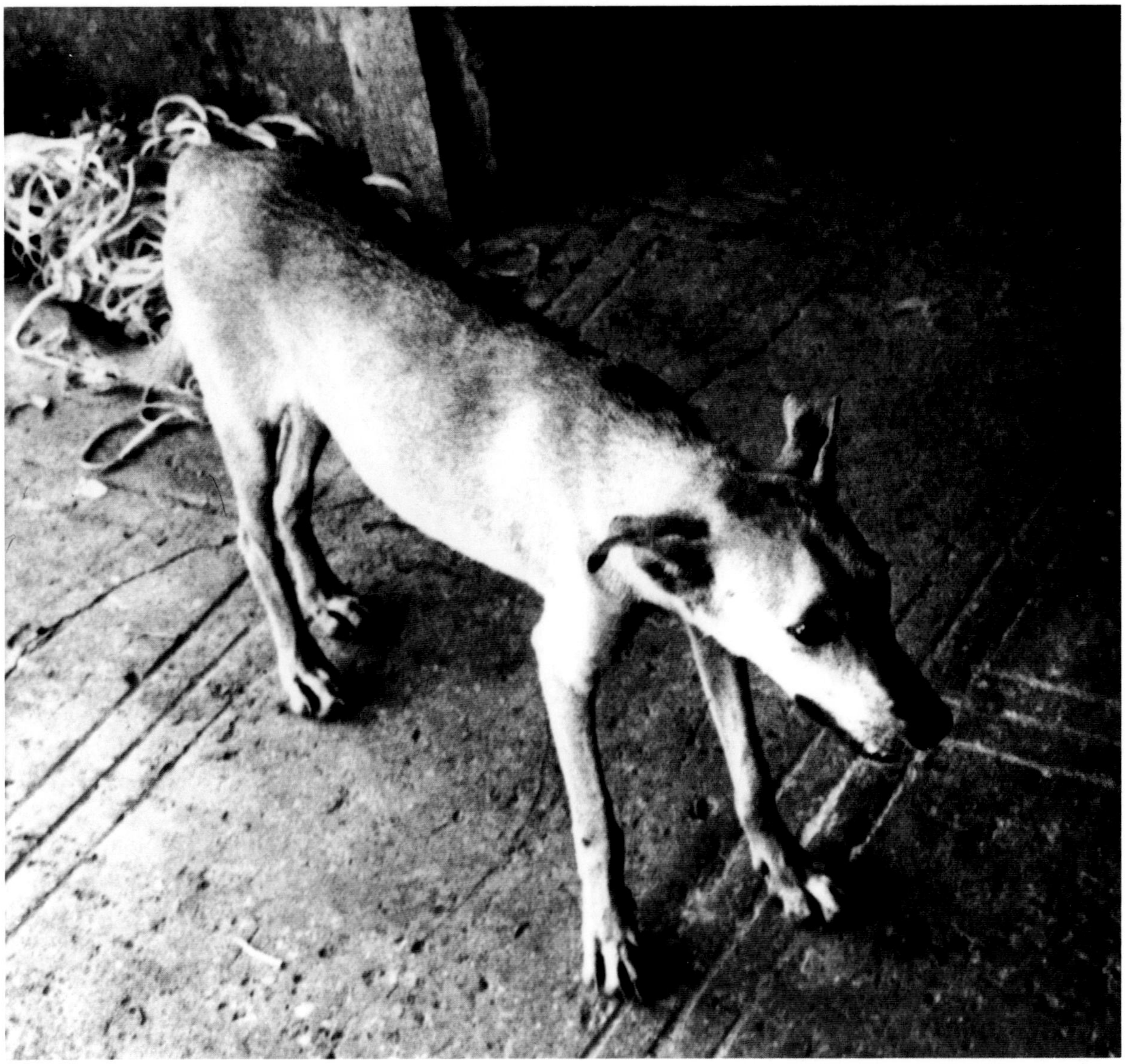

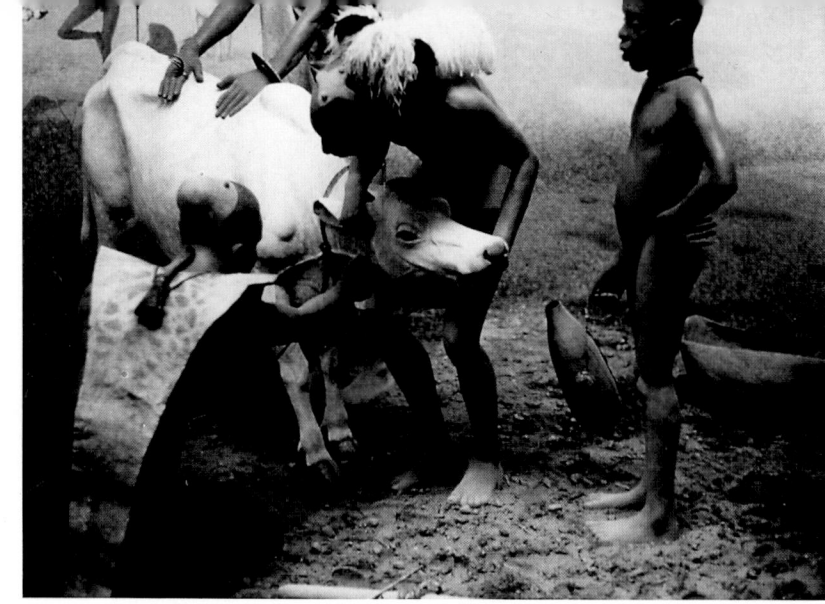

Are photographs just tiny windows looking into the world, frozen moments of it that lie flat and quiet without sound or smell or movement? Susan Whatsername said something about photographs being like small deaths which is maybe true. Maybe not. Maybe such a statement reflects that person's fear of being photographed. Certain people in certain places for ages have felt that a photograph steals a part of your soul, so when someone aimed a camera at them they were likely to throw a spear or cut the photographers throat or shoot them, or slug the photographer on the chin and demand a fifteen percent cut of the royalties. To me, photographs are like words and I generally will place many photographs together or print them one inside the other in order to construct a free-floating sentence that speaks about the world I witness. History is made by and for particular classes of people. A camera in some hands can preserve an alternate history.

> — David Wojnarowicz,
>   from *Close to the Knives*

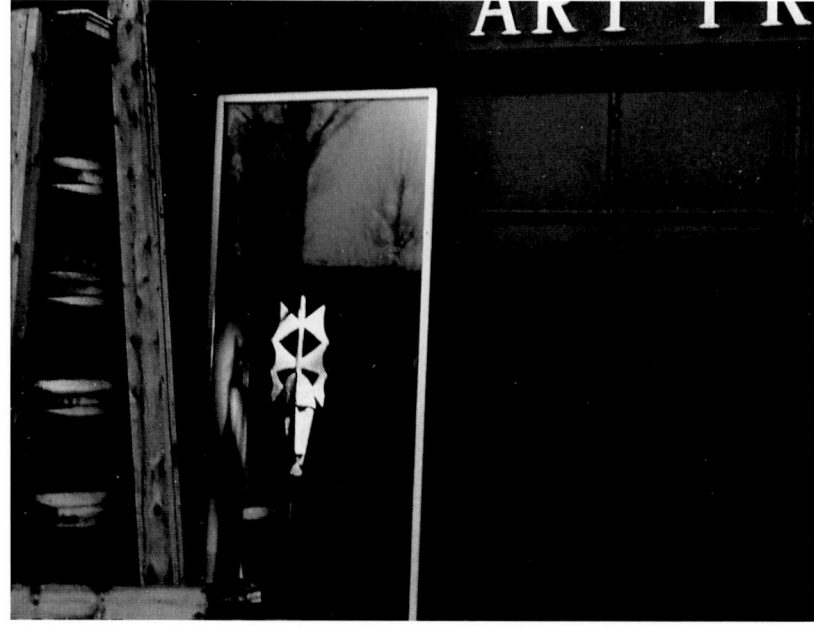

TRAVELS THROUGH AFRICA, *1988–89.*
Black-and-white and color photographs,
34 x 38" overall

54

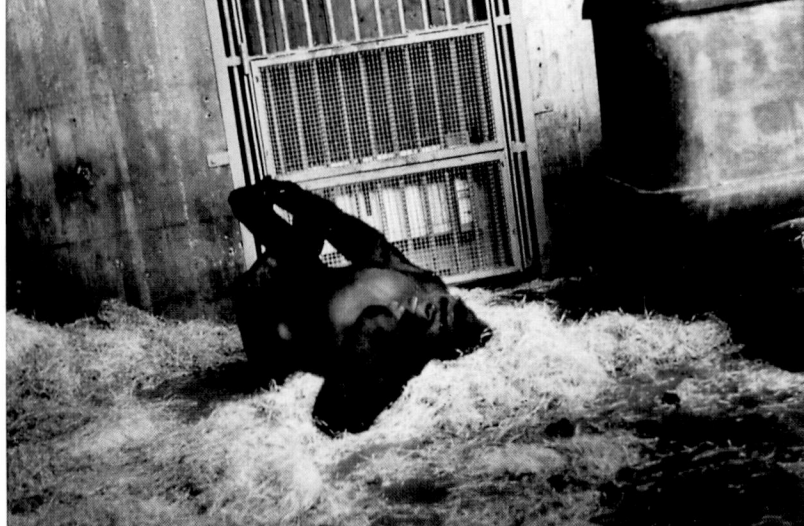

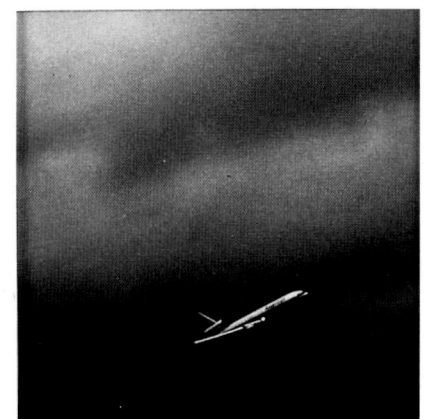
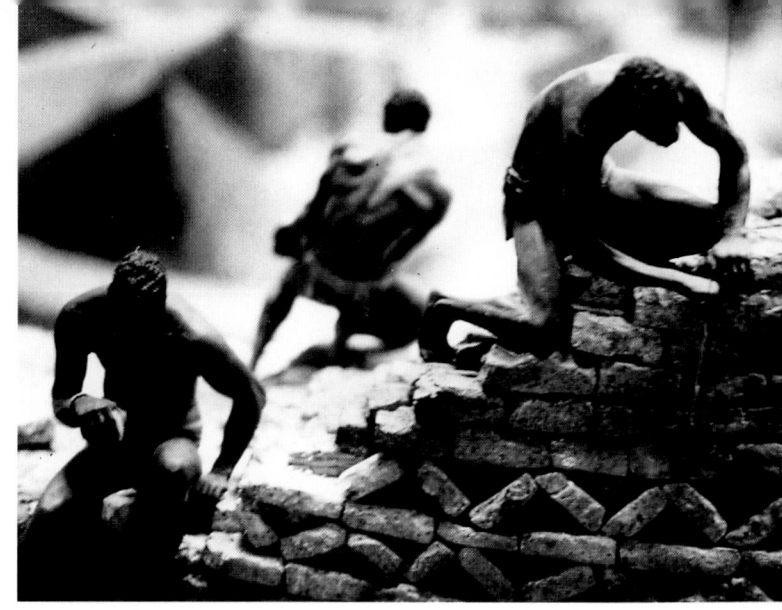
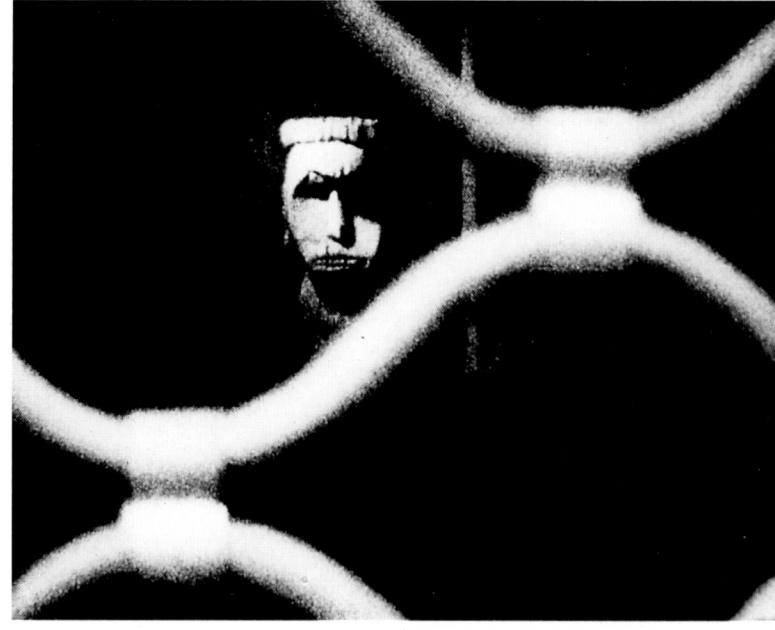
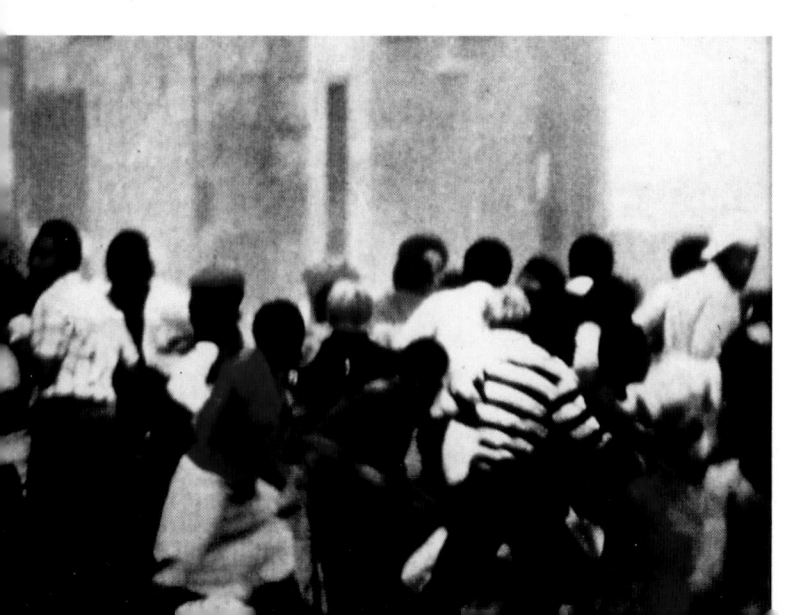
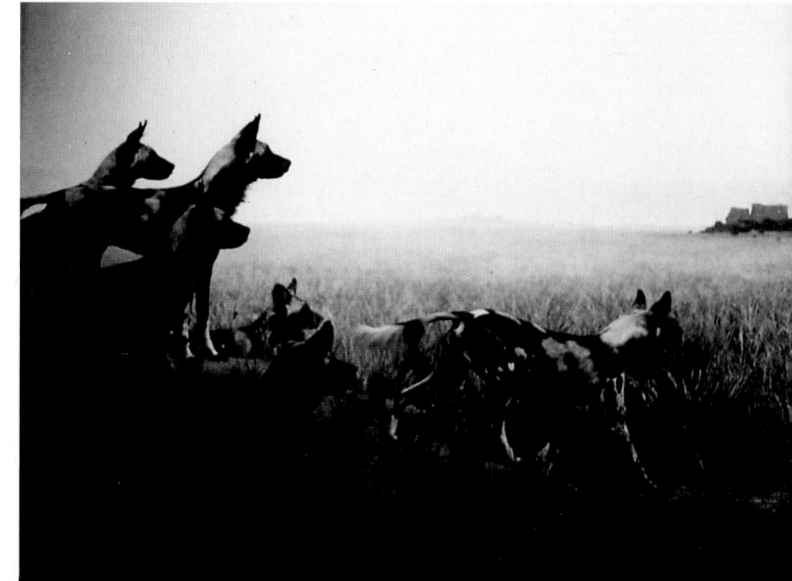

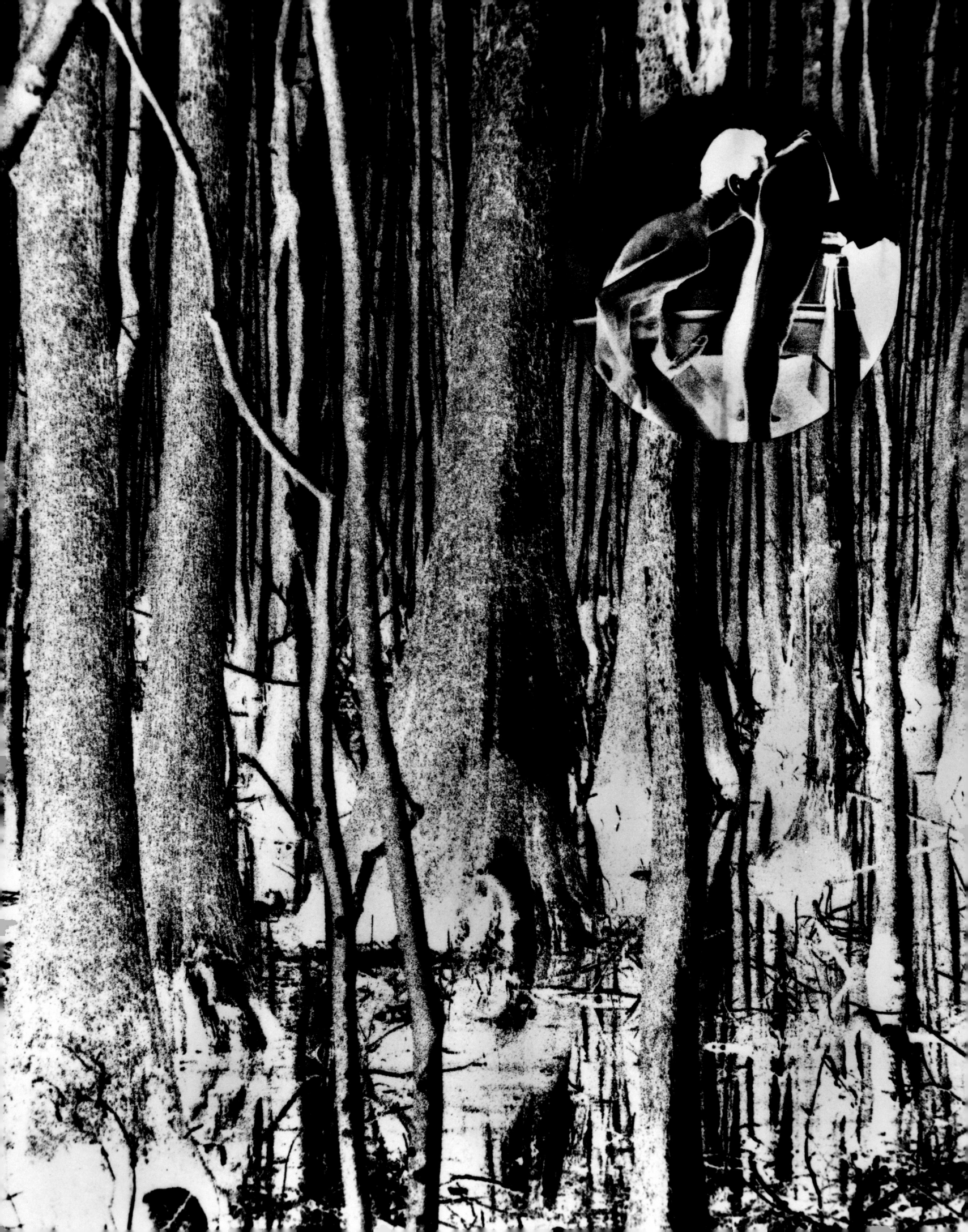

Love, sex, art, and death: in September of 1990, David

Wojnarowicz and photographer **Nan Goldin**, longtime friends,

sat down to a three-hour conversation....

This interview was commissioned by INTERVIEW *magazine and Brant Publications. Excerpts of the interview were originally published in* INTERVIEW'S *February 1991 issue.*

David Wojnarowicz: Nan is kvetching about the size of her calamari.

Nan Goldin: It's *tiny*.

DW: They yank these squids out of the deep blue sea and....

NG: They're like your sperm sculptures!

DW: Little *mutant* sperms! Nan's eating mutant sperm at a fashionable Lower East Side restaurant.

NG: How old are you now? Thirty-six?

DW: I'm turning thirty-six tomorrow.

NG: Happy Birthday! My birthday's the day after—I didn't know we were born so close together. And now you have a new book, *Close to the Knives*. Tell me about the epilogue. You've said it's your favorite piece of writing.

DW: Yeah. A few months ago, I went to Mexico and I was really sick. It was just after I found out that [the Reverend Donald] Wildmon had sent out that piece of appropriationist sex literature saying that it was mine—but I had to leave the next morning, I didn't have a chance to see it. I was in the Yucatán. I was feeling as sick as a dog, and I was with Tom and we found a poster for a bullfight in some dive neighborhood. He wanted to go and I was like, "Ohhh." I felt really sick, and I was lying in this hotel room

with Walt Disney Mexican Mouse cartoons playing in Spanish, which really unnerved me. I really thought I was gonna lose my mind. And I was feeling unbelievably horny—in a sense that I did way in the past, in terms of something like a teenager...you know that kind of bottom-line, sidewalk lust? So I went for a walk and found this pool hall at the end of a park in the middle of Mérida. I was lurking around the pool hall and watching some unbelievably beautiful guy unload a truck. And if you know the scene, you can go in and see this old guy in the back who gives out the pool cues—and for zero money you can rent out a little chamber. It's right next to the park, so that's ideally where you meet the boys, none of whom can afford condoms, so it's this major death scene waiting to hap-

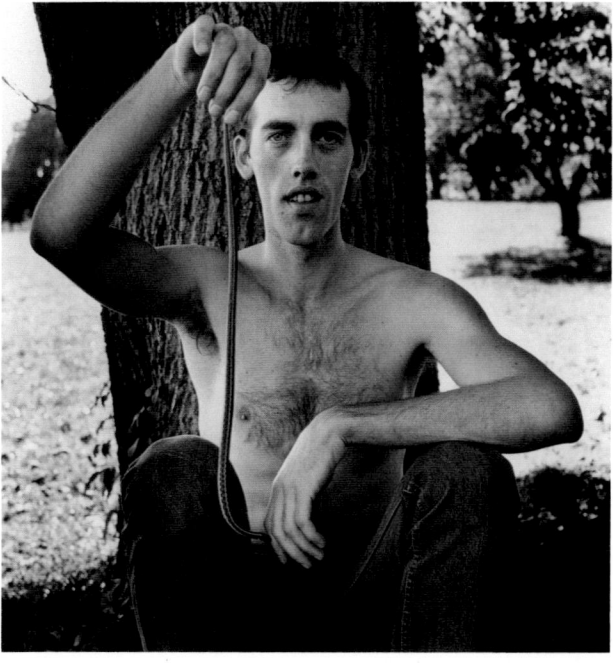

pen. I was feeling this intense lust, just standing on the street corner in a daze, having these thoughts of lustful sex, and…and it got very frustrating, so I went back and told Tom, "Okay, let's go to the bullfight." I figured maybe blood would wake me up, or snap me out of this daze. And during this bullfight I kept this journal which was horrifying. I mean, I'd seen a bullfight before on TV in Mexico City, and there was one guy who killed the bull—I suddenly understood what the sport was. Because it was one of the most unbelievable movements of the male body through space, so extraordinarily beautiful that the death was like a climax. And it made perfect sense in a very profound way. But *these* guys were like horrendous bullfighters, and they were totally carving up these bulls in the ring. So while I was there I started writing this piece, and it jumps between all the events of my childhood, from my first sexual experience as a six- or seven-year-old kid to the experience of my father, who was completely brutal and sadistic, to all these images of violence that I remember as a child.

My earliest memory is of hearing a police siren go by. And I remember running blocks to follow it and when I got there there was this guy in a white T-shirt on a front lawn with a gun to a woman's head. So my piece jumps into all these random violent scenes in Jersey, and then sexual scenes, and it's interspersed with this slow, tense buildup of the bullfight. I sat there and just notated every description and color and smell, all the dust and the heat. I wove in some of the fantasy stuff from the pool hall and the guy unloading the truck, following that through in my imagination and getting the key and going to the room and crawling across the bed at him….

NG: Listening to you it seems like there's no difference for you between then and now; your visual and verbal memories are so acute. I read your story about your trip to the meteor crater and it was like a road movie. I had the best sex after reading it.

DW: Wow, that's great! My strongest memories are always connected to really powerful images, images that I can drift on, that I can never forget. Years ago, a trucker told me that driving a truck was the one thing in the world that made the most sense for people to do because you're essentially at rest in the seat of the truck, and you're alone. You're encapsulated by the form of a vehicle—but at the same time your landscape is forever changing, so it's not the same thing as being at home. It's almost like the perfect state of being, to be floating through a landscape and at rest at the same time. I always love that feeling of riding in a car, except that the mental stuff gets very, very intense. Your brain starts chattering away. Plus it gets very sexual, very sensual. You start populating that car with men.

NG: Was that real, the story about meeting that guy at the rest station?

DW: Yeah. We were literally in the middle of nowhere, in a car. You could see hundreds of miles in any direction and not see a soul, and the fact that it was illegal for him to put his dick in my mouth seemed so completely absurd to me at the time, in that landscape. I wrote, "If a cop rolled up while I was lost in orgasm, and I had a gun, I would have shot him." And been justified. And it all happened down the road from this major tourist trap, where that meteorite, a twenty-seven-ton chunk of metal hit the earth 500,000 years ago, and now some jerk charges five bucks just to look at the hole. It's so perfectly American.

NG: So much of your work is about desire. Where does your sexual desire lie now?

DW: Well, an element of my sexuality has always been fantasy, or in the anonymous sex that I've had. It's something I've loved about growing up in the seventies, and going over to the warehouses occasionally, or in the parks, or in the subways, or four o'clock in the morning, on a train going to Brooklyn. There's this enormous projection of created biography that I would project on to the other guy that I was engaging in sexual activities with—the sum total of desires. It could be the line of the guy's neck, or a gesture they make, or the way they light a cigarette, or the way that street light falls on their face, or the way their pants hang on their hips. I would project a biography on the other person, and interact with some element of that, within the real physical touching of that sexual experience.

After my diagnosis I had to rearrange *how* I have sex—I mean there's a full expression of sexuality without ever having a dick in

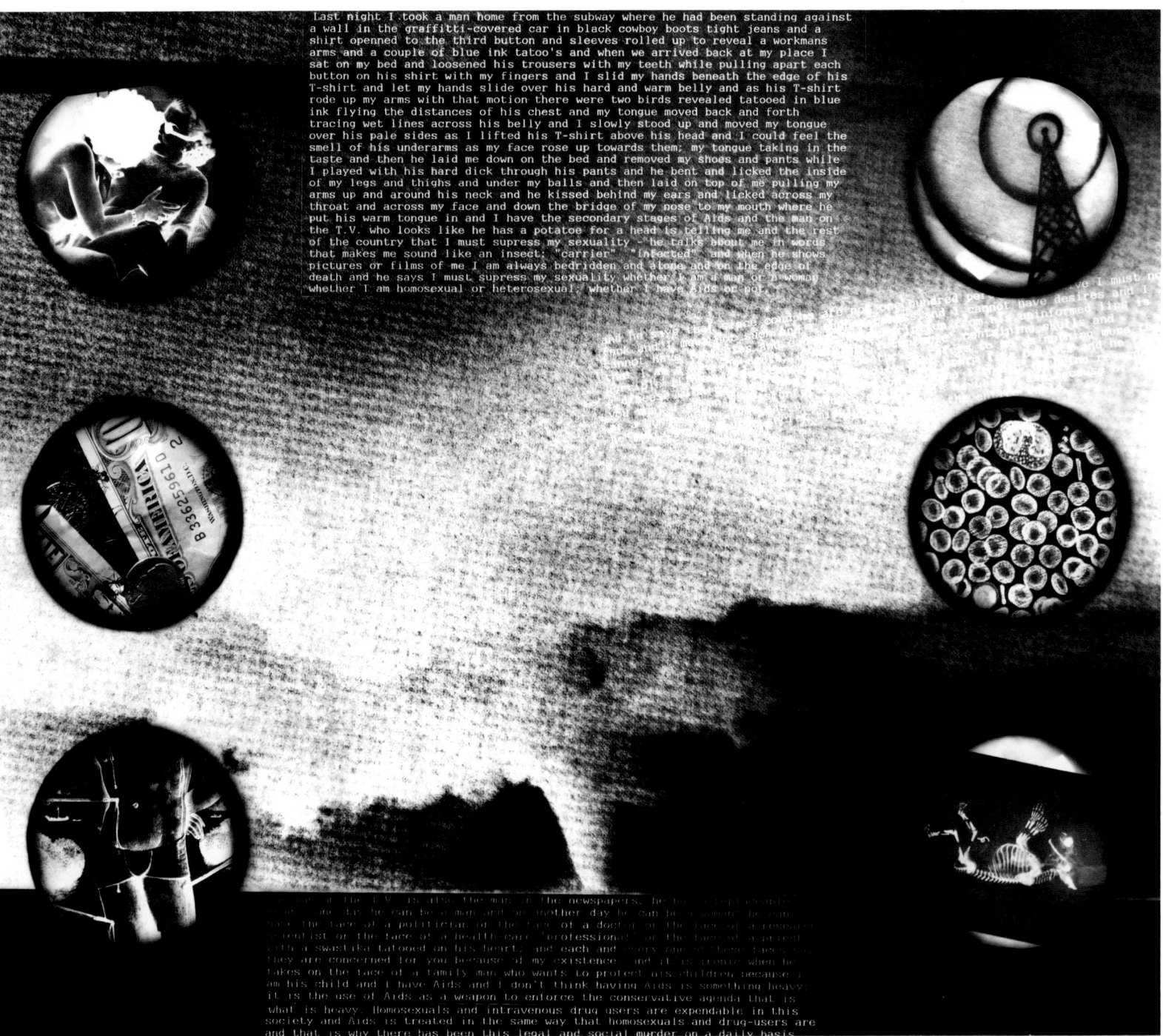

Last night I took a man home from the subway where he had been standing against
a wall in the graffitti-covered car in black cowboy boots tight jeans and a
shirt openned to the third button and sleeves rolled up to reveal a workmans
arms and a couple of blue ink tatoo's and when we arrived back at my place I
sat on my bed and loosened his trousers with my teeth while pulling apart each
button on his shirt with my fingers and I slid my hands beneath the edge of his
T-shirt and let my hands slide over his hard and warm belly and as his T-shirt
rode up my arms with that motion there were two birds revealed tatooed in blue
ink flying the distances of his chest and my tongue moved back and forth
tracing wet lines across his belly and I slowly stood up and moved my tongue
over his pale sides as I lifted his T-shirt above his head and I could feel the
smell of his underarms as my face rose up towards them; my tongue taking in the
taste and then he laid me down on the bed and removed my shoes and pants while
I played with his hard dick through his pants and he bent and licked the inside
of my legs and thighs and under my balls and then laid on top of me pulling my
arms up and around his neck and he kissed behind my ears and licked across my
throat and across my face and down the bridge of my nose to my mouth where he
put his warm tongue in and I have the secondary stages of Aids and the man on
the T.V. who looks like he has a potatoe for a head is telling me and the rest
of the country that I must supress my sexuality - he talks about me in words
that makes me sound like an insect; "carrier" "infected" and when he shows
pictures or films of me I am always bedridden and alone and on the edge of
death and he says I must supress my sexuality whether I am a man or a woman
whether I am homosexual or heterosexual, whether I have Aids or not.

the man on the T.V. is also the man in the newspapers, he has the reversible
head; one day he can be a man and an other day he can be a woman; he can
wear the face of a politician or the face of a doctor or the face of a research
scientist or the face of a health-care 'professional' or the face of a priest
with a swastika tatooed on his heart, and each and every one of these faces say
they are concerned for you because of my existence and it is ironic when he
takes on the face of a family man who wants to protect his children because i
am his child and i have Aids and i don't think having Aids is something heavy;
it is the use of Aids as a weapon to enforce the conservative agenda that is
what is heavy. Homosexuals and intravenous drug users are expendable in this
society and Aids is treated in the same way that homosexuals and drug-users are
and that is why there has been this legal and social murder on a daily basis

your mouth, or your behind. There's a whole range of sexual expression that I can enact with another person. But at the same time, I'm living in a country where in Reno, Nevada, there's a woman who is now serving a life sentence for agreeing to have sex with an undercover cop, as a prostitute, on the condition that he wear two rubbers, one on top the other, because she was HIV-positive and she felt that would protect him and her. And it *would* have. She got arrested and it

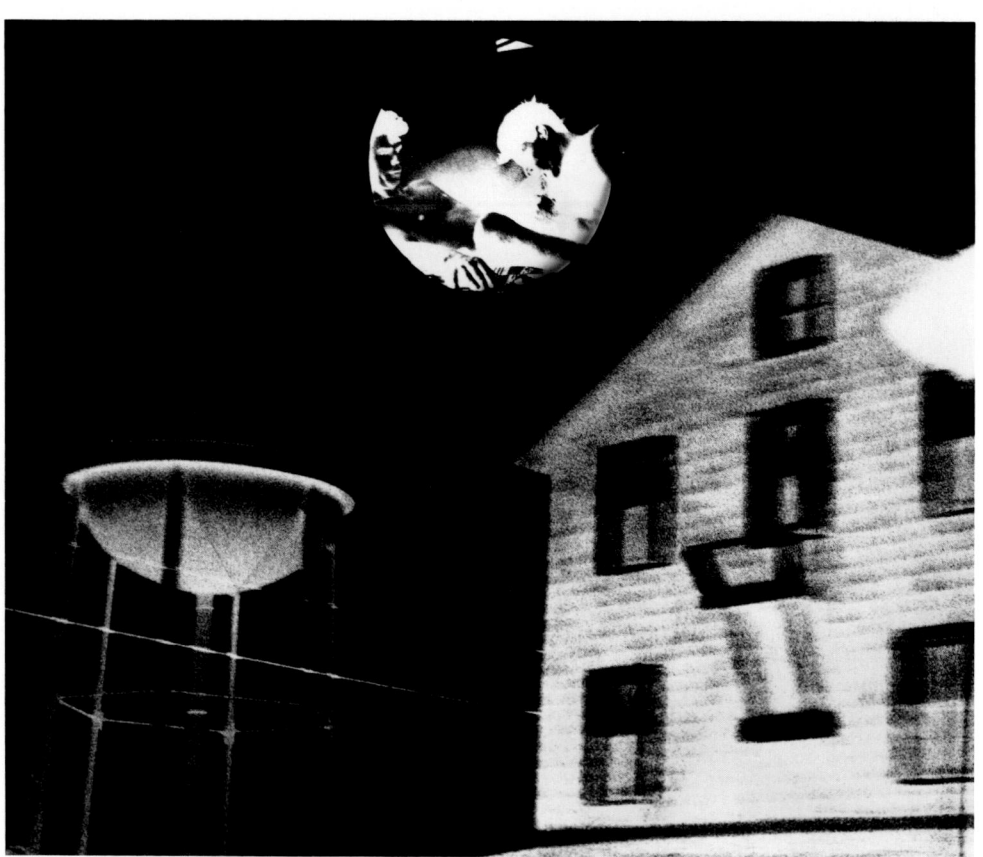

was a setup. And now she's serving a life sentence. So how can we even begin to deal with people with AIDS being just as sexual as anybody else? Some people have this idea that you're diagnosed with AIDS and all of a sudden you're just a disease on two legs, or you're just waiting for death, or that your life goes into suspended animation. Or that you're facing some death skull down the road, and it's just *bullshit*.

How do you tell a twenty-year-old kid who's diagnosed HIV-positive that he *can't* have desire, he *can't* touch others, he *can't* express his sexuality? Despite the epidemic, people are having just as much sex as ever. A condom, if used correctly, will prevent

transmission of disease. There's a full range of sexual expression that I've always tapped into ever since I was a kid. It doesn't all boil down to putting my dick in somebody's mouth, or vice versa. You could lick every square inch of somebody's body and have a *wild* fucking time, you know. I love the taste of flesh, the interaction of flesh. You know, living in America, it's like we're all used to getting fucked, but I prefer to feel the weight of somebody on me when I'm getting fucked, as opposed to what we experience from government.

NG: Did you know other people who were homosexual when you were a kid?

DW: Yeah. Thirty-year-old guys, forty-year-old guys. I've always said that I had my mid-life crisis when I was sixteen. Because I hung around with all these older guys who picked me up in Times Square. And I got to know their mental structures so well that I believed I'd never go through what they went through because of this proximity. I've never feared getting old—actually, I love the idea of getting old, especially these days. I'd be very happy to be a ninety-year-old coot with a cane, whapping someone on the head.

NG: You still might. Did you know that other boys had the same fantasies that you did?

DW: I didn't know until I got seduced by teenagers when I was six or seven. When I was little I always thought that a cock-sucker was like some species of caterpillar.

NG: At what point did you start feeling desire?

DW: My first sense of desire was sitting on a couch. My stepmother and my half-sister and my brother all got in a car to go pick up my father at the bus station. He used to go away for weeks or months at a time. I was sitting on the couch looking at a *TV Guide* and I came across a soap advertisement with this guy under a stream of running water, lathering himself up. And there was something about his face, his lips, his arms, the bicep—I went into a trance. It must have lasted an hour and a half. And all of a sudden, I heard the sound of a car coming in the driveway, and I *snapped* the magazine shut and hid it, and went up to my room. When I think back to that it's my first sense of desire and my first sense of guilt.

NG: You wrote in one of your books about that line between you and self-destruction. And how you were standing on one foot, with one foot over the line.

DW: I talk about that scene. I write a lot about what it means to come back from self-destruction. Essentially every person I've ever been friends with has been a fighter of some kind. And they are the people that have made this world worth living in. Their sensibilities are what give me comfort in my life. So to see people come back from drugs, or other compulsive behaviors—people who are fighting their way back from that.... There are not many things that I can say I'm really happy about in my life, but I really love seeing those people come back, and I feel like what they're coming back to do is to confront the state all over again, in a way that's not self-destructive to them.

NG: How do you manage to look head-on at all this stuff? What I feel about all your work and particularly your writing is that you go in with your eyes wide open, and you go as deep as you can. How do you feel safe enough to do that?

DW: If something makes me uncomfortable, or scares me, or threatens me, I get really pissed off. I'm angry about feeling all this outside pressure that demands that I feel guilty or afraid. The only way I can stop that sense is to surround myself with that fear and get to understand its shape. And once I know its shape, then it can't affect me. The only way I could survive all my life was to stick my fingers in it, even though I understood that to confront all this was somehow taboo. When I was younger I used to feel guilty that I looked at death, or that I looked at all that bad stuff around me and spoke of it. Even as a child, people would act like I was morose or weird.

NG: You've said, "Hell is a place on earth and heaven is a place in your head." In reading your work that comes right through. I mean, I can't avert my eyes anymore, because of your text. But how do you walk down the street without averting your eyes?

DW: I've done that since I was a kid. I

remember trying to describe this to someone. And I said, "The two of us could walk down the street and you would probably notice the fresh begonias in the window up there, that drift of cloud on the right, that building and maybe this attractive person. And I would come away seeing the bum's rotted feet, with the infections and the maggots and the stink and the smell, and I would come away with the full weight of what that block contained."

NG: And how do you translate that horror

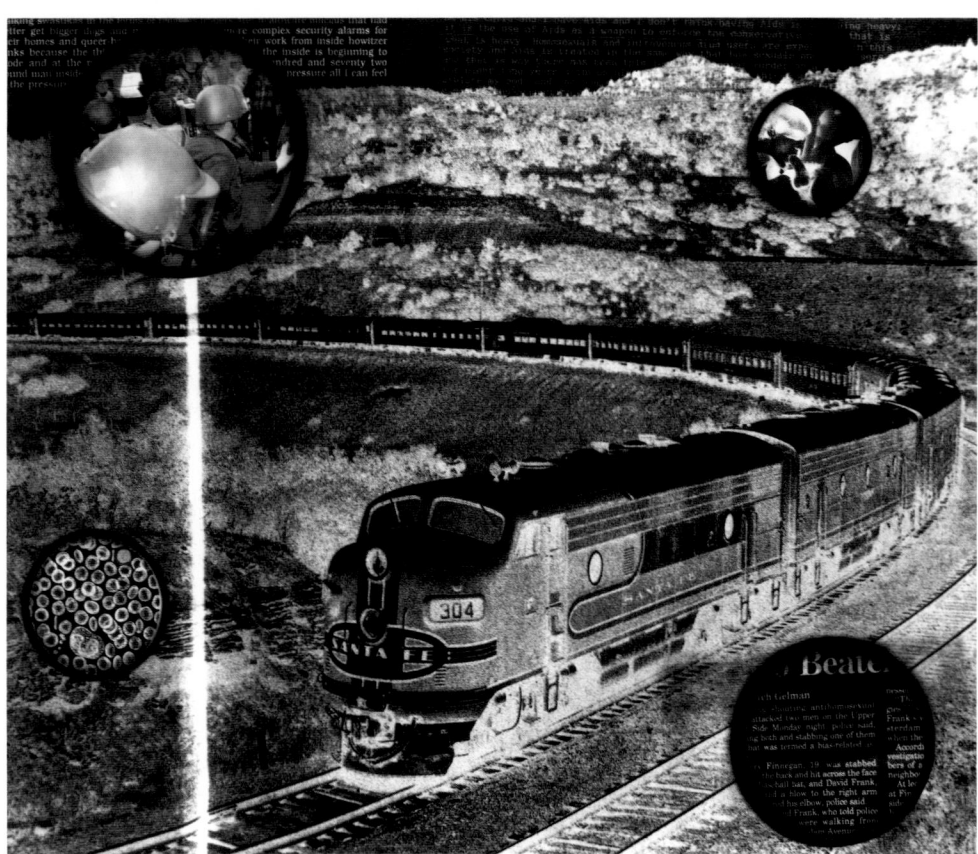

into something that you can live with? Through your writing?

DW: Yeah. And I think it quickly develops into rage. I've been in rage all my life at this thing we call "society."

NG: You talk about this line between you and the mass murderer as being very thin, that each of us has that potential in us, and that we're all capable of it. Do you feel in some way the book is your mass murder?

DW: I've always wanted to write a book that really talked about the things I've seen in this country. If I could write a book that killed America, I would have done it.

NG: Did you find that things were different when you moved to Europe?

DW: I thought I'd live there for the rest of my life. I loved it. I mean, only 'cause a whole new collection of men were there. [*Laughing*] Boy, were they hot! But Europeans are practically crushed under the weight of their history. At least we are free to invent anything.

NG: You write for relief from your own perceptions, but is it also because you think it's important to leave a record? I think America is the land of revisionist memory.

DW: Absolutely. My two biggest impulses for writing the book were: if some kid gets a hold if it and would feel less alienated, great. I really suffered as a teenager, because I never had any indication that there was anything out there that reflected myself. But I also wanted to leave a record. Because once

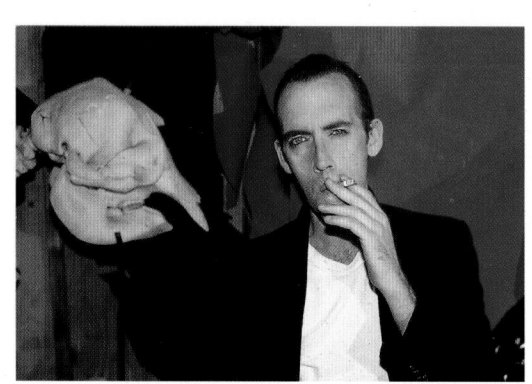

this body drops I'd like some of my experience to live on. It was a total relief to have put words to what I put words to, an enormous relief.

NG: How did you go from living on the streets to living on the Lower East Side?

DW: I went to this halfway house for ex-cons. They thought I was so desperate that I'd become a convict it they didn't take me in. Then I worked in manual labor here in New York and in custodial jobs. I mean, the same shit I'm doing now, you know. [*Laughing*] In the art world. Just shifting through society's garbage.

NG: Were you writing at the time?

DW: Yeah. I've been writing since I got off the streets. I started out writing bad poems, and then I started with the monologues in my early twenties. I've also made things since I was a kid. I used to make sexual "Archie" comics out of collage and then throw them down the incinerator whenever I'd hear my family coming home.

NG: When did you start showing your work publicly?

DW: Around 1982. Some jerk-off in SoHo actually called up Peter Hujar and asked him if he knew who had done these stencils on abandoned cars on the East Side. When I lived on the Bowery, whenever there was a car wreck, they dragged the wreck right outside my apartment and they'd leave it there for eight or nine months. Then I discovered

that if I stenciled all these images of war all over the wrecks, they'd tow them overnight. So for a while, I did that, and then I started stenciling on the walls and then I went through SoHo and spray-painted all these gallery doors with burning houses. I was doing these action installations, along with Julie Hair, where we took a hundred pounds of bloody cow bones and threw them down the staircase at Leo Castelli's, and stenciled an empty plate and knife and a fork on the wall, and then we ran off. This was right in the middle of a Saturday afternoon. Nobody raised an eyelash.

NG: How do you feel about the art world now?

DW: If the art world was reduced — if conditions in this country increase in the direction they've been going, and suddenly all art was made to look like tiny refrigerators, the art world wouldn't falter for a moment. I think that the real power structure, the money structure, the collector structure, the boards of museums and institutions, 98 percent of those people would be happy to keep a market alive for small refrigerators. And those are the people that should be held accountable for the state of things in this country. They've never collected real culture in this country. Their mirror is completely tarnished. The only thing they reflect is their investments and their private collections.

NG: What would you like your work to do?

DW: I want to make somebody else feel less alienated — that's the most meaningful thing to me. I think part of what informs the book is the pain of having grown up for years and years believing I was from some other planet.

NG: A lot of people I know still see you as kind of the moral conscience of our time. How does that make you feel?

DW: I want people to hear me. I want to be understood and acknowledged to a certain extent. But do I think that something I say might have the weight to shift something? I don't know.

NG: It does for me. It does for a lot of people.

DW: Good, but then you also have that effect on me. We can all affect each other, by being open enough to make each other feel less alienated. We all are able to have a profound affect on each other, a positive effect that sustains us....But I ain't no Jesus. [*Laughs*] 🌀

Nan Goldin, DAVID WOJNAROWICZ AT HOME, NEW YORK CITY, *1991. Cibachrome print, 30 x 40"*

For most people with Aids in this country their only alternative to the highly toxic AZT is the possibility of getting into a government/drug company sponsored drug trial - most women are excluded from these trials for no apparent reason; 1/3 of one percent of all women with Aids manage to gain access to these drug trials. Lesbians are completely excluded and even the government statistics on Aids will not recognize lesbians as either existing or vulnerable to the disease of Aids. Puerto Ricans, Blacks, Haitian and other people of color are excluded from these drug trials. The drug companies insist that in order to be eligible for inclusion in the drug trials one must have a private physician who can monitor the amounts of the drug you take. This automatically excludes the poor or those on welfare since their healthcare usually takes place in clinics where the doctors are constantly rotated. So this means that only white middleclass men have some chance of receiving drugs for the treatment of Aids if they are unable to handle the toxicity of AZT. Word is out that many poor minorities are unable to get a diagnosis of Aids from clinic doctors because if given a diagnosis then hospital beds have to be made available to them in the event of severe illness such as P.C.P. pneumonia. A poor person with P.C.P. stands a good chance of a clinic doctor telling them they only have the flu and being given ineffective antibiotics and told to come back later if it doesn't improve. Obviously this means they will die a short time later at home or in the hotel they live in or in the shelters.

Homeless men or women are not diagnosed even though city statistics acknowledge there are between five and ten thousand homeless people with Aids living on the city streets or in shelters where they are susceptible to the more than 300 opportunistic infections people with Aids can get. T.B. and pneumonia is rampant in the shelter sytem. Shelter doctors are likely to purposefully not diagnose homeless people with Aids because hospitals are overcrowded and the beds are saved for people with insurance or money. Intravenous drug users have to be completely clean of drugs for a period of seven years before they are elegible for drug trials. The waiting period for most addiction treatment centers is one to two years; so this means a drug-addict who has Aids has to kick his or her habit and then stay alive some how for seven years before being considered for the drug trials. It has taken eight years for the city government to begin information campaigns aimed at intravenous drug users and only recently have some small ads on the subway begun to use the spanish language even though an enormous amount of heterosexual people with Aids are from minority communities. They also say the homosexual community is so well informed that there need be no ad campaigns aimed at homosexuality and safe sex - once again this is nonsense; there are large percentages of men who engage in homosexual activity but because they simple fuck some guy or get blown by a guy they don't consider themselves homosexual. And although the gay baths in lower Manhattan were closed down the baths in harlem have been allowed to remain open and city health officials still won't acknowledge that Lesbians can get Aids.

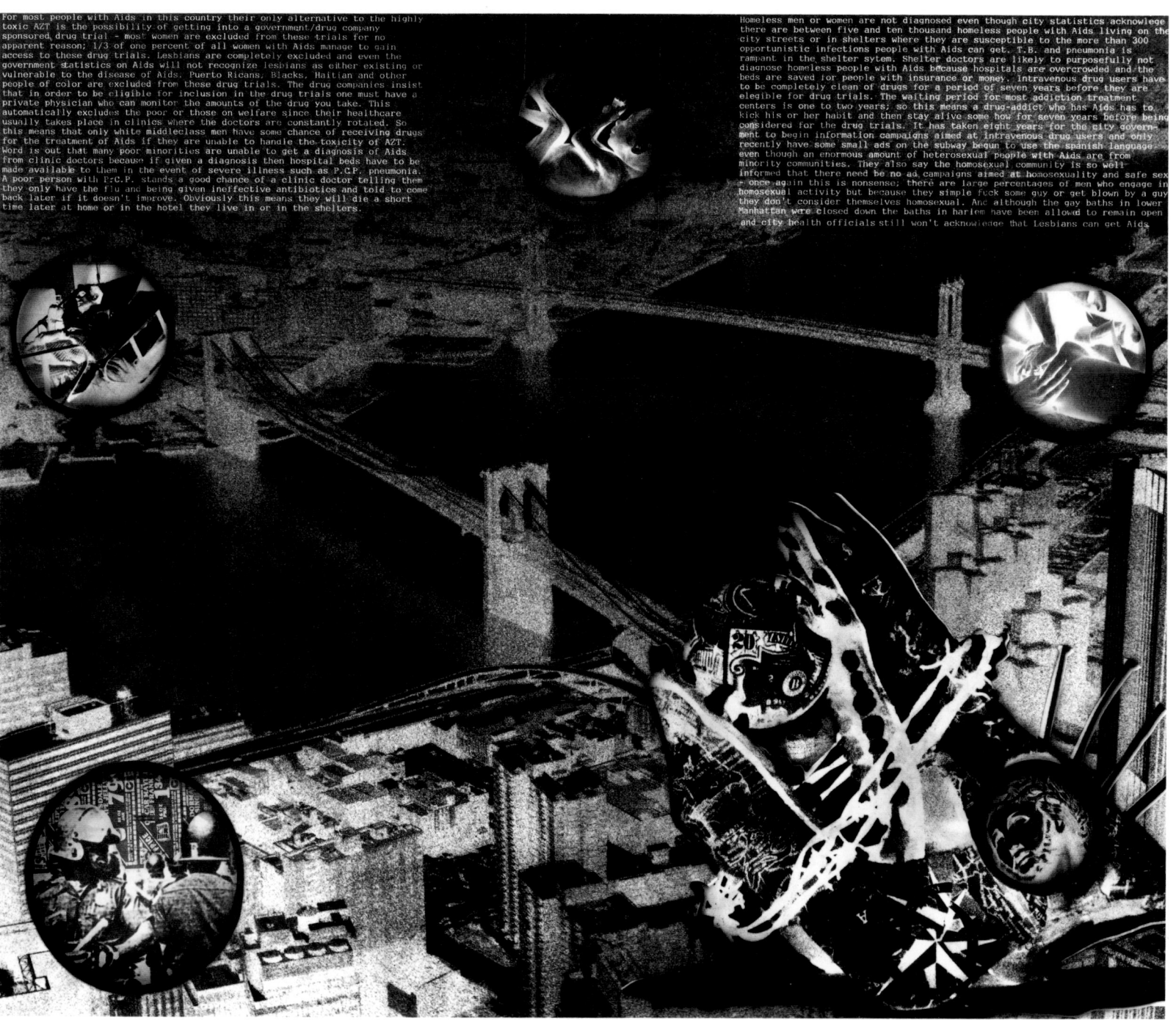

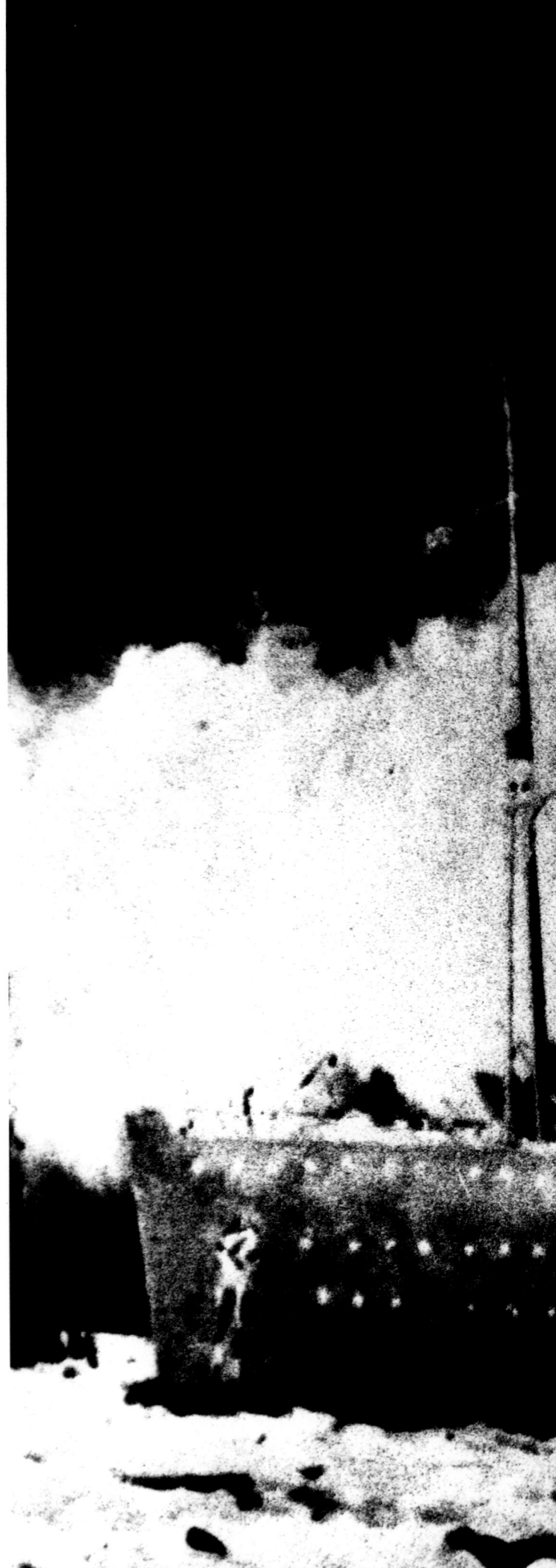

Step back a few hundred miles into space; in the air above all this it all looks like ants in a clockwork maze of pre-invented structures. By mixing variations of sexual expressions there is the attempt to dismantle the structures formed by category; all are affected by laws and policies. The spherical structures embedded in the series are about examination and or surveillance. Looking through a microscope or looking through a telescope or the monitoring that takes place in looking through the lens of a set of binoculars. Its about oppression or suppression. Its about sexuality in this age of Aids and the attempted suppression of sexuality. Are you comfortable looking at these images of obvious sexual acts in a crowded room. Do you fear judgement if you pause for a long time before an image of sexual expression? Can you sense absurdity or embrace in the viewing of images.... I'm in the throes of facing my own mortality and in attempting to communicate what I'm experiencing or learning in order to try and help others I am effectively silenced. I am angry.

    —David Wojnarowicz, excerpted from his text
      on the "Sex Series" in *In the Shadow
      of Forward Motion,* 1988–89

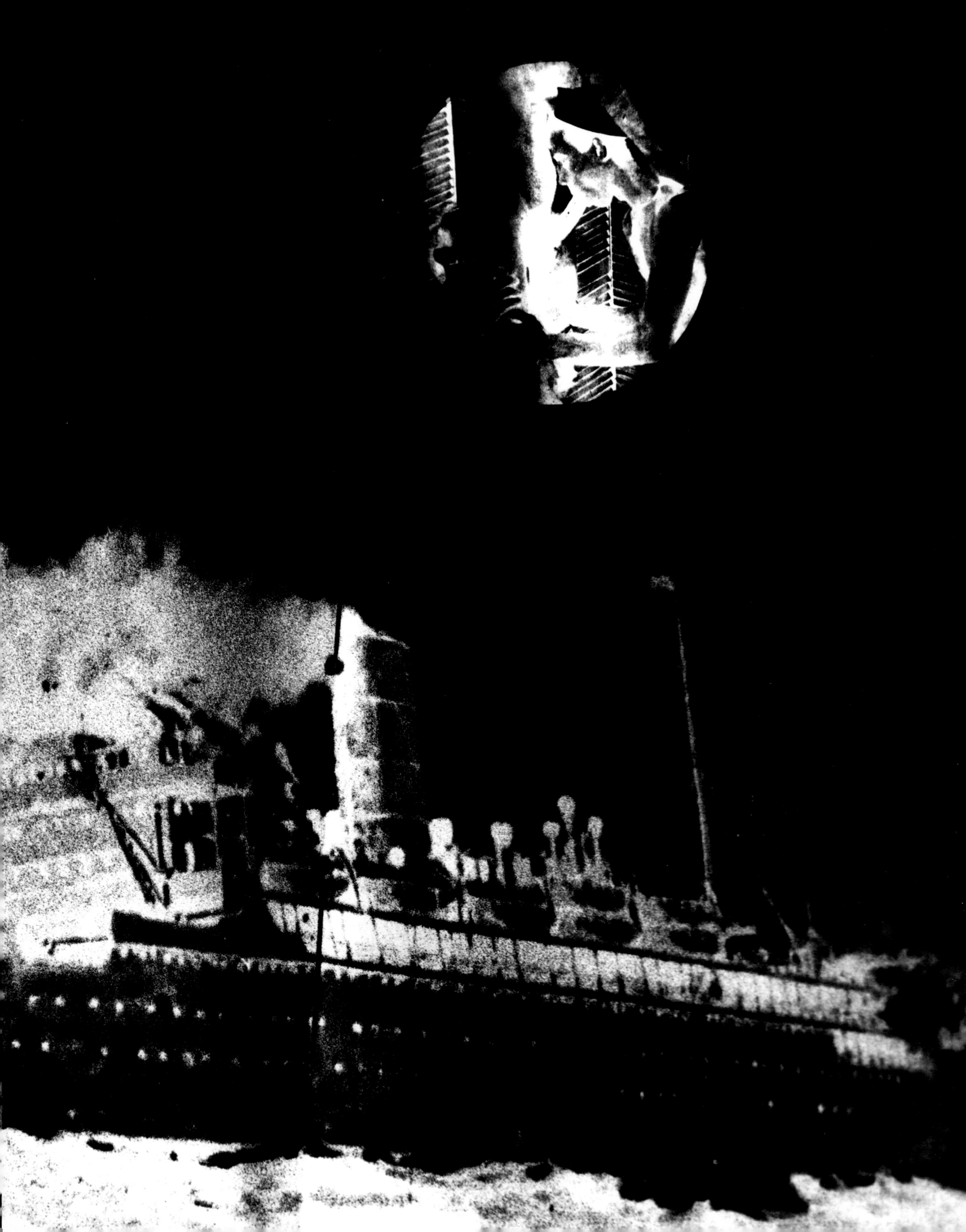

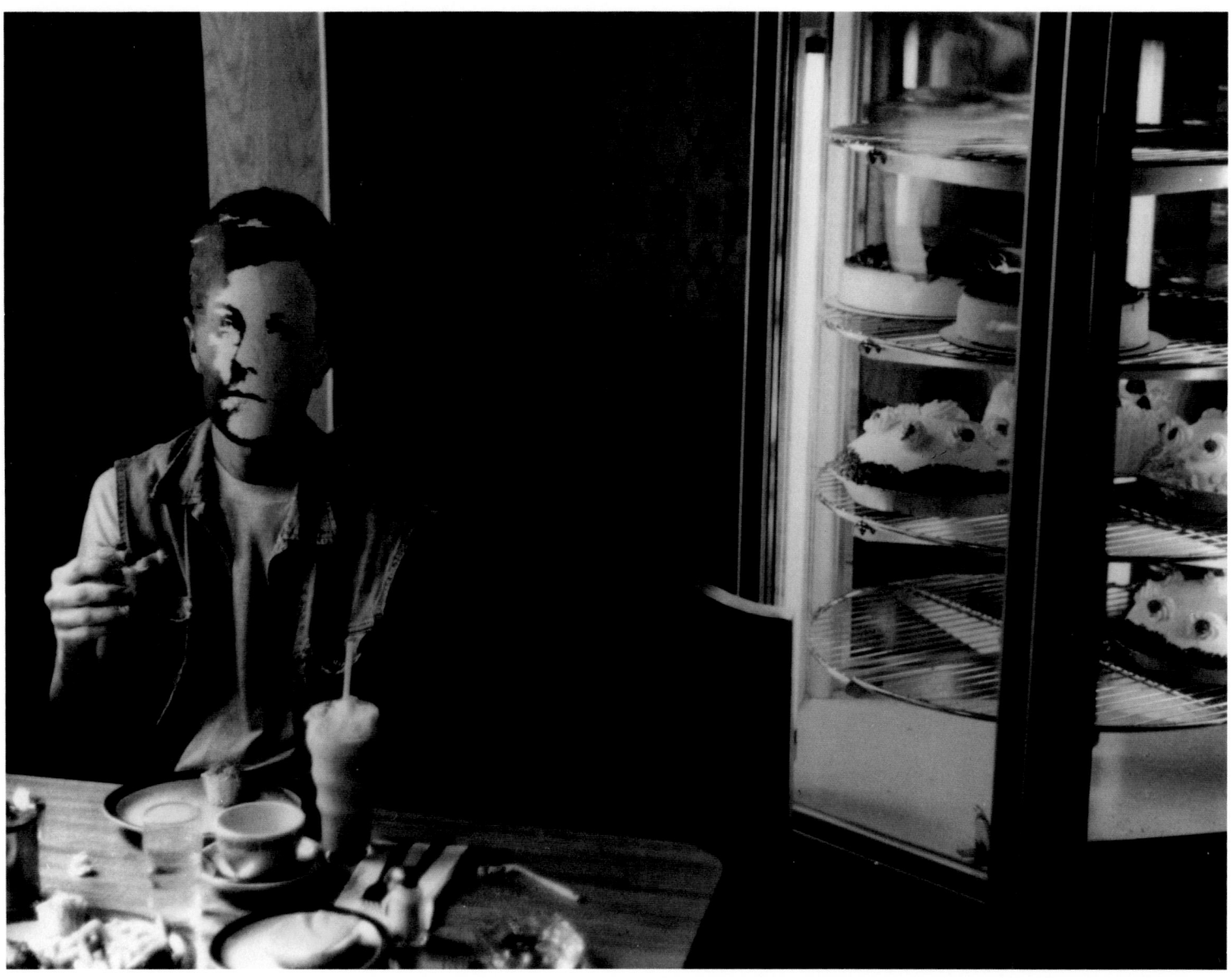

Pages 66–69: all **UNTITLED**, *from the series "Arthur Rimbaud in New York," 1978–79. Gelatin-silver prints; pages 66–67: 8 x 10"; pages 68–69: 10 x 8"*

IT'S THAT LATE MORNING LIGHT *that bathes everything in the landscape giving it an apparition of warmth. I'm sitting at a second story table of a restaurant, behind the plate-glass windows of some crummy piece of architecture feeling dark. Maybe it's what we call sadness, maybe it's darker than that and all I can think about is the end of my life. In the far distance at the edge of the runways is a thin wedge of horizon made up of dead brush, maybe trees—it is formless other than that enormous oil*

refinery thing and a couple low-set buildings made up of blond concrete and shadows. What does it all mean? What's going on in this head of mine? What's going on in this body, in these hands that want to wander that guys legs over there? I just had a fight with my boyfriend in the middle of the airport twenty minutes before board-ing a plane to Mexico. I console myself with the sight of the construction crew down below in the fenced off area of the runway. I count eight or nine of them and I feel like shit. I guess years

ago I could start thinking of the interiors of those construction trailers with the drafting tables and cheap oak furniture and calendars and ringing phones and one of the crew members taking me inside and locking the door and a ratty couch over to the side and him removing his sweater and thermal undershirt all in one move so I could reach over and put his sweat on my palms but that is a drift of thought that takes a lot of effort right now and I don't care about making that effort. What does it mean, what for and

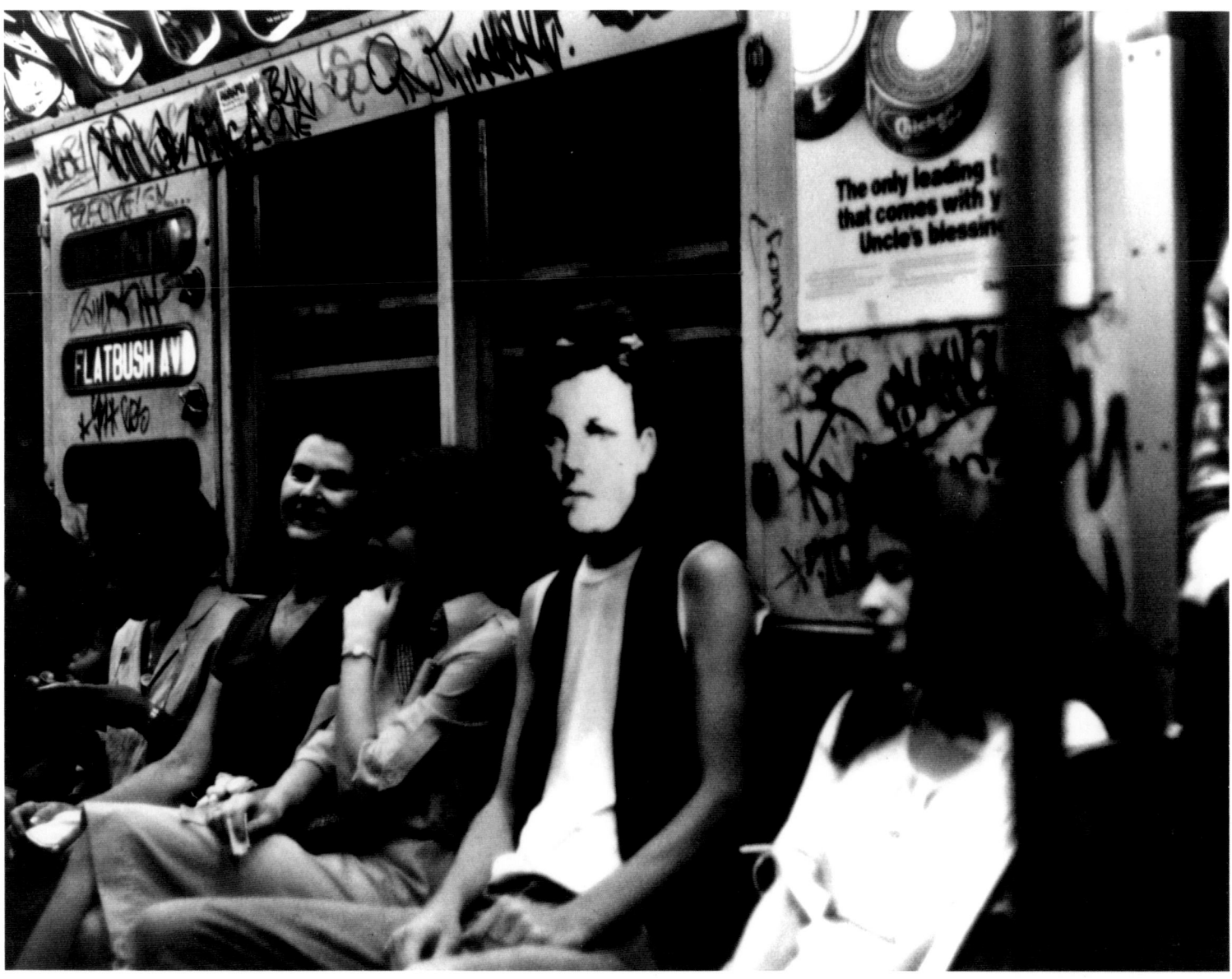

why? *and the red tail fins of some of the planes parked nearby have white crosses painted on their sides and I think of ambulances—ooh love is wounding me and I'm afraid death is making me lose touch with the faces of those I love; I'm losing touch with the current of timelessness that drove me through all my life til now. I maybe won't grow old with a fattening belly and some old dog toothless and tongue hanging low in the house. I won't grow old and maybe I want to. Maybe nothing can save me despite all my*

dreams as a kid and all my dreams as a young man having fallen to their knees inside my head.

I wished for years and years that I could separate into ten different people; ten versions of myself in order to give each person I loved a part of myself forever, and also have some left over to drift across landscapes and maybe even go into death or areas which were dangerous, and have enough of me to survive the deaths of one or two or three of me. This is what I thought was appropriate for all of my desires

and I never figured out how to manage it all and now I'm in danger of losing the only one of me that is around. I'm in danger of losing my life and tell me exactly what gesture can convey or stop this possibility, what gesture of hands or mind can shut it down in its invisible tracks—nothing, and that saddens me.

A friend of mine recently killed himself and I can't let go of him; he has followed the first flight to Miami and now it is going towards dusk and I'm sitting in a replica of the earlier

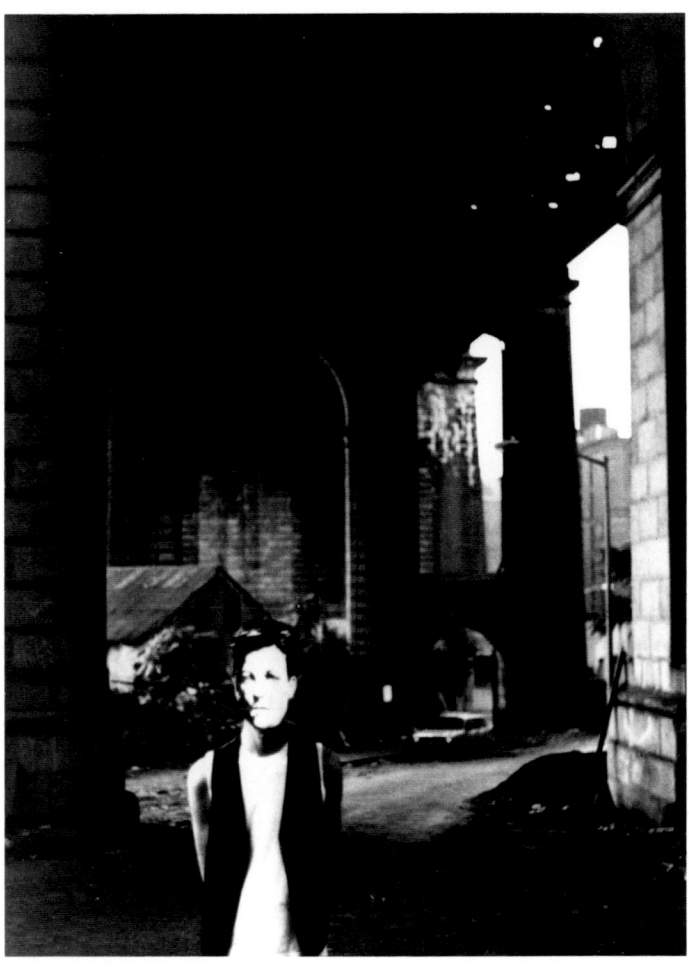
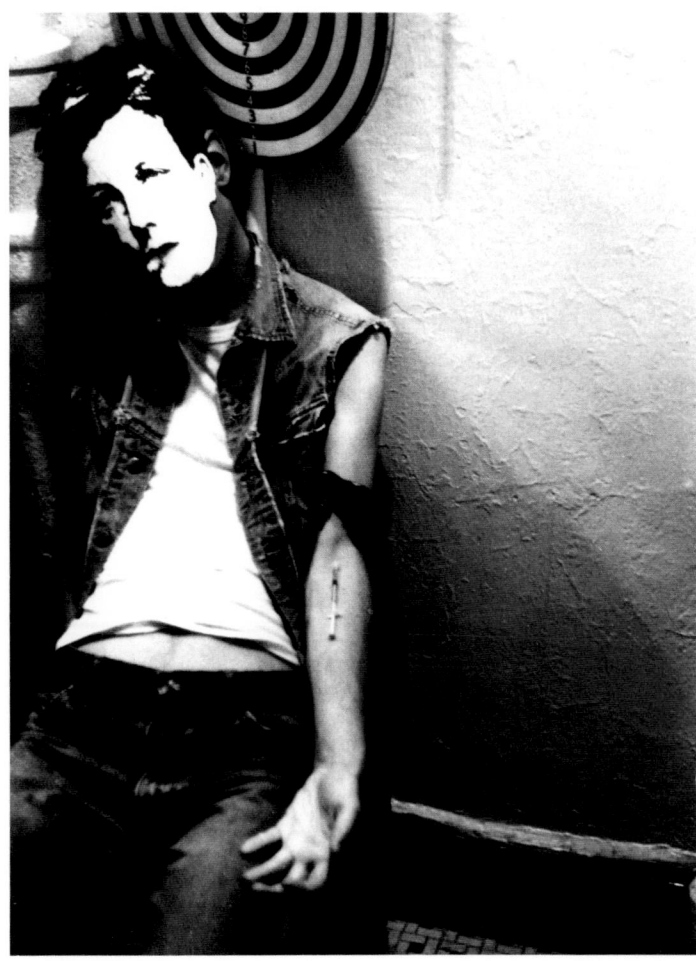

waiting room waiting for the plane to be announced. My boyfriend Tom is wandering the billion shops of the air-port and I am smoking a cigarette and thinking about Death. A man on the balcony takes a kodak picture of the sunset and uses a flash attachment—what does he hope to illuminate? If I could I'd descend the stairs and run with my eyes closed all across those runways to the far horizon and break through the screen of dusk as if it were a large screen of paper held vertical, and enter a whole other century or life. If I could I'd jump into the warm ocean and swim until I disappeared like a cartoon dot on the horizon. Once, years ago in a warehouse along the hudson river I wrote on an aban-doned wall about a man who flew a

single-prop airplane out over the ocean until it ran out of gas and I envied that man so much it hurt. That was years and years ago so does that mean up until now I have been living on borrowed time? Should I count back-wards like the Mayans so that I never get older? Will the moon in the sky listen to my whispers as I count away?

Text from the mixed-media work
WE ARE BORN INTO A PRE-INVENTED EXISTENCE, *1990*

I FEEL A VAGUE NAUSEA *stroking and tapping the lining of my stomach. The hand holding the burning ciga-rette travels sideways like a strong cloud drifting the open desert; how far can I reach? I'm in a car traveling the folds of the southwest region of the country and the road is steadying out and becoming flat and giving off an energy like a vortex leading to the horizon line. I hate arriving at that destination. Transition is always a relief; destination means death to me. If I could figure a way to remain for-ever in transition, in the disconnected and unfamiliar, I could remain in a state of perpetual freedom. After hours and hours of driving in solitude I moved into a section of countryside that is controlled by the marine corps*

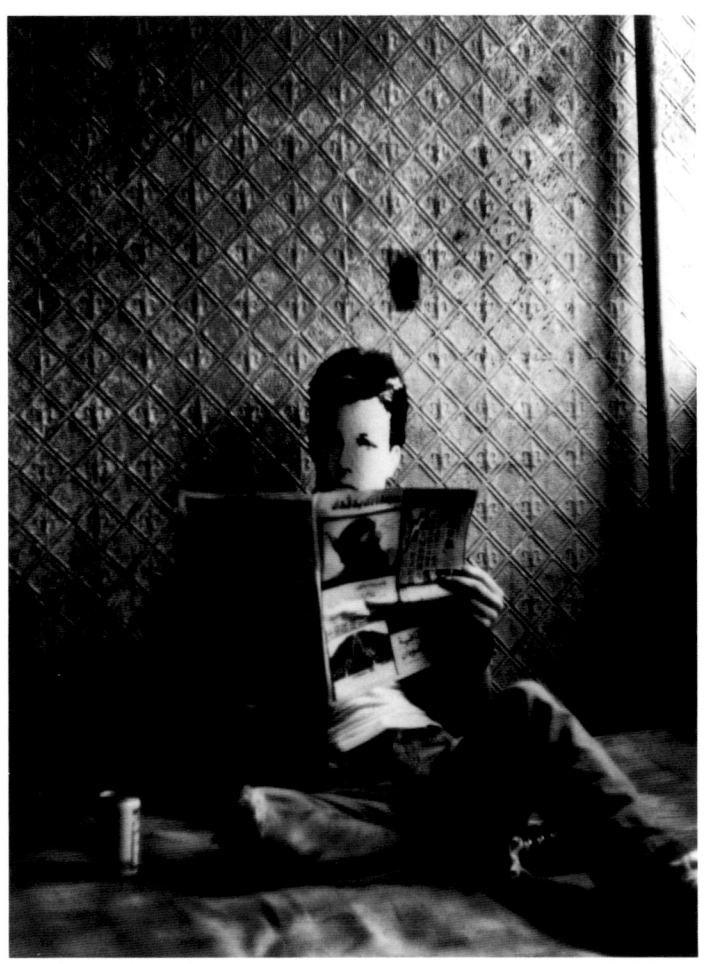
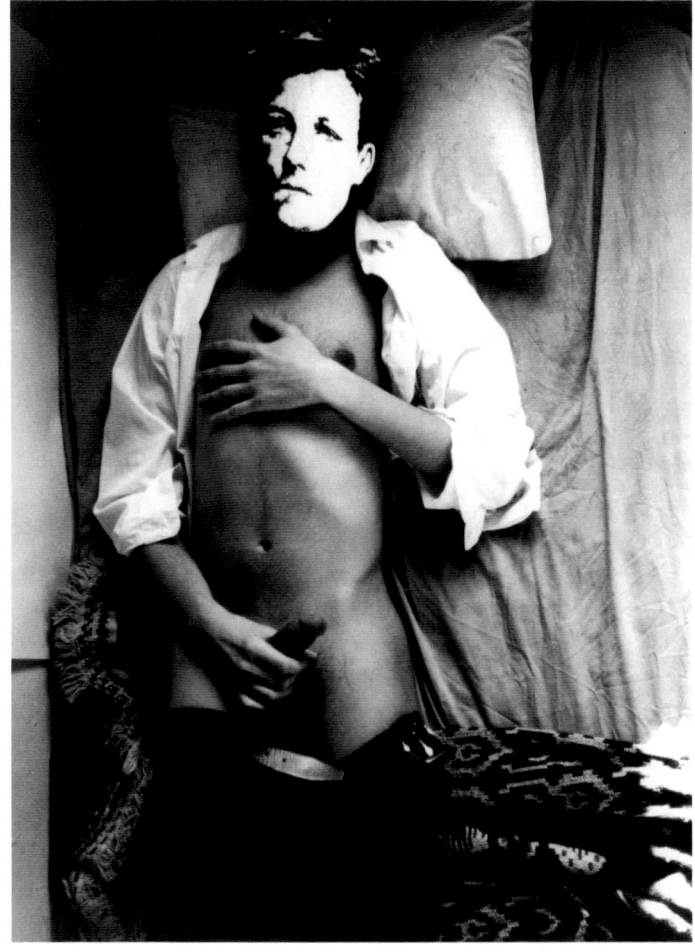

air station. Civilization and its approach is beginning to make me feel jittery. I feel something concrete slipping off the ledge back there behind my eyes. I was, up until this moment, a member of the industrialized tribe; the illusory tribe that catapults this nation, this society, into something thick and hallucinogenic. My hand with the cigarette is slowly making its way back across the hip of the horizon; its slow motion drift creates dark spot below it like a cloud shadow on the landscape that travels at the same speed. The hand with the cigarette is drifting for hours and hours back to my waiting lips. What is it in these wrists that grab the steering wheel; what blood flows through these arms and hands; what color and sensibility in that blood? What textures and images are coded and locked into those genes, those cells, those bones that drag the world towards my eyes? What do these eyes have to do with surveillance cameras; what do the veins running through my wrists have in common with electric wiring? I'm the robotic kid with caucasion kid programming trying to short-circuit the sensory disks. I'm the robotic kid looking through digital eyes past the wind-shield into the pre-invented world. I'm the robotic kid lost for a fraction of evolutionary time in the outskirts of tribal boundaries; I've slipped through the keyhole of an enormous psychic erector set of a child civilization. I'm the robotic kid lost from the blind eye of government and wandering edges of a computerized landscape; all civilization is turning like one huge gear in my forehead. I'm seeing my hands and feet grow thousands of miles long and millions of years old and I'm experiencing the exertion it takes to move these programmed limbs. I'm the robotic kid, the human motor-works, and surveying the scene before me I wonder: what can these feet level, what can these feet pound and flatten, what can these hands raise? 🏠

Text from the mixed-media work I FEEL A VAGUE NAUSEA, *1990*

Close friend to both David Wojnarowicz and

Peter Hujar, writer **Fran Lebowitz** renders

an intimate portrait of both artists....

Melissa Harris: How did you and David meet?

Fran Lebowitz: I met him through Peter Hujar because Peter was very intent on me meeting him. Peter didn't like that many people. He liked more people than I do, but still not that many. And he was extremely enthusiastic about David in every respect. I really put off meeting David, probably because he was very young. And I suppose I just thought he was a trick that Peter particularly liked—which was not necessarily a draw as far as I was concerned.

But finally, I did meet David, and I actually paid very little attention to him because of having this preconceived notion of him. And then when Peter got sick, because Peter had no money (and I mean no money, not a dollar), Peter's friends took care of him. This was a small number of people, who had to do everything for him, because he had no money, no insurance, no anything. And David was one of those people. And so was I. So we were thrown together in this intensely emotional, arduous situation. And that's how I really got to know him; in fact, I got to know him in a way that I would never have gotten to know him under other circumstances.

And as soon as I got to know David, I instantly felt very emotionally attached to him. Peter was an extremely close friend of mine. And David even picked up

Opposite: UNTITLED, *1988–89. Black-and-white photograph, acrylic, text, and collage on Masonite, 39 x 32"*

"If I had a dollar to spend for healthcare I'd rather spend it on a baby or innocent person with some defect or illness not of their own responsibility; not some person with Aids…" says the healthcare official on national television and this is in the middle of an hour long video of people dying on camera because they can't afford the limited drugs available that might extend their lives and I can't even remember what this official looked like because I reached in through the t.v. screen and ripped his face in half and I was diagnosed with Arc recently and this was after the last few years of losing count of the friends and neighbors who have been dying slow vicious and unnecessary deaths because fags and dykes and junkies are expendable in this country "If you want to stop Aids shoot the queers…" says the governor of texas on the radio and his press secretary later claims that the governor was only joking and didn't know the microphone was turned on and besides they didn't think it would hurt his chances for re-election anyways and I wake up every morning in this killing machine called america and I'm carrying this rage like a blood filled egg and there's a thin line between the inside and the outside a thin line between thought and action and that line is simply made up of blood and muscle and bone and I'm waking up more and more from daydreams of tipping amazonian blowdarts in 'infected blood' and spitting them at the exposed necklines of certain politicians or government healthcare officials or those thinly disguised walking swastika's that wear religious garments over their murderous intentions or those rabid strangers parading against Aids clinics in the nightly news suburbs there's a thin line a very thin line between the inside and the outside and I've been looking all my life at the signs surrounding us in the media or on peoples lips; the religious types outside st. patricks cathedral shouting to men and women in the gay parade: "You won't be here next year – you'll get Aids and die ha ha…" and the areas of the u.s.a. where it is possible to murder a man and when brought to trial one only has to say that the victim was a queer and that he tried to touch you and the courts will set you free and the difficulties that a bunch of republican senators have in albany with supporting an anti-violence bill that includes 'sexual orientation' as a category of crime victims there's a thin line a very thin line and as each T-cell disappears from my body it's replaced by ten pounds of pressure ten pounds of rage and I focus that rage into non-violent resistance but that focus is starting to slip my hands are beginning to move independent of self-restraint and the egg is starting to crack america seems to understand and accept murder as a self defense against those who would murder other people and its been murder on a daily basis for eight count them eight long years and we're expected to pay taxes to support this public and social murder and we're expected to quietly and politely make house in this windstorm of murder but I say there's certain politicians that had better increase their security forces and there's religious leaders and healthcare officials that had better get bigger dogs and higher fences and more complex security alarms for their homes and queer-bashers better start doing their work from inside howitzer tanks because the thin line between the inside and the outside is beginning to erode and at the moment I'm a thirty seven foot tall one thousand one hundred and seventy-two pound man inside this six foot frame and all I can feel is the pressure all I can feel is the pressure and the need for release

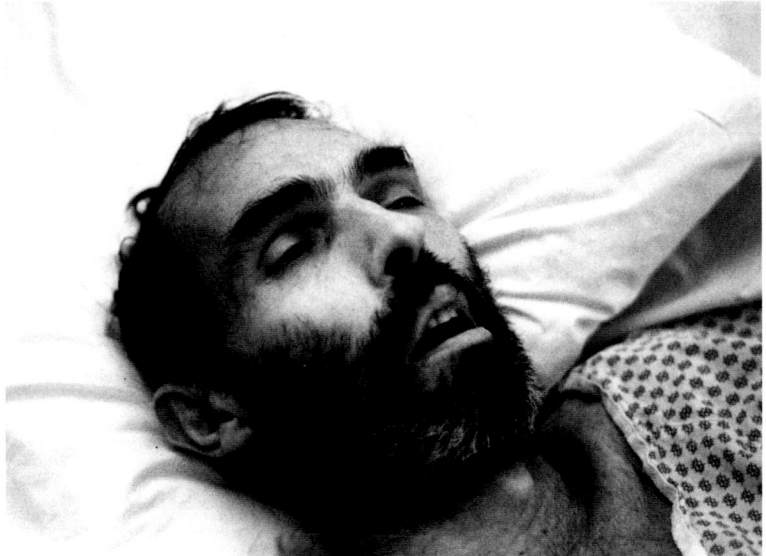 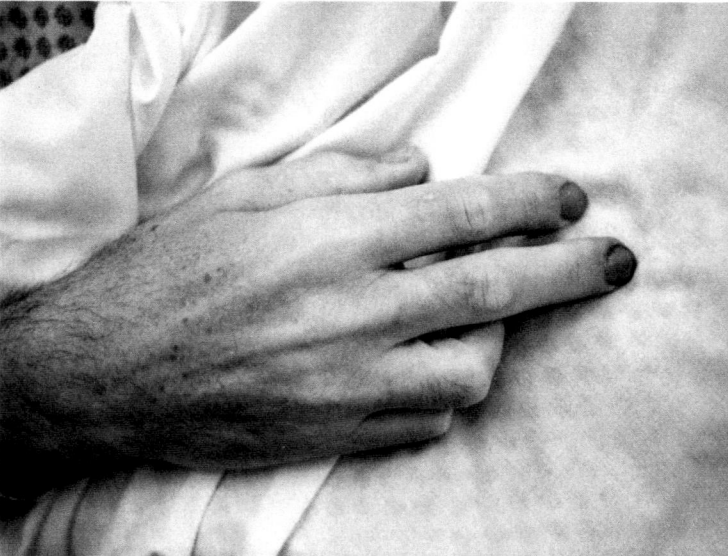

some of his mannerisms. At first, I was not conscious of the fact that he reminded me of Peter. And so, because I loved Peter, I kind of put him in that category. David was very interested in everything about Peter, too, and therefore he had quite an interest in me.

Anyway, when Peter was really sick, David and I had to do a lot of things for him together, one of which was so horrifying, and also something unimaginable before AIDS. Peter planned his funeral before he died. This is not uncommon with people who have AIDS. But it certainly was before AIDS—not only an uncommon experience, but an inconceivable one. Now, Peter was alive and I went to buy the coffin for him. David offered to go with me—which I was very grateful for, because naturally it's not the sort of thing you want to do alone.

MH: Did David know he was HIV-positive then?

FL: I don't know whether he knew. I didn't. I have to say I assumed that he was. But he didn't tell me that he was. I would doubt that David knew, frankly, because he doesn't strike me as the sort of person who would want to know.

Also, David, even if there had been no such thing as AIDS, had such an unhealthy way of life that he hardly looked different at the beginning of his illness than he did when he was dying. David lived entirely on coffee and cigarettes. He had had a very poor childhood, which was reflected in his general health, having nothing to do with AIDS. He never looked like a glowing, healthy young guy.

At any rate, it was a horrible experience for both of us to go and buy this coffin. And then we went out to eat. I mean, these kind of experiences are…they are science fiction. You go to a funeral home and you pick out a coffin for a friend who is alive, and then you go to a hamburger place and have lunch. And we stayed in that coffee shop for hours, I mean really hours. And that was the first lengthy conversation I had with David, where he told me a lot of things about himself and about his background that I didn't know before.

And then after that, in a certain way, he became, to me, a very close person, although not in the usual way—not like a person that I went to the movies with all the time…. But there was a point of connection that was really, in my experience, unique, because of the odd way in which it came about.

MH: What did you talk about?

FL: We talked about everything. And especially his childhood, which was hair-raising.

UNTITLED, *1989.*
Gelatin-silver prints, triptych,
10 x 14" each

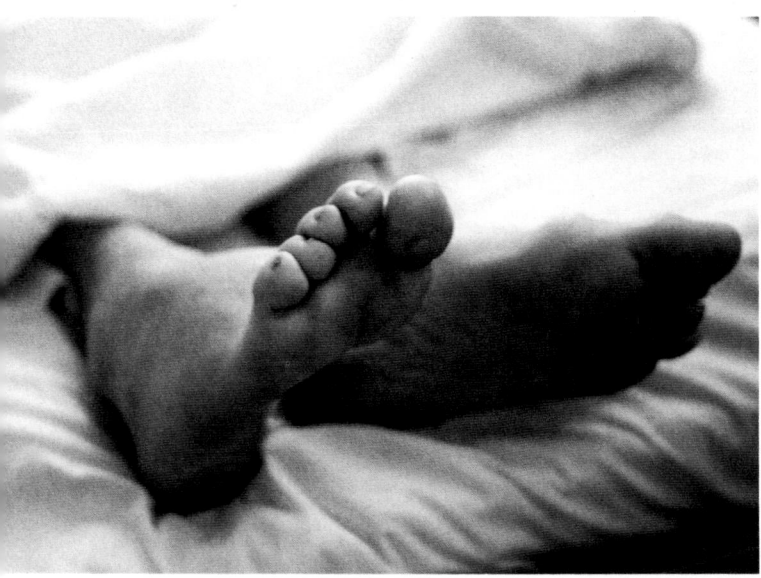

Peter also had had a hair-raising childhood. And that may have been the thing that initially brought those two together.

We had fun in our conversations. David was very articulate, very receptive; he understood things, he got it…I talked to him on the phone all the time. And we talked about everything. I didn't see him all the time. After Peter died, I saw David several times for a meal. But not while Peter was alive.

M H : In what way were he and Peter similar?

F L : Well, after a while, I started to think of him as Peter's son. That's kind of what he seemed like to me. And I think that David may also have had that feeling about him, in a way.

Now, of course, a lot of this was just wishful thinking on our parts. Peter would have a son, and then we would have some part of Peter. Still, I think that Peter influenced David perhaps in a kind of paternal way. And—I think it was Peter who taught David about photography.

I also know that Peter only had two cameras, and that he gave one to David before he died—he gave his other camera to the photographer Lynn Davis. Lynn is like a saint. She took care of Peter when he was sick, and then Robert [Mapplethorpe]. It's a

testament to Lynn—that one person could be close to Peter and Robert, two of the most difficult people imaginable. It's amazing. When David was very sick he called Lynn and asked her to come down to his house, and didn't tell her why. She went down there and he said, "I'm never going to be able to use this again, and I know that you should have it." It was Peter's other camera.

Anyway, Peter and David were especially similar in their level of rage, although David handled it much, much better than Peter did. They were similar inside of that rage.

M H : About what? Their childhoods?

F L : Although David was much younger than Peter (*much* younger than Peter), he was much, much more mature. By which I mean David had to navigate the world in a way Peter never could. David was a more conventional person really. I mean, that's not a thing you would ordinarily say about David, but he was more conventional emotionally than Peter was. He wasn't as damaged. Even though he had a childhood just as damaging, he was much stronger. That would be my opinion of it. And he wasn't nearly as emotionally marginalized, or as tortured as Peter.

The sort of background that David came from is a classic background for a serial

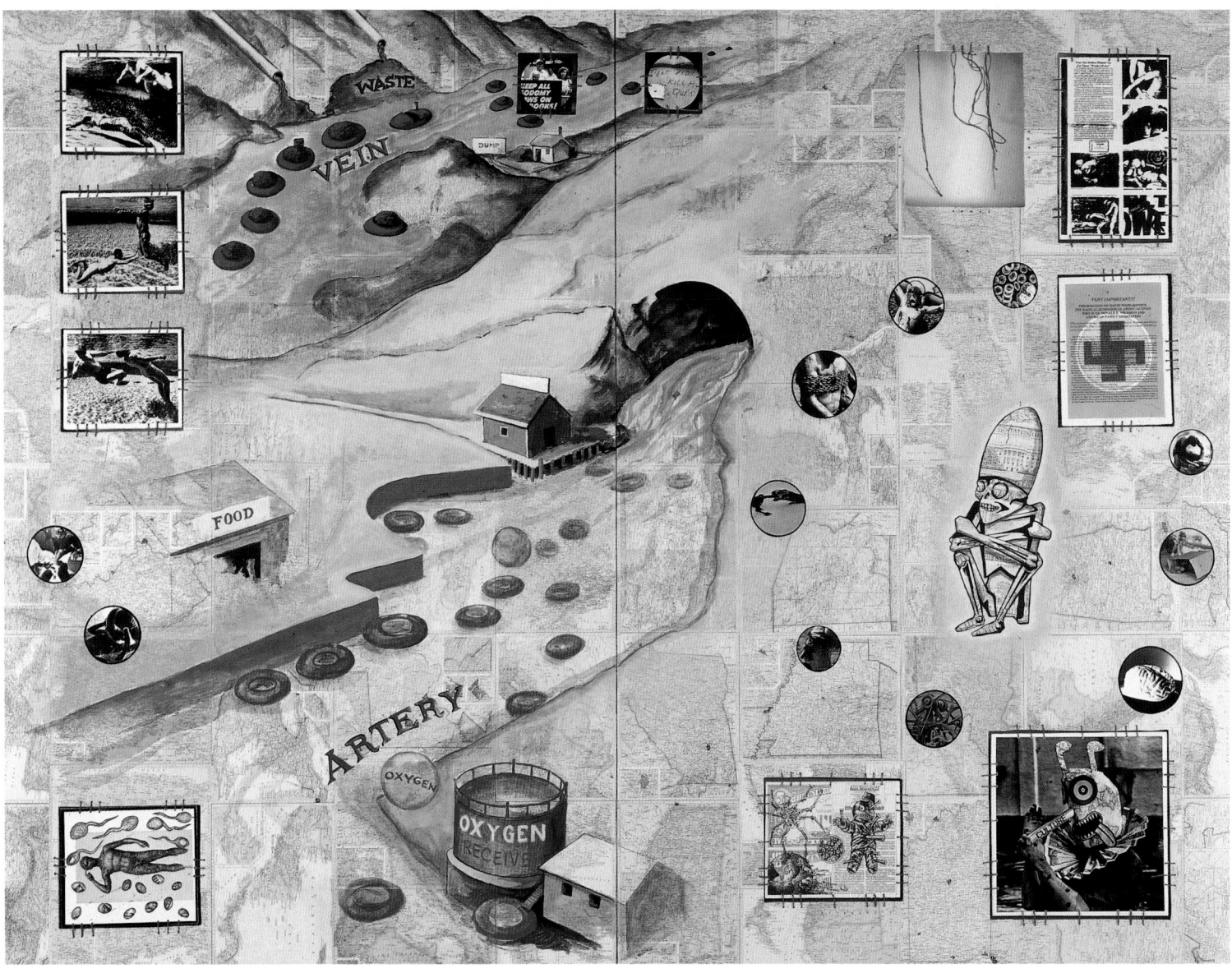

WHY THE CHURCH CAN'T/
WON'T BE SEPERATED FROM
THE STATE. OR. A FORMAL
PORTRAIT OF CULTURE, *1991.*
Black-and-white photograph,
acrylic, spray paint, photostat,
lithograph, string, and collage
on Masonite, 8 x 12′

Opposite: SUBSPECIES
HELMS SENATORIUS, *1990.*
Cibachrome, 12¼ x 19″

killer. When someone commits a horrible crime, and then someone wants to make an excuse for them, they point out his childhood. I never feel that that's an excuse for criminal behavior, but it is an explanation. David, instead of turning into a serial killer, turned into an artist.

Now, this has entirely to do with David's exceptional character, and character is something I believe to be innate. You know, some people are good and some people are not good. I mean in a moral sense. And David was. He was a person who was concerned about other people.... When Peter was dead, and David was very grief-stricken—and David was sick—he called me about my cold, or asked me how something was going, how

some problem of mine was going. He really thought about people in a very generous way.

I like David's work, but my primary interest in David is not his work. My primary interest in David was his heroism. I mean, I would say that David is the most heroic person I have ever known.

MH: Why?

FL: Rising above the damage that's been done to you— I think that's heroic. And no matter how good your character is, it certainly takes a tremendous amount of courage to do that. And I don't mean so much his behavior in the face of having AIDS, because in fact, a great many people turn out to be astonishingly courageous in dealing with this illness. That wouldn't set him so far apart.

But the way that he dealt with his life when he was well, the life he made for himself, and the invention of his sensibility, you know—there was definitely something heroic about him.

The lack of self-absorption in David was palpable, especially in an environment where everyone is so concerned with themselves. The lack of selfishness. His ability to have a vision of life that was really inclusive of other people's feelings and other people's states of mind.

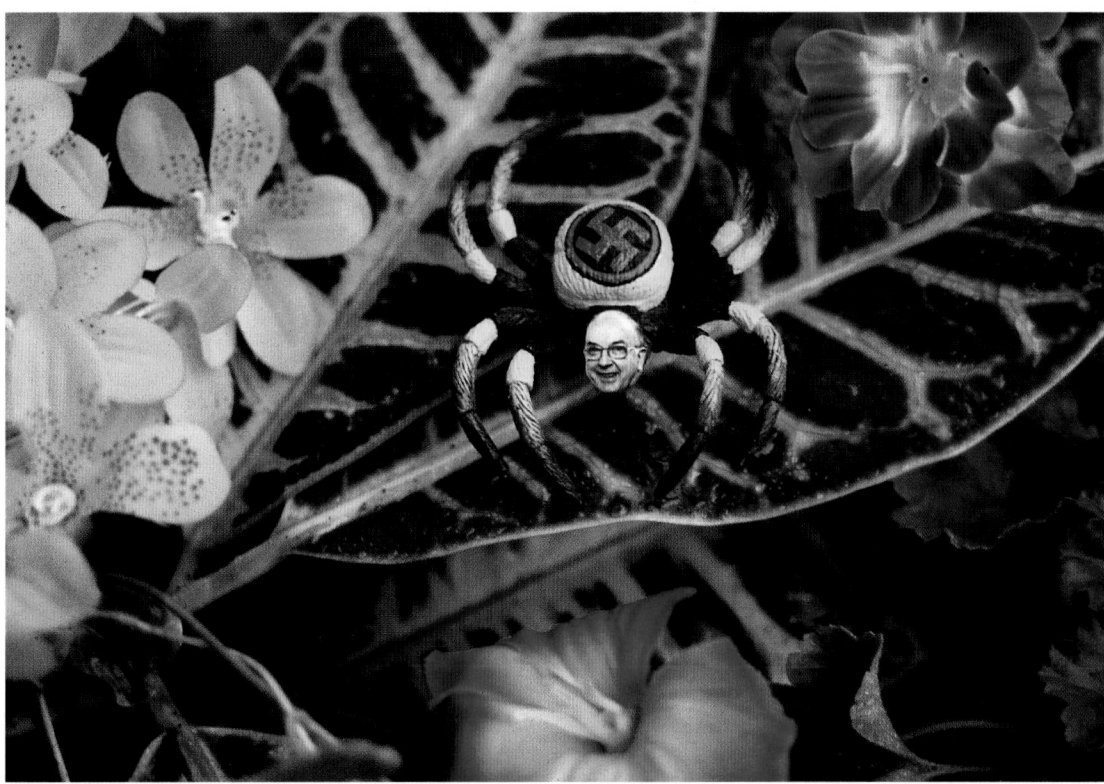

I would have thought that about him if there was no such thing as AIDS. Even his relationship with Peter, you know. I'm sure that initially in that relationship, because he was so much younger than Peter, he was seeking a kind of direction and protection and stuff like that, which I'm sure he got to a certain extent, because Peter was very smart and much older and much more experienced.... But David was by far the stronger of the two. And in the end, he took care of Peter. And I don't mean when he was sick, but I mean, in the end, he could see more than Peter, he was more at home in the world, and I think...I'm sure there was an aspect, a moment, or a time in that relationship where that was a disappointment to David. I mean, you're seeking the father, and then you've got to be the father.

MH: How was he able to change roles? Was he capable of loving unconditionally?

FL: Well, not unconditionally. No, not unconditionally. But because he was in a state of grace. He was like what a priest is supposed to be. He is what Catholic doctrine is supposed to be about. That's really what he was like. He could see things that way. Most people can behave kindly or be attentive to other people when things are going well for themselves. Expansiveness usually comes from success, it usually comes from not feeling fearful, etcetera. In the face of fear to behave that way, in the face of your own problems, that's really difficult.

Most people protect themselves from knowledge of themselves, since most people are not so swell, and they would rather be unaware of that fact. And David, who was pretty swell, was very analytical about himself, and really quite easy on other people, unless they were doing something to him. I am not easy on other people. I am hard on a person who passes me in the street. I am suffused with being judgmental. And he was not that way.

Now, on the other hand, David was a real warrior. Some of the aspects of this I tried to subdue in him. This fight he got into with Donald Wildmon, I felt, and would feel if it happened to someone else, was a waste of energy. This is really hitting your head against a wall. When David was involved in that, and other kinds of fights like that, I thought of him as very young. I think you learn not to fight these implacable enemies, these automatic enemies. You have to skip them.

MH: What did he say to you when you said that to him?

FL: He would listen to me and then do what he wanted. He sought a lot of advice from me—not that he took it. Partially, I think that once Peter died, he associated me with Peter. There was a lot of that going on in my relationship with David—I became some

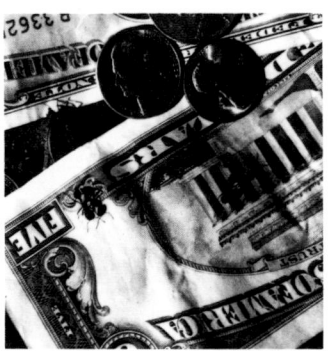 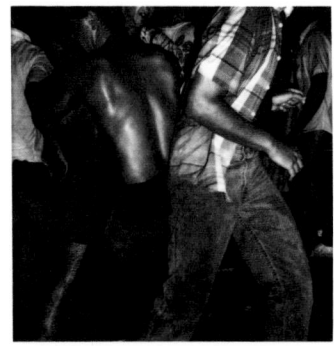 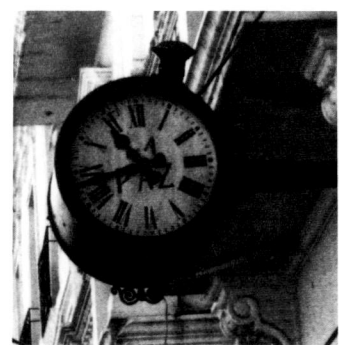

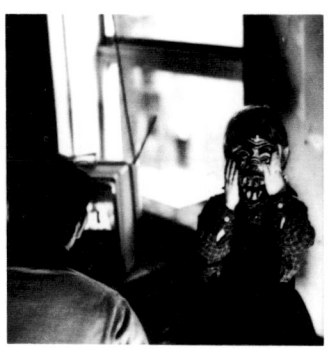 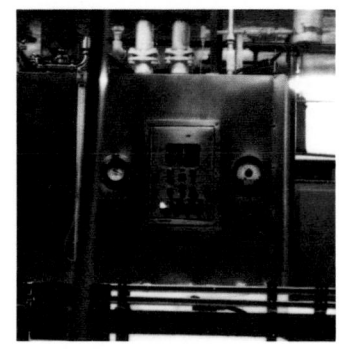 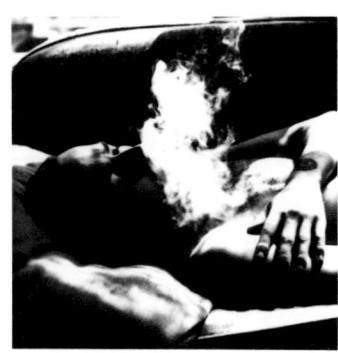

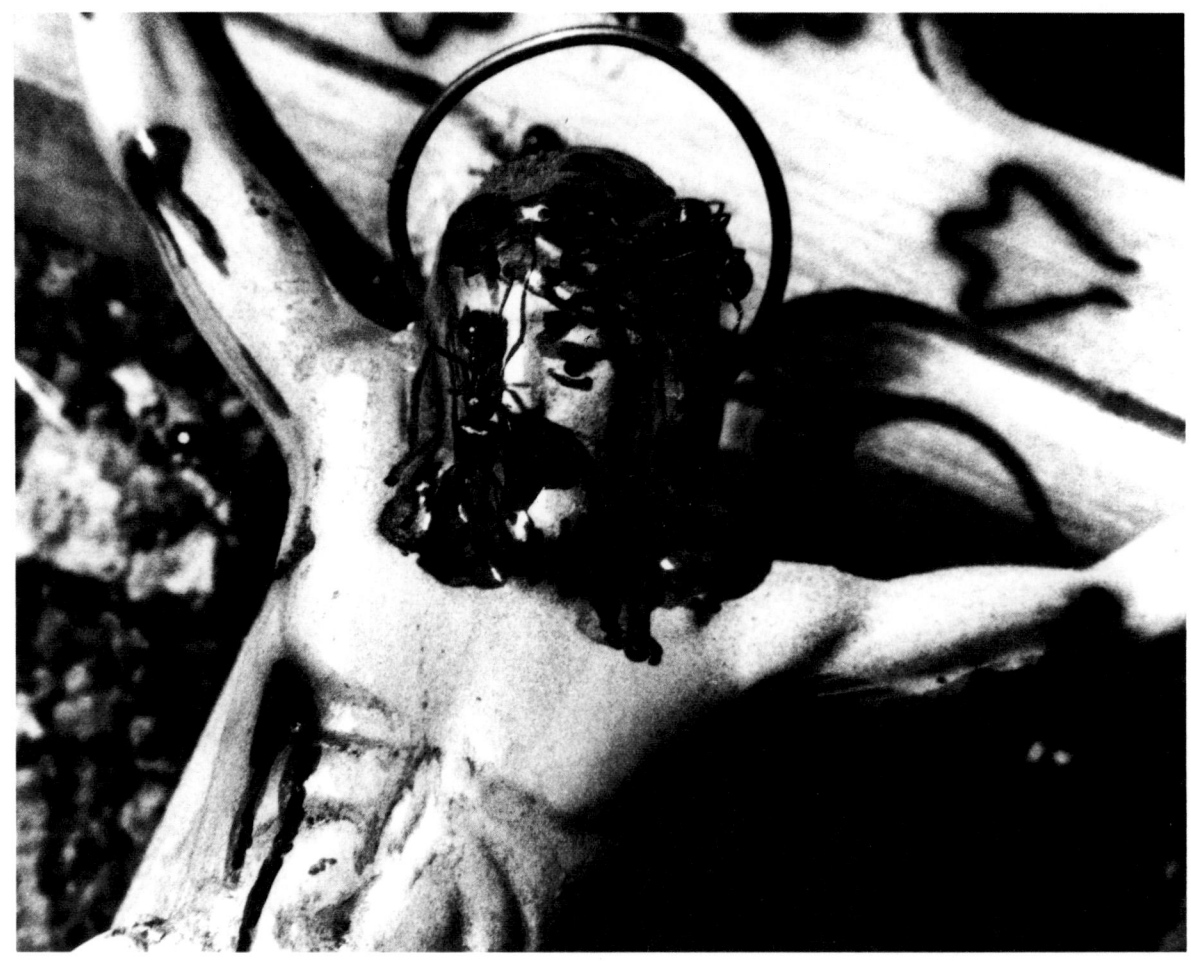

aspect of Peter for him, too. And he missed him very much. Anyway, with these kinds of fights, he didn't listen to me. He fought with the people who owned his building. I mean, that was ridiculous. You can't win against these people. Of course, once he decided to do this, I tried to get a lot of people to help him. But especially since he was sick, I did actually say to him, "You don't have the years, to waste two years in some stupid lawsuit with some slumlord. Get out. Move. It's not worth it. It's just an apartment. Don't commit your energies to that kind of thing."

M H : Why do you think he did it? Was it his anger? Tenacity?

F L : Because he couldn't not do it. Because that was his response. And that was to me, although a very attractive feature of his personality, a childlike one. He was right. So what? I mean, it didn't matter that he was right. He was dying. And he never learned that you don't win anyway against these people.

And especially this Wildmon guy, you don't fight with these idiotic fanatics. But David's rage was murderous. He won the suit and got a dollar or something. Maybe he saw it as a moral victory. I don't know.

The thing is, it's not a debate. It's not like you're going to change their minds.

Also, I feel these aren't the real foes of art. The real foes of art are people who think bad artists are good artists. I'd say, "David, there are probably a lot of people who are fans of your work that are much more dangerous to art than this guy. You know, bad curators, bad museum directors, bad editors—these are the foes of art." The real foes of art are not people who just…you know, who hate sex.

M H : Even if they are using art for their own political agenda?

F L : David didn't agree with me on this.

M H : Did he take Wildmon's attack very personally?

F L : Well, I think he took it personally in a certain way, in the way that your work is you. But I also think that David believed in sides in a way that I don't. And this guy was on the other side. David had a lot of conventional hatreds — the Catholic Church and these kind of things, that to me are, in a way, banal hatreds. There are more subtle things to hate

than these things. These are obvious, and you don't fight with them. These people are Believers; you don't fight with Believers.

M H : You think his work was infused with that kind of rage?

F L : Yes. His writing especially. I mean, his writing is direct. His visual work also has his eye in it, and I think all plastic arts are much more abstract than writing, so there is always something else operating in David's visual work — whereas the writing is almost pure rage.

The playful quality that's in his visual work is entirely absent in his writing, and the playful quality that was in him is entirely absent in his writing. I remember when Peter went to Columbia-Presbyterian once, and we scammed him into the Harkness Pavilion, which is a place for rich people. A great doctor just secretly put him in. No one knew he wasn't paying. Peter loved this. He felt like a zillionaire. And there was, on the wall of his room, a terrible painting—you know, like you would see in a hotel or something. And David drew on it. And every time he'd come, he would draw another of his little animals and stuff like that. It really entertained Peter; you know, it added a lot. Every day, it was the one pleasurable note in going to visit Peter in the hospital. I would look to see what David would make, and then I would talk to him about it.

I think that the salient virtue of David's work is the authenticity of it, by which I mean it's so clearly honorable, the intent. Which is really in direct opposition to ninety-nine percent of all work being made now everywhere in the world. And I think that really makes it stand out. It's a real vision, it's a real idea.

I don't like its primitive quality. It is opposite to my sensibility. But his attachment to it went hand in hand with his attachment to his insistence on fighting with people head-on. I think he lumped all these things together. And I think that he was genuinely suspicious and contemptuous of any sort of style or polish. He saw it as the enemy.

M H : Do you think he also saw it as somehow institutional?

F L : Yes, in some way institutional, and in some way authoritarian, and in some way

Opposite: SPIRITUALITY (FOR PAUL THEK), *1988–89.*
Gelatin-silver prints on museum board, 41 x 32½" overall

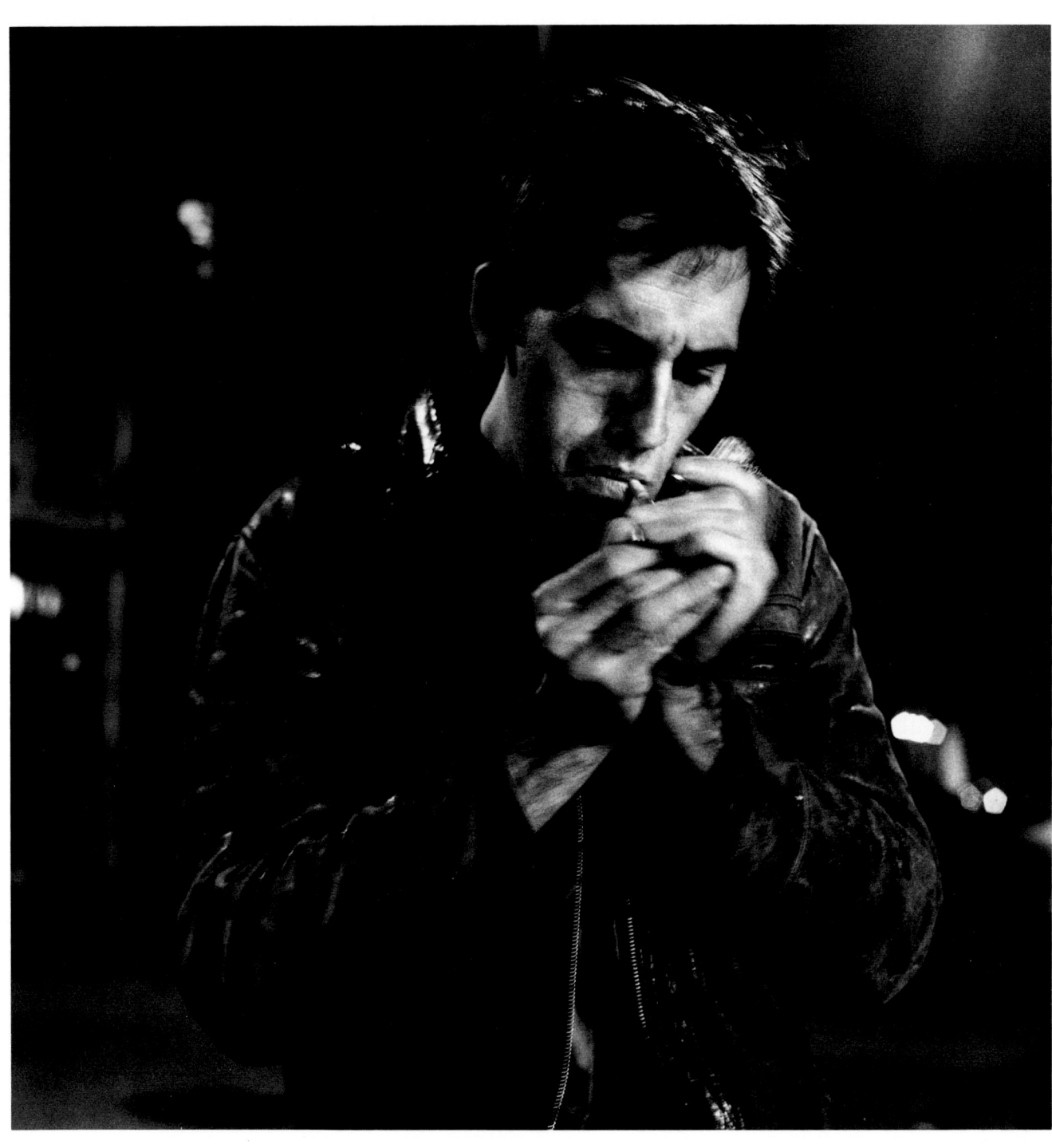

Peter Hujar, **DAVID LIGHTING UP***, 1985. Gelatin-silver print, 14 x 14"*

Opposite: **UNTITLED (GENET)***, 1979. Xeroxed collage, 8½ x 11"*

glossy, not serious…. David in every respect was the opposite of the dandy. There was also nothing about David of the professional. He didn't try to make a certain amount of work or think he had to work *x* amount of hours or whatever. I never had that impression…I never heard David say, "I've got to get work done," or "I have to try to work," or "I have a show coming up," "I have a book due out…." It didn't burden him, you know. He just did it. He had a childlike urge to do it. This was the thing about David that I just envied tremen-

dously, because I find it impossible to work, and I feel it totally as a burden. And he did it all. I think he enjoyed doing it. And when he wasn't feeling well, he tried to work. Not because he felt guilty about not working, but because he wanted to work. And I think he had the idea that if he worked, he would feel less as if he were sick. Also, with his writing, I don't think David found it hard, because I don't think he saw it as writing. I think he just did it.

MH: The way people talk…?

FL: Yes. I once tried to talk about his writing with him and said, "You know, if you do this, if you do this, if you do this"—and he wasn't interested. David had a lot of verbal ability. I thought that he should read Edith Wharton. I realize that very few people would think David Wojnarowicz and Edith Wharton would be a perfect match. But we were talking about something, and I said, "Well, that's like so-and-so; did you ever read this?" and he said "No." And I said, "Well, I think you should read this; you would like it, dah-da-dah," and I gave him a Wharton novella. I don't think he read it.

But actually, why shouldn't David like Edith Wharton? Because she's a very good writer, and anyone should like her. I mean, it's far from his sensibility, but I think his life could only have been enriched by reading Edith Wharton. I would still recommend it to him.

I think of David like the Beat poets, whose work he loved. Their work was very rough and…I also think David liked that way of life. David loved to drive places. It was a real thing with him, but it was also a kind of Kerouac thing. He liked to have adventures, you know, and experiences. And he would drive, not because he couldn't afford a plane ticket…but because he just liked the road, the myth. When he was really sick, and couldn't drive, he wanted to go someplace in the Midwest, and I offered to drive him. The number of times I've offered to drive someone to the Midwest is one. I think he had a kind of created notion of Bohemia. Even though he was a genuinely marginal character.

Yet he felt a real sense of community with other people. There were a lot of other artists David liked, and whose work he liked, and who he felt liked him. David was genuine. You know, he would see a guy dressed in a certain way and take it at face value. I would be walking down the street with him and see a guy dressed this way, and think "This guy goes to NYU." "This

guy asked his parents to buy him a CD player." David would think he was Jean Genet.

MH: Do you think that David was political?
FL: Very. Very. Although not always in a direct way. But that's how you would characterize his thinking. Because he saw the world politically, by which I don't mean party politics or even politics in terms of conventional issue politics. But his basic take on things was an adversarial relationship between him and institutions, or himself and authority, and that's a totally political way to look at life. You know, he hated cops. Cops. Not this cop, or that cop. Cops.

MH: Because of what they represented?
FL: Because they're cops. Because when he was a little boy, he was beaten up by a cop. He and another little boy were twirling around on that bar that's in the middle of the subway car. And then a cop told them to sit down, and they sat down, and then the cop came walking through the car and hit David in the head with a nightstick.

So he had a hatred of cops. He had a hatred of any concentration of power at all. Because it always had been his enemy. Peter was exactly like this, by the way, so that was a big point of connection between them.

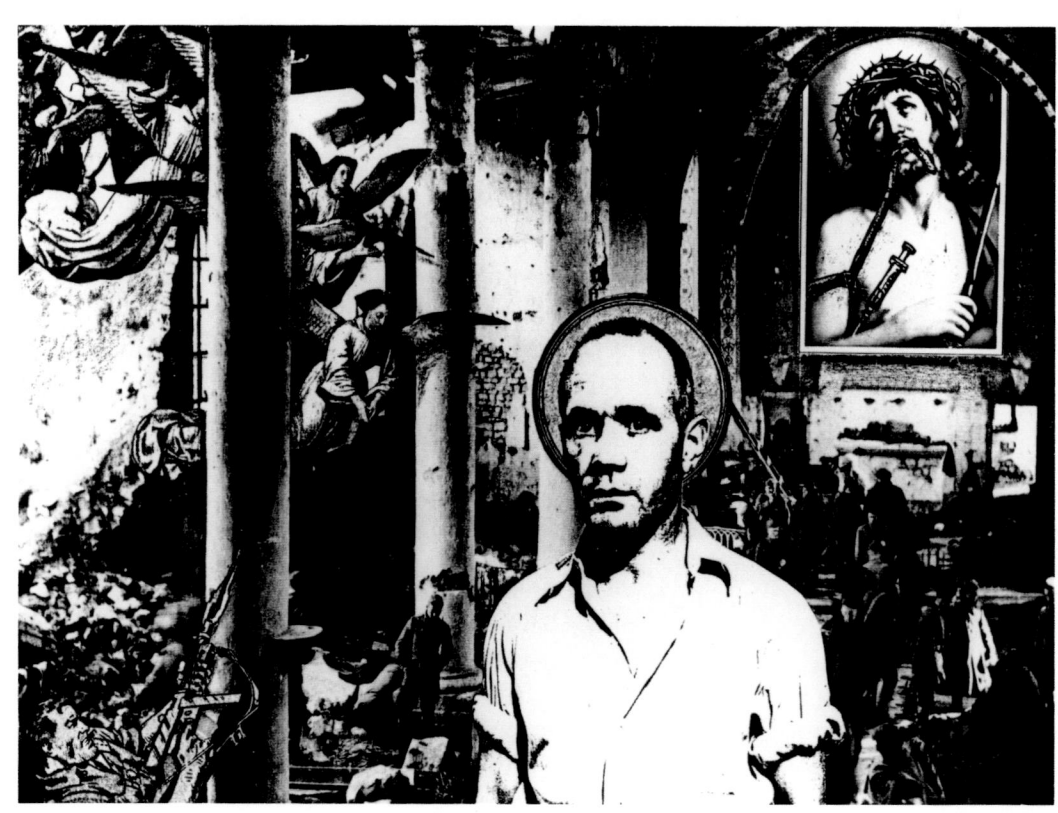

MH: And David's ideas about "other" and "difference"...do you think that he was simply interested in protecting the rights of any marginalized group of people?

FL: Well, I think that maybe it came to that. David doesn't strike me as a person who would have been interested, say, in homosexual politics, gay politics, without AIDS. People seem to forget, people in New York didn't care about this gay rights stuff initially. It was a West Coast thing in the early seventies—a soft-headed, dopey West Coast thing. People in New York had a life—they had things to think about. New York was far from a hotbed of homosexual activism.

MH: Did David's work and his writing and everything change when he got sick, or when Peter died, or when Peter was sick...?

FL: I don't think so. I mean, maybe it became more urgent. But I didn't notice it. But I'm not a scholar of David's work.

The only change that I noticed in David was an increase in his level of rage, which was already very high: he exhibited more combative behavior as he felt more and more threatened. It's very, very threatening, first of all, to lose someone you're very close to. It's more threatening to know you yourself are going to die. And then, he constantly placed himself in situations to be further threatened, so that his life became a total war.

David had no sense of proportion, in my opinion. Each thing was experienced by him at the same level of intensity. That didn't abate or modulate as he became more and more threatened, but increased. He became more fanatical, not less.

MH: And it took a lot of his energy.

FL: That was my only objection to it. First of all, it's none of my business. What do I care what he does? If he hadn't been sick, I wouldn't have paid any attention to it at all. I don't go around telling people how to live their lives. But he often sought my advice, especially about the apartment. When I saw, for example, he insisted on staying there, I tried to get other people who were more like his landlord to help him stay there, because he wanted to so much.

I did not approve of him staying there, for a number of reasons, one of which is they were working on the building. It wasn't a very healthy place to stay. It was noisy. It was hard to sleep. They were making noise, doing construction...they were building a movie theater underneath him. Even if you were in perfect condition, it was not a healthy environment. They were kicking up a lot of dust and debris and stuff. It was an old building—and I thought it was an unhealthy place for him to live, period. But since he was insistent on staying there, I tried to help him stay there. I can hardly think of a way in which I am like David, so when we talked about the NEA and all that kind of stuff, I was not in agreement with him about it in general.

MH: Why? Regarding the NEA, what did he think and what did you think?

FL: He had the standard, capital-A Artist reaction to it. "These philistines," "This Jesse Helms." And first of all, my reaction to it is, of course these people are like that. Are we supposed to be surprised that Jesse Helms is like this? That whole thing with Robert [Mapplethorpe] and the Corcoran...it seemed unbelievable to me that people were surprised by this.

But also, for someone with the kind of rage David had and the kind of black-and-white way of looking at the world—in personal relationships, he was capable of a lot of subtlety and had great ability to see variations in motivation of behavior and people. He was a very humane person in that way, not at all knee-jerk—except when it came to things like the government, cops, the church...he did have that response.

MH: I understand that Peter, very near the end of his life, asked a priest to come to his house. What if any, were David's religious beliefs?

FL: David hated the church, the Catholic Church, and in particular Cardinal O'Connor.

I don't know what David's religious background was. I assumed he was a Catholic. I could be wrong. But I don't think that he had any religious upbringing, because I don't think he had much of an upbringing at all.

MH: No. He was both abandoned and beaten....

FL: Yes. And, it wasn't like anyone was sending him to Sunday School every Sunday or taking him to church, or whatever. David had the kind of hatred of the Catholic Church that people who go to parochial school have. People who go to Catholic school from the

Opposite: **SOMETHING FROM SLEEP IV**, *1988–89. Gelatin-silver print, acrylic, and collage, 16 x 20½"*

time they are little, and hate the nuns because the nuns beat them up.

And David chose O'Connor to concentrate on, and O'Connor makes himself a target because O'Connor becomes involved in secular politics. That's the reason I don't like him. And David and I discussed O'Connor a lot. For me, what O'Connor does in regard to the Church, I feel, is none of my business. I'm not Catholic. He can do whatever he wants. I get angry at O'Connor when he dictates what the public school system should do. When he talks and puts pressure on public issues. That is not allowed. Not allowed. That I profoundly believe.

MH: No mixing of Church and State.

FL: This is big-time not-allowed. The cardinal is not allowed to say anything about public schools. If I was the Pope, I wouldn't let him say anything about it.

But David…no, he didn't make the separation. He's a bad cardinal not only because he says what the public school system should do, but because he tells Catholics what to do. So I would say to him, "Well, that's his job, David. His job is to tell Catholics what to do." His job is to be an authority figure. That is his profession. You could disagree with him. But he's not out of line. He's well in line to tell Catholics, "No, you can't use birth control," or whatever he tells them.

To David it was all one thing. He took all this stuff personally. You know, O'Connor wasn't telling the TV camera this; he was telling David.

MH: How could he have such a hatred for institutions, yet feel connected enough to them to take their dictates personally?

FL: David and Peter were both like orphans. And there's a particular quality to that. So I think that this sets up a thing where you're unconsciously seeking something from these people, institutions that the rest of us—who don't feel like orphans— don't seek from them.

Peter was not political at all, but had a profound distrust of any kind of authority, including someone who even owned a small art gallery. You know, he couldn't make a distinction between someone who owned some little photography gallery and the Pope. But David was much more directly political, more involved. And yet David could also get along

with people. David was able to function somewhat in a group. Peter wasn't. Even a group of two.

David was not a difficult person to get along with. He was a very good friend. A very conventional person emotionally. You know, you didn't have to read him, figure him

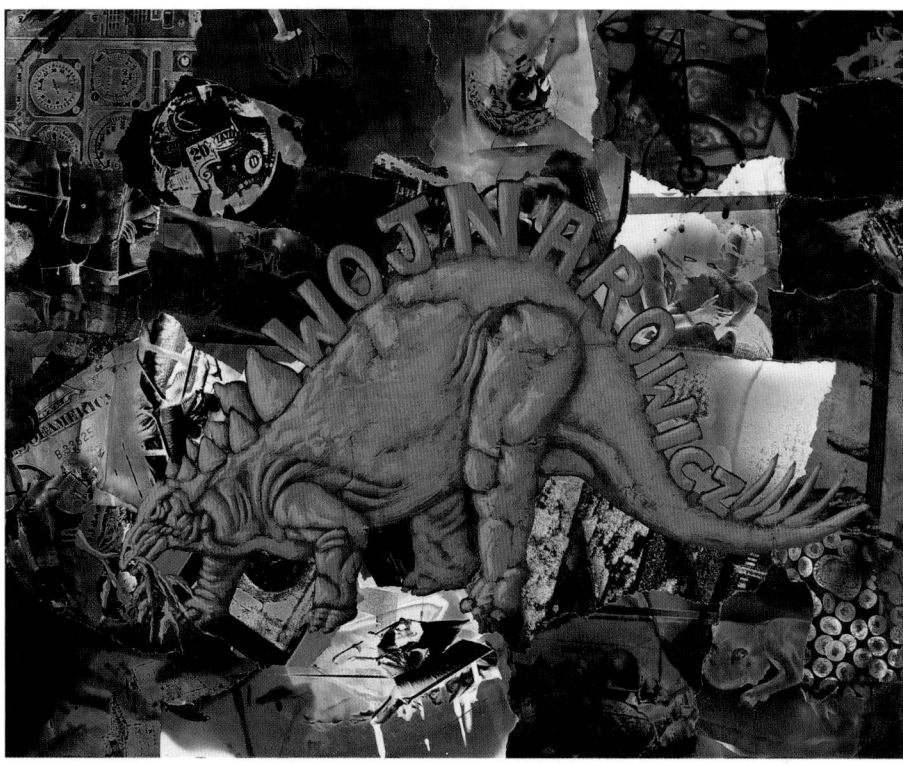

out…. A very straightforward person. And a person who thought about other people in a real way, and aside from his views, or his prickliness…could have probably gotten along even with Jesse Helms if he had wanted. He did not want to. But he was a very easy person to get along with. Peter was an impossible person to get along with.

Peter was a very admired person. And everyone was in love with Peter. In a particular scene he was a central icon to at least two generations. But he was not popular in the usual sense, because he was hard to get along with. And he also scared people. Whereas I don't think that David scared people or intimidated people in any way. I think he was a very accessible person.

MH: Was David very sexual? His writing certainly is.

FL: Excessively, by which I mean it embodies the sexuality from his childhood as well. David had childhood sexual experiences, as

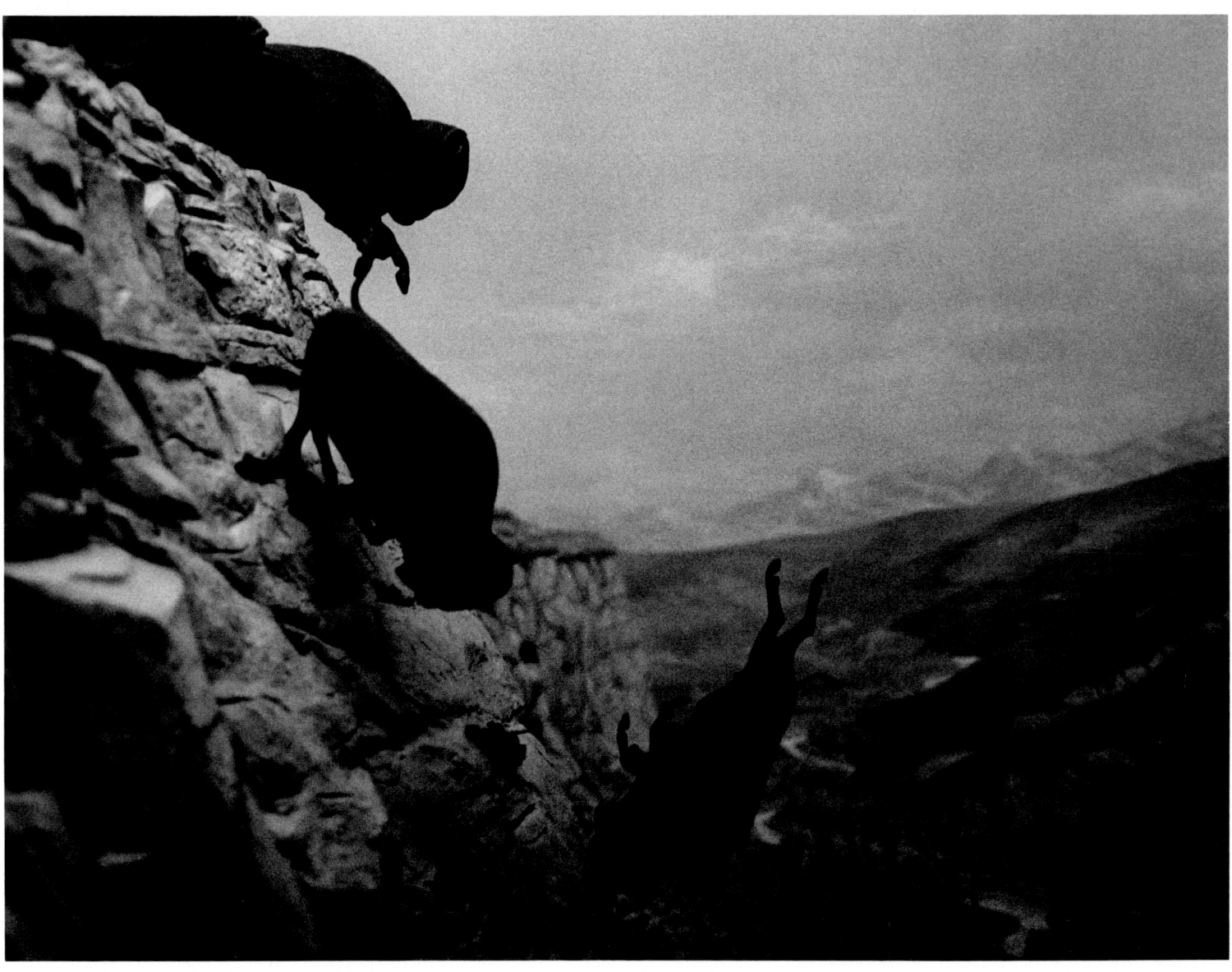

UNTITLED, *1988–89. Gelatin-silver print, 27½ x 34½"*

Opposite: UNTITLED, 1992. Gelatin-silver print and silk-screened text, 38 x 26"

did Peter. Peter believed that he was a willing partner in this, because people who don't have childhoods don't believe in childhood. People who are forced to take responsibility for themselves from the time they're children, people who aren't protected by adults, don't get to be children. So they always believe that they were in charge of their lives at a time when they weren't.

M H: They believe they always acted willfully.

F L: Yes. They always acted willfully. Because they don't understand the difference in the state of consciousness between a child and an adult.

Now, Peter didn't have the experience of being a hustler, like David did. David understood the ways in which adults abused children…. But I think he believed that there

were some people who weren't like that.

M H: David believed that some of the people he was hustling were being kind?

F L: Yes — that it was alright because they were nice to him. They didn't beat him up, or they didn't steal…. Yes, David thought there were good and bad users of eleven-year-old hustlers. I make no such distinction.

David was like a person who brought himself up…. He performed all of the functions for himself that everyone else needs a whole society to provide. He was his mother and his father and his school and his Sunday school and his neighbors and his aunts and his uncles — and he invented himself. This is a heroic effort. This is a massive effort and act of courage. Tremendous. And when he was sick with AIDS, he would call his friends to see how they felt. 🏠

Sometimes I come to hate people because they can't see where I am. I've gone empty, completely empty and all they see is visual form; my arms and legs, my face, my height and posture, the sounds that come from my throat. But I'm fucking empty. The person I was just one year ago no longer exists; drifts spinning slowly into the ether somewhere way back there. I'm a xerox of my former self. I can't abstract my own dying any longer. I am a stranger to others and to myself and I refuse to pretend that I am familiar or that I have history attached to my heels. I am glass, clear empty glass. I see the world spinning behind and through me. I see the sculptures and mundane effects of gesture made by constant human relations. I look familiar but I am a complete stranger being mistaken for my former selves. I am a stranger and I am moving. I am moving on two legs soon to be on all fours. I am no longer animal vegetable or mineral. I am no longer made of circuits or disks. I am no longer coded and deciphered. I am all emptiness and futility. I am an empty stranger, a carbon copy of my form. I can no longer find what I'm looking for outside of myself. It doesn't exist out there. Maybe it's only in here, inside my head. But my head is glass and my eyes have stopped being cameras, the tape has run out and nobody's words can touch me. No gesture can touch me. I've been dropped into all this from another world and I can't speak your language any longer. See the signs I try to make with my hands and fingers. See the vague movements of my lips among the sheets. I'm a blank spot in a hectic civilization. I'm a dark smudge in the air that dissolves without notice. I feel like a window, maybe a broken window. I am a glass human. I am a glass human disappearing in rain. I am standing among all of you waving my invisible arms and hands. I am shouting my invisible words. I am getting so weary. I am growing tired. I am waving to you from here. I am crawling and looking for the aperture of complete and final emptiness. I am vibrating in isolation among you. I am screaming but it comes out like pieces of clear ice. I am signalling that the volume of all this is too high. I am waving. I am waving my hands. I am disappearing. I am disappearing but not fast enough.

LUCY R. LIPPARD is a writer, teacher and activist, author of sixteen books on contemporary art and the novel *I See/You Mean*. She has created performances, comics, street theater, and has worked for twenty years with artists' groups as co-founder of: Printed Matter; The Heresies Collective and journal; Political Art Documentation/Distribution and its journal *Upfront*; Artists Call Against U.S. Intervention in Central America; and Boulder Women's Action Coalition. She is active in the Alliance for Cultural Democracy, and was co-editor of "How To '92," in its "Campaign for a Post-Columbian World."

Her books include: *From the Center: Feminist Essays on Women's Art*; *Eva Hesse*; *Get the Message?: A Decade of Art for Social Change*; *Overlay: Contemporary Art and the Art of Prehistory*; *A Different War: Vietnam in Art*; *Mixed Blessings: New Art in a Multicultural America*; *Partial Recall: Photographs of Native North Americans*.

She has received a Guggenheim Fellowship, the Frank Jewett Mather Award for Criticism, two National Endowment for the Arts grants in criticism, the Claude Fuess award for public service, a citation from New York City's Mayor David Dinkins, and the Smith College Medal, among many other honors and awards.

VINCE ALETTI is the photography critic and a senior editor at the *Village Voice*. His collection of American physique photography from the 1950s will appear in book form before the century is over.

C. CARR is a staff writer for the *Village Voice*. Her book, *On Edge: Performance at the End of the Twentieth Century* (Wesleyan University Press/University Press of New England) includes several pieces on David Wojnarowicz.

DAVID COLE, along with Peter Weiss of the Center for Constitutional Rights, and Kathryn Barrett, Jonathan Olsoff, and John Gutoff of Skadden, Arps, Meagher, Slate & Flom, represented David Wojnarowicz in his case against Donald Wildmon and the American Family Association. Cole is now a professor at Georgetown University Law Center.

KAREN FINLEY is a New York–based artist whose recent projects include the installations *Moral History* and *Written in Sand* and the performance *A Certain Level of Denial*. She has also made numerous dance records and has written and directed plays, among them *The Theory of Total Blame* and *The Lamb of God Hotel*. Finley is the author of two books: *Shock Treatment* (City Lights, 1990) and *Enough is Enough* (Poseidon, 1993). In 1986, Finley and Woj-

narowicz collaborated on the film *You Killed Me First*, directed by Richard Kern.

NAN GOLDIN's photographs have been shown worldwide. Her ongoing multimedia project *The Ballad of Sexual Dependency* was published in book form by Aperture in 1986. Goldin has also curated a number of exhibitions. Several other books of her work have been published, including *Vakat* (Walter König); *The Other Side 1972–1992*, and most recently, *A Double Life* (both Scalo/Parkett, Zurich).

ELIZABETH HESS is a writer living in New York City. Her work has been published widely, including in the *Washington Post*, *Art in America*, and *Artforum*. She currently writes a column on art for the *Village Voice*, and is preparing a monograph on the artist Ida Appelbroog (forthcoming from Rizzoli).

TESSA HUGHES-FREELAND is a filmmaker and writer living in New York City. Her films have been shown throughout Europe and the United States, and include *Playboy*, and most recently *Dirty* (with Annabel Lee) and *Nymphomania* (with Holly Adams).

FRAN LEBOWITZ is the author of *Metropolitan Life* and *Social Studies*. She is currently working on a novel entitled *Exterior Signs of Wealth*, and her children's book *Mr. Chas and Lisa Sue Meet the Pandas* is forthcoming this fall from Knopf.

CARLO McCORMICK is a writer and Associate Editor of *Paper*. His work has appeared in numerous publications, including *Artforum* and *High Times*, and his subjects range from comics to tattoos to strip shows. McCormick has written many articles on David Wojnarowicz, including "Fables, Facts, Riddles & Reasons in Wojnarowicz's Mythopoetica," in the "Tongues of Flame" exhibition catalog.

TOM RAUFFENBART worked for twenty-five years at New York City's Child Welfare Administration, and retired in 1992 on a disability pension due to AIDS. He met David Wojnarowicz in January 1986 in the basement of a porno theater and was his boyfriend for the next six and a half years. He now lives in New York, and is the executor of the Wojnarowicz estate.

KIKI SMITH is an artist whose work is well-known internationally. Since 1979, she has been using images of the human body and its processes in her sculptures, installations, print works, and photographs. She and David Wojnarowicz were close friends and colleagues in the mid 1980s.

CREDITS

Note: Unless otherwise noted, all works are courtesy of P•P•O•W Gallery, New York, and the Estate of David Wojnarowicz.

Contents page, pp.3, 4–5, 56, 59–61, 63–65 private collection, subsequent edition of 12 at 16 x 20″, various collections; p.6 collection of Tom Rauffenbart; p.9 collection of New York Public Library; p.10 collection of Barry Blinderman; p.11 collection of Justin Frankel; p.12 collection of Penny Pilkington; p.13 collection of Jean Foos; p.14 private collection; pp.16–17 collection of Phillip Briet; p.19 collection of Barry Blinderman; p.20 bottom: collection of Robert M. Ransick; p.21 private collection; p.22 collection of National Gallery of Canada, Ottawa; pp.24–25 private collection; p.27 private collection; p.28 edition of 3, various collections; p.29 edition of 10 (printed posthumously by Wojnarowicz estate), various collections; pp.30–31 collection of Michael Lynne; p.34 courtesy of Pace Gallery, New York; p.38 collection of Josef and Marcy Mittelman; p.39 courtesy of Estate of Paul Anderson; p.40 collection of Jill and John C. Bishop Jr.; p.41 collection of Dr. Robert Friedman; p.43 collection of Penny Pilkington; p.44 2 editions of 5 each, varying sizes, various collections; p.45 2 editions of 5 each, varying sizes, various collections; p.46 right: collection of Glenn Goldberg; p.47 collection of National Gallery of Canada, Ottawa; p.48 collection of Sondra Gilman and Celso Gonzalez-Falla; p.49 collection of Penny Pilkington; p.53 collection of Tom Rauffenbart; p.57 courtesy of James Danziger Gallery, New York and Estate of Peter Hujar; p.62 courtesy Nan Goldin and Matthew Marks Gallery; p.66 private collection; p.67 private collection; p.71 collection of Steve Johnson, Walter Sudol, and Burt Minkoff; pp.72–73 collection of Library of Congress, Prints and Photographs Division; p.74 collection of Arthur Newman; p.75 edition of 10, various collections; p.76 collection of Don Hanson; p.78 courtesy of James Danziger Gallery, New York, and Estate of Peter Hujar; p.81 collection of Luis Cruz Azaceta; p.82 edition of 5, various collections; second edition of 5 at 16 x 20″, various collections; p. 83, edition of 4, various collections.

PUBLIC COLLECTIONS:
Brooklyn Museum, New York; Richard F. Brush Art Gallery, St. Lawrence University; Denver Art Museum; Elvehjem Museum of Art, Madison, WI; Hallmark Cards; Jersey City Museum; Library of Congress, Washington, D.C.; Los Angeles County Museum of Art; Metropolitan Museum of Art, New York City; Milwaukee Art Museum; Museum of Contemporary Art, Chicago; Museum of Modern Art, New York City; Museum of Modern Art, San Francisco; National Gallery of Canada, Ottawa; New Museum of Contemporary Art, New York City; New School for Social Research, New York City; New York Public Library, New York City; Princeton Art Museum; Virginia Museum of Fine Arts, Richmond; Whitney Museum of American Art, New York City

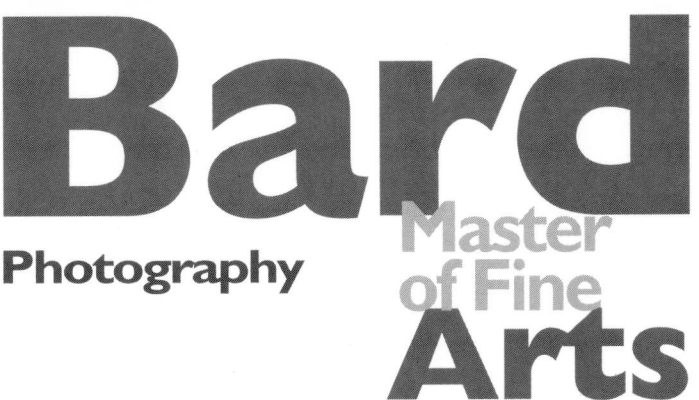

Bard Photography **Master of Fine Arts**

Summer MFA Photography Program at Bard College

At the Milton Avery Graduate School of the Arts of Bard College, a Masters of Fine Arts degree can be earned in three summers of intensive work.

The Photography program is located within a broad arts environment emphasizing interdisciplinary critiques and access to artists working within Film/Video, Music Composition, Painting, Sculpture, and Writing.

Current faculty includes:

John Divola, Stephen Shore, and Anne Turyn in Photography; and, in the other disciplines, Peggy Ahwesh, Ron Baron, Nancy Bowen, Alan Cote, Petah Coyne, Lydia Davis, Cecilia Dougherty, Stephen Ellis, Jean Feinberg, Arthur Gibbons, Reginna Granne, Joan Jonas, Ann Lauterbach, Jackson Mac Low, Nicholas Maw, Keith Sanborn, Leslie Scalapino, Jessica Stockholder, Lynne Tillman, and Tom Woodruff.

For more information contact:

The Milton Avery Graduate School of the Arts

Bard College

Annandale-on-Hudson, NY 12504

(914) 758-7481

Institute of Design
Illinois Institute of Technology

Graduate
Fellowships
Photography

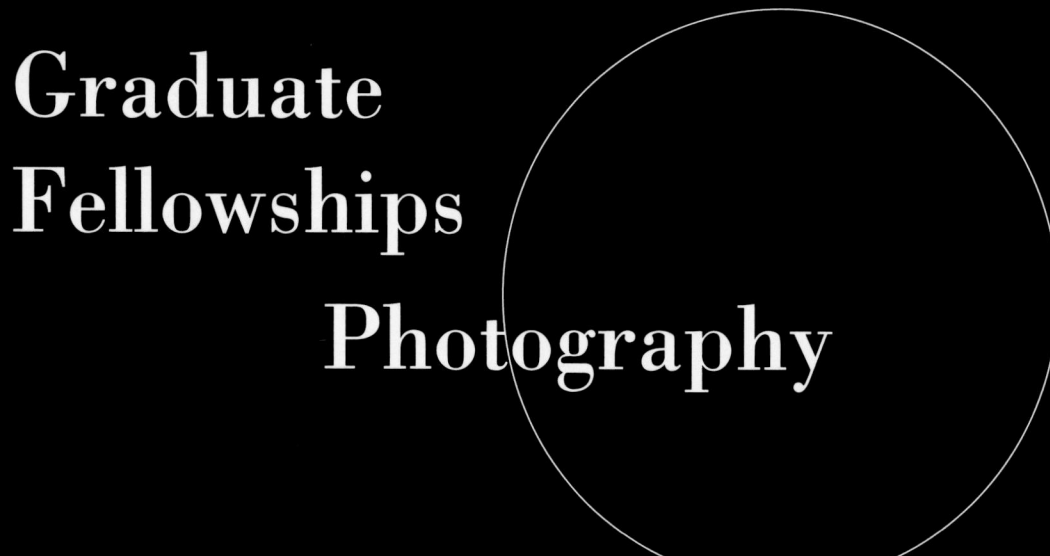

Image makers, image imaginers, and image users from the
arts, design, sciences, and humanities are all invited to apply.
Our photography program offers project-oriented graduate
studies in documentary methods, electronic imaging, and
communications design. The philosophy at the Institute of
Design demands the highest appropriation of both traditional
and advanced technologies in the undertaking of intelligent
images of conscience and social critique.

Under the direction of distinguished faculty, and with the
assistance of subject matter specialists from other fields
within IIT and the entire Chicago area, students have the
opportunity to explore diverse issues within an intellectual
and professional environment.

For more information contact:
Graduate Admissions
Institute of Design
Illinois Institute of Technology
10 W. 35th St.
Chicago, IL 60616   USA
1 • 800 • 496 • 7251

VISION *Editions*

VE

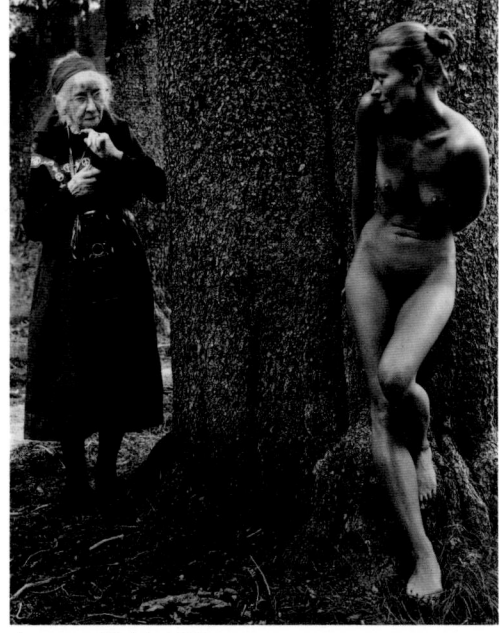

Imogen and Twinka, 1974

Judy Dater

single print
edition of 40
6 5/8" × 8"

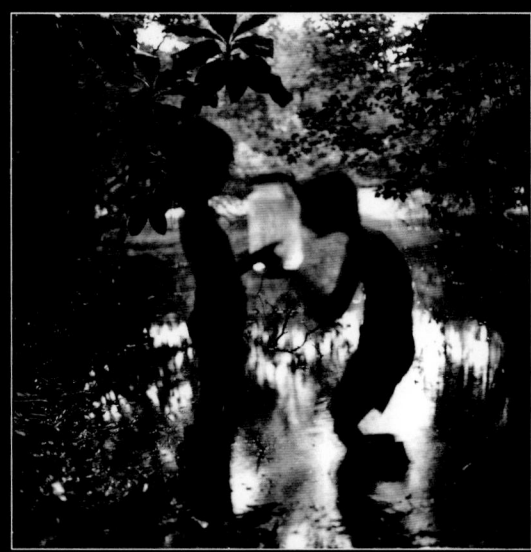

Fireflies, 1992

Keith Carter

single print
edition of 40
10" × 10"

A continuing series of limited edition platinum/palladium prints and portfolios

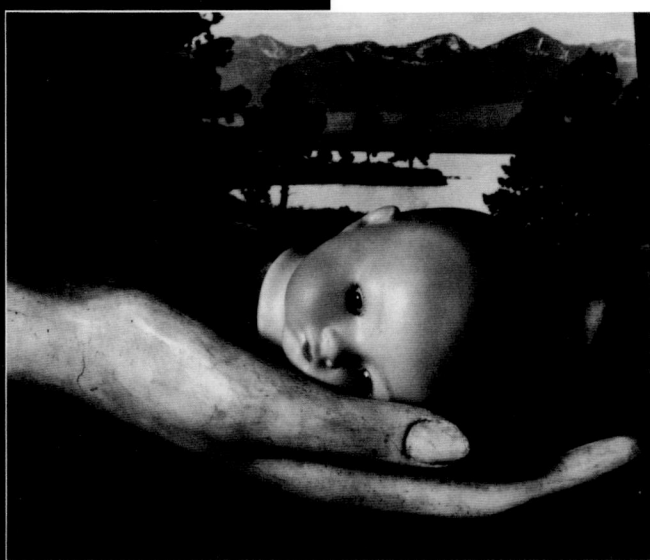

Ruth Bernhard
Gift of the Commonplace

portfolio of 10 images
edition of 40
5" × 7" to 6" × 7 3/4"

Creation, 1936

VISION GALLERY • 1155 Mission Street • San Francisco, CA 94103 • (415) 621-2107 fax (415) 621-5074

VE

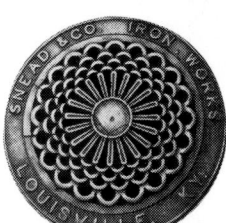
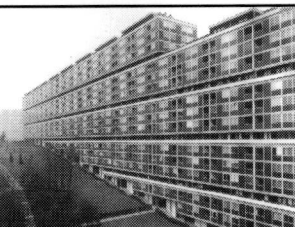
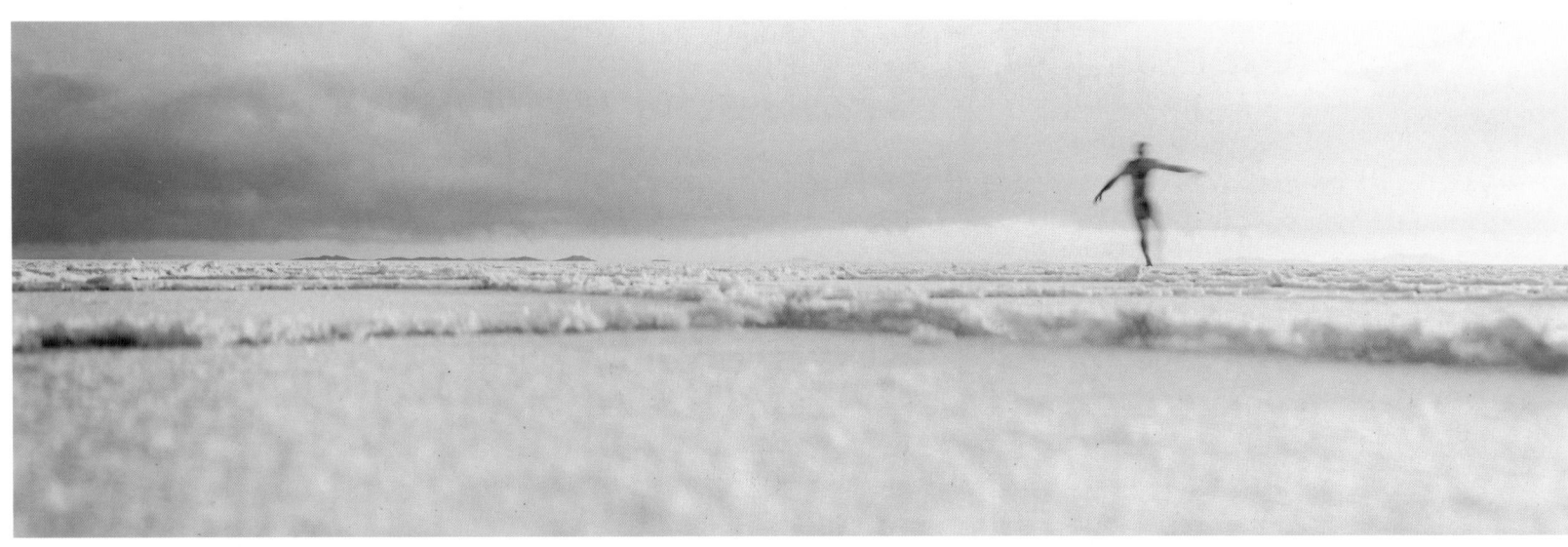

UNTITLED # 232, BY NICK WAPLINGTON. FROM *OTHER EDENS*, PUBLISHED BY APERTURE, FALL 1994.

AVAILABLE IN AN EDITION OF FIFTY PANORAMIC PRINTS AND FIVE ARTIST'S PROOFS, ON 20-BY-45-INCH PAPER, SIGNED AND NUMBERED BY THE PHOTOGRAPHER. THE PRINTS ARE BEING OFFERED AT $950 UNTIL JANUARY 30, 1995; THEREAFTER, $1,250. FOR MORE INFORMATION OR TO PLACE AN ORDER, CONTACT APERTURE, 20 EAST 23RD STREET, NEW YORK, NY 10010. PHONE: (212) 598-4205; FAX: (212) 598-4015